CHAPTER 1

Stepping Up to a Challenge

My name is Sally Crystal, and I am a freelance reporter. Making a living this way is not easy or very profitable. Nowadays, colleges are graduating journalists in higher numbers than ever before in history, which creates a few problems for the new kids on the block. Everyone coming out of college hopes for one of the few top job openings that are being offered. After graduating, most of us are expected to hone our craft for a couple of years before anyone will even take a serious look at us as a member of their newspaper, television news team, or radio talk show. I have never understood why being a journalist was so important to me; somehow, it got into my blood at a very young age, and I couldn't shake it.

Today this was not where I wanted to be sitting on a beautiful summer's afternoon, here in a drab, windowless lunchroom of the newspaper office that has been accepting my freelance pieces. I'm now proofreading an article on the positives and negatives of Common Core, an educational system that was to be voted on soon by Congress. Time was of the essence, for it needed to be in the copy room in a few minutes if it was to be part of tomorrow's news headlines at all. The door to the lunchroom opened, and Mr. Korn, my boss, walked in. How could I tell him not to sit down? Or that I was in a hurry and had no time to talk. My silence did nothing to hinder his plans of pulling up a chair and making himself comfortable right across the table from me. The cup of hot coffee in his right hand conveyed his desire to stay for a while.

"Sally, my brother and I can't agree on which one of our two freelance reporters that we want to offer an opening on the paper to this fall. You see, both the people are equally qualified for the position, and both want a permanent in-house job. This job offer could propel each of their careers into the national limelight," he said, pausing.

I could hardly keep myself from yelling, "Go faster—who have you picked? Is it me?" I struggled to keep a calm and serene look about my face while melting into an emotional basket-case inside.

"Sally, the only thing we could come up with was to offer both you and Jake Bates a weekly column for the summer. Whichever one of you gets the most readers interested in your column and our paper over the summer months will get the position. Are you interested?" he asked.

"Yes! Yes, of course," I said, jumping up out of my chair with excitement and knocking it over on the floor behind me.

"Calm down, girl!" Mr. Korn said while laughing at me. "You don't even know what is being asked of you yet."

I picked up my chair off the floor and repositioned it, then sat back down to listen to my boss's idea.

"Your assignment, if you should take it, is to write a column for the summer on Black Hawk Harbor. You must write on everything that you find of interest there. It will take all your skills as an investigative reporter to pull this one off. If you're as good as I think you are, you will become a new member of our office and staff. Sally, don't believe for one minute that this will be a cakewalk, for those in Black Hawk Harbor are wise and very private, especially when it comes to reporters," he said as a warning of sorts.

"Sir, would it be all right for me to write my column using a pen name? That way the readers will never know it's a woman writing it. I'll be freer to get into places that wouldn't otherwise allow a reporter, like private parties and dinners. As you just said, sir, they don't take to talking to people like us," I reminded him.

"Sure, I can see no reason why your column can't be written using a pseudonym. It shouldn't bother my brother or the reporter that he is backing, for it won't change the outcome of the challenge.

Although, I would think you'd profit more using your real name, for it will propel you and your writing into the limelight if it is well received," he added, a bit concerned.

"Many famous writers that are well-known now started as ghostwriters and went on to do wonderful things in both national news, books, and television. You won't be sorry, sir, I promise," I said with excitement.

"Okay, okay, we'll try it your way." He paused for a second and then added, "I'm excited about this summer project, too. We've never done anything like this before. I, for one, believe that we are in store for a great adventure. I can hardly wait for the first installment of your summer column," Mr. Korn stood up, then added, "I know you will do me proud, Sally." He was smiling while he walked out of the lunchroom door.

Wow! I could hardly believe what just happened and pinched myself to make sure I wasn't dreaming. I was almost too excited to think about anything else. I remained in the lunchroom for a few more minutes to calm down and finish my proofreading. I couldn't stop myself from pondering over the possibilities of what this could mean to my career. When I walk out of here today, I will be starting a new chapter in my life. This gift my boss had just offered me could turn out to be the most important one in a lifetime—or a terrifying Pandora's box.

I quickly gathered up my things and headed down the hallway to the pressroom. I had no sooner stepped through the doors there than I heard someone call out my name from across the room.

"Sally Crystal!"

"I hear that only one of us can obtain the position opening up in the newsroom as a column reporter in the fall. You're still young, your break will come, hang in there" Jake Bates said in a boastful manner while he was leaving the room by another door, without giving me a chance to reply.

"Well, you old fart!" I thought while handing off my piece on Common Core to the printers while still in a bit of disbelief. "My grandmother had a name for people like you. She would have given you a lesson in manners if she were here." I am sure he thinks he is all that and his winning is a foregone conclusion, at least in his mind. After all, it is true he does have ten years of experience over me, most of it in sports and city government. Where mine has been as an investigative reporter in all the dark and questionable places between here and the nation's capital, it's only as a freelance writer that I was able to report on these things, for women were very seldom given these kinds of assignments on any paper. Times, they are a changing; you can bet your bottom dollar on that.

Looking back now, I can remember where and when the seeds of journalism were planted in my life. I was in the fifth grade and had just lost my mother to cancer; it was an excruciating time in my life and full of sadness and horrible pain. Upon returning to school a week later after her funeral, we were doing career week, and we had a speaker in to share her career choice with us.

Miss Walker was a pretty, tall, skinny colored lady in her twenties, and I was mesmerized by what she said her job was. She called herself an investigative reporter and journalist, who had traveled the world, worked with presidents and kings. Now, this reporter was telling us about freedom of the press and how important it was in a democracy, to keep us a civilized society. Without honest reporters, a country could fall to evil, corrupt men and women. She shared many careers where a good journalist could be employed. The seed she planted that day in me caused me as a child to become an avid newspaper reader. I grew up wanting to do the kind of work that she enjoyed all those years ago.

While in college I had enjoyed the time, I spent working on the College Beat for a local paper. The small newspaper job paid me a little, helping me buy a few things I needed that weren't covered by my scholarship, plus helping me hone my craft. After college, I went on to make a modest living as a freelance writer, right up until this morning. This summer could become the most considerable part of my journey and a dream of a lifetime. I must always remember and respect the private lives and affairs of all those who live in Black Hawk Harbor. There is a fragile line that I dared not cross while writing about others; if I didn't respect it, my writing career and life as a reporter could come to a sudden end.

SUMMER CHALLENGE

So here I go again, I thought as I drove down the highway to Black Hawk Harbor. It was already three in the afternoon on May 16, 2015. My life was about to go through a drastic change, one that I could never have foreseen.

CHAPTER 2

A Picture from the Past

Upon entering Black Hawk Harbor, I noticed a newspaper stand in front of a restaurant on Main Street. I quickly pulled my car up in front of it and jumped out to grab a copy, leaving my motor idling. I slipped my seventy-five cents into the slot provided for it, and the door flipped open; I retrieved a copy, closed the door, and returned to my car. Once back behind the wheel and before moving my car, I quickly pulled the paper apart trying to find the rental ads and threw the rest of it to my back seat. My eyes scanned down the page as I looked feverishly for someplace in this area to live. I had hopes of finding something I could afford on my meager income. If I was being honest with myself, this time of year in the harbor one couldn't rent a dog house. There was nothing under a thousand dollars a month, and the amounts listed didn't include utilities. I looked further down the page near the bottom and found a thick black framed box that read, "Room for Rent 1060 Beach Street, see Miss Marple."

"This may be the only way I can afford to live here in the harbor for the summer," I said aloud to myself.

I quickly added the address to my GPS and followed the directions being given to me by a female's voice; within five minutes, I was sitting in front of the house. The GPS must have malfunctioned, for this couldn't possibly be the right place. People who live in homes like this don't rent out rooms to strangers. It was a huge old Victorian house, and even from the curb, I could see three large fans in the

Summer Challenge

A Mystery of Unquenchable Desire

D'Maule

Copyright © 2019 D'Maule
All rights reserved
First Edition

Fulton Books, Inc.
Meadville, PA

Published by Fulton Books 2019

ISBN 978-1-63338-970-0 (paperback)
ISBN 978-1-63338-971-7 (digital)

Printed in the United States of America

ceiling of its old plantation-style porch that surrounded the entire front of the house. The house itself sat on a professionally manicured knoll that was encompassed by beautiful flowering trees and colorful flowering beds that were in bloom around the house, all gracing the upper shoreline of Lake Michigan. It looked like a house right out of the *Victorian Living* magazine.

I shut off my car and stepped out onto the curb next to the sidewalk. After straightening my clothes, I gathered up my courage and made my way up the beautiful stone walkway that led to the door. I caught myself hesitating just before pushing the doorbell button.

What if it's the wrong house? I thought. Then I noticed out of the corner of my eye a small sign, tucked back just out of sight to the right in the lower window: "Room for rent. Inquire inside."

I had not taken any real time to think all this through.

What am I going to say to the person that comes to the door? Why do I need a room? What will I tell her I do for a living? I questioned myself.

My boss had warned me about the people in the harbor and their dislike for reporters. They vacationed here to get away from such things. They valued their privacy and chose this beautiful location when they had enough money to live anywhere on earth.

I must be truthful if I am going to gain the trust of these people for more than a minute. It will be the only way I'll get juicy enough news to keep my readers interested. My ability to blend in and get invited to their parties and other social functions was crucial. I thought. *So it all starts right here.* I slid my finger over the top of the bell button and pushed it down. I could hear it ring out and see through the glass in the front door a short elderly lady approaching. I watched her as she made her way to the door.

She looked like a character out of an old English mystery novel that I had seen on TV.

I believe that the main character in one of those stories was a woman called Miss Marple. This woman coming to the door had silver hair wrapped up into a bun atop her head, which appeared to be secured somewhere in the back, and a pencil protruded out of the right side of her old-fashioned hair bun.

Had I just interrupted her doing crossword puzzles or her writing? I wondered.

The lady who was standing looking back at me just inside the door sent a sudden chill running through my body like a high-speed Amtrak train; I quickly stepped back on one foot to keep my balance as she opened the door.

"Oh, Mother! What am I getting myself into?" I almost said aloud.

As the door swung open, I could now see her powder-blue eyes that were surrounded by her delicate ivory-toned skin, which seemed almost flawless. Could I only venture a guess about her age maybe seventy- or eighty-something? She stood all of five feet tall in her black granny heels and wore a gray skirt that flowed down to the tops of her shoes. Her beautiful pink ruffled silk blouse edged in lace brought out the rose color in her cheeks, while the strand of white pearls glimmered in the sunlight as they graced her elegant white cardigan sweater; her look spoke of another place and time. She certainly looked like the mystery sleuth Miss Marple in those books, but this lady is a real person and very much alive. If there were ever really another Miss Marple, she would surely be dead by now. Only time will answer all the many questions that swarmed around in my head.

First things first, I thought to myself, *I must first get the room.*

I needed to live in the harbor, if I were to win the challenge and the column in the offering, even if it meant having to live with some real live characters for a while. *Wait a minute. how do I know this is the lady of the house and not her housekeeper?* I asked myself.

"Hello, my name is Sally Crystal, and I am looking to rent the room spoke of in the paper. I am looking to get some R&R over the summer here in the harbor. I am a writer by trade and haven't had any time to enjoy a summer in years. Other living quarters around here are very costly, much more than I can afford. While I was looking at the paper, I noticed your ad, so I decided to come and check out the room mentioned. You do still have the room for rent, don't you?" I asked, now almost entirely out of breath.

"Yes, but first let me show you the room I have, then you can tell me if it's what you're looking for. If so, then I will tell you about the house rules and the price," she responded in a calm, soft voice.

She swung the door open a little further so I could enter the porch and house; then I followed her up the stairs and down one of three hallways, to a room on the right side of the house with the number 3 on the door. She opened the door and stepped aside so I could have walked through it. It looked like I'd entered a hotel more than a residential home. It was a large room right out of the turn of the century, with curtains from floor to ceiling, a four-poster bed, even the flowered wallpaper spoke of times past. Light maple furniture and handmade linens graced the bed. There was a beautiful desk and chair, three lamps of varied sizes, and scone lights on the walls, making it a very warm and welcoming room. The elderly lady opened two doors to the right and showed me the spacious walk-in closet with a small apartment-size refrigerator turned on, sitting at one end of the closet. *A strange place for a refrigerator*, I thought.

Then we walked across the room to a set of French doors that she opened, and to my surprise, I was looking at a magnificent view of Lake Michigan from a two-chair balcony.

"Yes, this is perfect, more than I could have imagined. But what is your price?" I asked, looking into the compassionate eyes of the little lady to my left while trying to ward off the fear of not being able to afford it.

"Is it something you think you could be comfortable in for the whole summer? You see, I don't have time to rerent it again if you should change your mind? For all who would likely be interested in renting, it would already have found other places," the lady said cautiously.

"Yes, yes, this is perfect," I replied with excitement.

"Then it's settled, I'll rent it to you for the discount price of 250 a month. You must supply your food unless I invite you to eat with me. You must also supply your detergent, toiletries, and things for your personal needs. All my guests have the run of the house just as if it were their own home. You'll find a fully stocked reading library and a comfortable TV living room. You are encouraged to eat your meals in the kitchen when possible. Everyone is expected to clean up after themselves; there are no maids here. You will be able to use the laundry room on the third day of the week, which coincides with the number three on your door. You have the third stall in the carriage house, in which to store your things and park your bike if you have one." The lady paused, and I reached down into my purse and brought out my checkbook.

I quickly wrote out the amount on the check, then stopped and investigated the face of the lady in front of me and asked the right spelling of her name.

"I can't remember you telling me your name, is it Miss Marple?" I asked.

A huge smile lit up her face with a heavenly glow and sprinkled stardust in her eyes.

"Yes, that is my name," she replied.

I quickly added the name to the check, feeling almost ashamed for asking her such a question; after all, that is the name that she put in the paper.

"I guess I'll be calling this home," I said upon handing her the check. "Miss Marple, thank you. This is better than anything I could ever have hoped for," I added.

Miss Marple handed me a key ring with three keys on it.

"These are the keys you'll need for the back door, your room, and the carriage house," she said, releasing them into my hand, then added "So tell me, dear, when can we expect you to move in?" she asked.

"I must go back to my old apartment, pack up, and do a little cleaning there so I can get my deposit back from the landlord. I should be able to get back here and settle in in about two days at most," I replied.

"That sounds good," she said as we walked back to the front door together. I opened it this time, then went out and down the steps to the curb where I had left my car. After getting into my car, I turned around and looked out my car window to mouth goodbye to her as she waved me off.

I was surprised that Miss Marple hadn't asked me for references of any kind; I found that a bit peculiar, but it saved me from answering questions.

It took me all the two days to clean, pack and retrieve my deposit.

"Sally, I am so glad that you found another place, for I've already rented this apartment to someone else, for your lease ended, and you didn't speak to me about renewing it. You might be interested in knowing that I also had to raise the amount of rent by seventy-five dollars," the landlord said.

Boy, was I ever glad that I had found that place in the harbor or I would have been out on the street. Everything works out—if it's meant to be, I thought, and I was more than satisfied with my choice. I couldn't have been more excited than I was at that very minute, squeezing the last item into the trunk of my car and closing it. I then ran around the car, got in, started it up, and then turned around and waved goodbye for the last time. I drove away from that address, not feeling any sadness about it; it was a load off my mind, and within ten minutes, I was pulling into Miss Marple's driveway. I could hardly wait to get all my things out of the car and put it away. Somehow the items went into the car faster than they came out. I had carried everything up to my room that I needed right away; the rest of my belongings went into the carriage house storage building.

It was two o'clock in the afternoon, and I lay down on the bed exhausted; once my head hit the pillows, I was out like a cheap flashlight. I woke up some three hours later to someone knocking on my door and calling out my name. I sat up on the edge of the bed to get my bearings, then stood and moved slowly to the door.

"Who is it?" I asked before opening the door.

"Sally, my name is Kenny, and Miss Marple asked me to come up and ask you to come to dinner," he said before I opened the door and smiled at him. "She thought that after a full day of moving you might like to eat a meal someone else made. What should I tell her?" he asked.

"What time did she say that I should come?" I asked him.

"She likes to eat at seven sharp," he replied.

"Yes! Tell her yes. I'd love to have dinner with her," I said. He quickly turned and walked away, leaving me standing in my doorway.

That only gave me two hours to scope out the village and find out where this story might get started.

I want to find a nice restaurant where I could go for breakfast in the morning, a place that had a broad mix of people of all ages and nationalities where I'd be able to pick up on something that would arouse the imagination of my readers.

The day had turned warm, so I slipped into a pair of shorts, a pictured T-shirt, and biking shoes. It wasn't long before I was out on my bike tooling down the roadside of the village. It appeared to be a busy village, full of tourists from all around the world. Between the cars and people, I found it hard to get around even on a bike at this time of the day. I soon racked my bike in front of a café called the Stain Cup. The advertisement in front of the restaurant boasted of excellent-tasting coffee and delicious breakfasts. It spurred my imagination enough for me to go inside and get a better look for myself. Right across from the entrance door was a large coffee bar, one that had signs inviting patrons to step forward and help themselves, then pay a waitress at the end of the counter. You could then leave with your coffee or take a seat at one of their many tables inside and out, or you could sit down and let a waitress wait on you.

Perfect, I thought, *my story will start here.* But it was still a mystery to me what that story would be. I made myself a cup of coffee and paid for it before taking a seat outdoors for a few minutes to scope out the different people around me. Without my earbuds, I was unable to hear those around me, yet the expressions on some of their faces spurred my curiosity. Oh, I know eavesdropping is considered rude in some places, but sometimes it's the only way for a reporter to get interesting facts about their surroundings. Tomorrow I will come more prepared. After finishing my coffee, I climbed back on my bike and started my ride back home along the waterfront. Time had flown by, and I still had to shower and dress for dinner. I pulled up to the carriage house and deposited my bike before heading up to my room. Once I was through the back door of the house again, I could hear Miss Marple call out to me.

"Sally, is that you?" she asked.

"Yes, Miss Marple, it is," I answered while standing at the bottom of the stairs.

"Please, would you come in here for a second? I have something that I want to ask you about," she said.

Her words sounded almost demanding, which caused me a bit of concern. I turned from the stairway and walked out to the side porch where she was sitting.

"Good afternoon, Miss Marple," I said, taking a deep breath before taking a seat in the white wicker chair across from her.

"Sally, I realize that we got started as a whirlwind. It seems that I forgot to get or talk to you about your references. So when you come down for dinner tonight, could you please bring me something to put into my files? Are we expected to ask for these things by law? It will also help me know how to relate to you like my border. I don't think for one minute that this should cause you a second of concern, darling, as you seem like an honest, law-abiding young lady to me," she said with a broad smile.

Little did she realize that her request had just sent my brain into overdrive!

"I'll write something for you, Miss Marple," I replied, then quickly stood up and scurried off while trying not to show any disrespect.

Once back in my room I quickly sat down at my computer to compose a reference letter. The letter told about parts of my life, right up and through college and how I had worked at newspapers as a freelance writer for the past two years. It also spoke of the kind of journalist I am and some of my future. What the letter did not tell is why I was here. Hopefully that would not become a question; after all, I had already told her that I was seeking some R&R. I placed the letter into the copier, then ran into the bathroom to shower. After dressing, I sat and jotted down some notes about the village and the Stain Cup that I didn't want to forget. Then I quickly ran back into the bathroom to put on a little makeup and a few pieces of jewelry. One is a flower pin that had an audio chip in it. The chip allowed me to record a conversation without someone else knowing about it. The pin was merely one of the many tools of my trade. I was planning to interview Miss Marple about her life, for there was a lot about this lady that I found fascinating. I would never use any information I got this way to break the law, but I have used it many times to nab the bad guys.

I picked up the reference letter off the copier and headed down for dinner. The table in the dining room was laid out in a manner where everyone could help themselves.

A large slow cooker sat at one end of the six-foot-long table, almost flowing over with chicken alfredo. There was a large tossed salad, a plate of garlic bread, lemonade, and various kinds of dessert.

Miss Marple and I quickly prepared our plates, then I followed her back to her parlor where we were out of ear range of the other house guest.

"Please, dear, close the door behind you. I want our time together to be private tonight," she said before setting her plate down on the library table and directing me to do the same across from her. We pulled up a couple of chairs and got comfortable; then we ate for a couple of minutes before she broke the silence.

"You were going to bring me something?" she asked, putting down her fork and looking up at me.

"Oh yes!" I replied as I reached down into my pocket and pulled out the letter I had prepared for her. I continued eating as she read. I was famished and couldn't remember the last time I had eaten. She scanned up and down the letter quickly reading it, then folded the letter and tucked it away into the pocket of her long, flowing skirt.

"So you call yourself an investigative reporter? No wonder we took to each other so quickly. I, too, was young like you once and sometimes noisier than smart. Oh, the tales that I could tell you would curl your hair," she said, spurring on my curiosity even higher while she took another bite. There was a brief pause in the conversation before she added, "I would not be bragging at all." She laughed. "I did get myself into some pretty deep predicaments and thank God. Somehow I was always saved. I used to blame my curiosity on the name I received at birth. To be truthful about it, it was never really the name but an unquenchable desire that ran through my blood that drove me to seek out evil and conquer it, thereby protecting the innocent. I guess I have a hero complex; it may all seem crazy-sounding coming from a woman of my age. It was God who gave me all my talents, and my mother branded me with the name of a real character sleuth, that being Miss Marple. Oh, my goodness, look here, child, I've gone and done all the talking again. Please tell me more about yourself," she said as she took another small bite from her plate.

"Where do I start? You're right. There is a hunger in people like us to track down evil. This is something I've found in myself, sometimes beyond my control. The eagerness we have for pulling at the loose thread of a mystery is sometimes the one thing that gives us our greatest joy, for without a mystery to solve, we are like a wet blanket at a picnic. I am about to share something with you that no one else can know," I said, leaning forward as if to whisper.

Miss Marple stopped eating and looked up into my eyes and with the stillness of a statuette so as not to miss a single word.

"Maybe we can solve some mysteries together in the harbor if something should spark our interest during the summer," I said teasingly.

"Wow! Are you kidding? You would share something like that with me, and let me be a part of solving another mystery? Well, it's been a year since my last one—no, decades," she said, laughing. "Yes! I think I've still got it. I will keep my ears open for anything out of the norm, and my eyes peeled for any unusual comings and goings around the harbor. I have a lot of friends that tend to gossip or share personal things. We can compare notes," she said, with a look of renewed youth and excitement in her eyes.

"Yes, your help will be priceless to me. I do not doubt that," I replied. We talked on for an hour or so before calling it a night.

CHAPTER 3

Preparing for an Encounter

The sound of my alarm clock going off at 5:00 a.m. caught me by surprise. I jumped up and ran around the bed and over to my computer desk to turn off the loud buzzing sound. I had set the clock near the computer, so I couldn't just reach up and turn it off. It's true that as a freelancer I could set my schedules, yet I still had a deadline to meet. You miss the deadline; you can lose the chance for your work being accepted at that paper again. Your name in this business was only as good as your work ethic. I was eager to get this day started, for it was the beginning of my research for my new column.

To get my day started, I decided to do a few bodies stretches. Then I moved across the room to pull the drapes and open the French doors in hopes of getting some fresh air; upon doing so, I almost fell to my knees in awe.

"Is this what a real sunrise looks like?" I whispered almost in reverence as if a higher power was listening.

The sun was a deep red-orange hue—so bright that I had to retrieve my sunglasses from the desk to look at it. It was so enormous that it took up the whole sky in all directions. The reflection of it fell across the rippling waves of the water below, making it look like waves of blood. I couldn't take my eyes off it while I quickly moved to take a seat in one of the deck chairs.

"Oh my god, what a sight to behold," I caught myself saying.

My body now seemed to be infused with an extremely high degree of excitement that flowed freely through me; this was nothing like I had ever experienced before. Within just a matter of a few minutes, the sun seemed to be sucked upward and pulled back from the earth, only to be surrounded by a brilliant blue summer's sky. They say, "You never know what you've missed if you've never seen all that is." This morning was one I'd never forget.

I retreated into my room and took a seat at the computer, turned it, on and logged in. I started to make a written record of everything that had happened since I last talked to my boss, which now seemed like a lifetime ago. It was hard for me to believe how far I had come in just three days. Look at me! I was living here in someone else's home; how crazy was that? I quickly finished up and put away my thoughts of days past and headed for the bathroom to shower and dress, then readied myself for the bike ride to a restaurant that I wanted to visit. I had told Miss Marple that I wouldn't be around for breakfast because I would be having breakfast at the Stain Cup.

I put my backpack on the bed, opened it up, and threw in a few things that I would need—things like earbuds and sunglasses which could pick up audio and video from a short distance. I would also need my iPad, and of course, what girl doesn't need her iPhone? I slipped my wallet inside the smallest compartment of the backpack and zipped it up, then tied its outer flap down. I pulled on my pink hoodie sweatshirt and a pair of sweatpants, then I ran out of my door, locking it behind me and down the back steps. I put my pack on my back and mounted my bike. I could see a large group of bikers approaching and was surprised to see so many families with such small children out so early in the morning. Those with youngsters rode in family units or clusters, heading all in the same direction. The faster riders all kept to one side of the road so as not to mix in with the others. There were no written rules, only unspoken respect for one another. Most riders carried backpacks and water bottles that they could grab without stopping.

I soon found myself deep in the mix of fast riders, those that seemed to enjoy their speed more than the scenic views that caught others' attention. I pulled away from the pack as we drew closer to the restaurant, while the others continued up M119 to the north. I quickly parked my bike in the rack next to the Stain Cup restaurant.

By eight, café tables most of them were full. I quickly slipped past the people seated outside and went into the restaurant. I made my way back to a little two-chair table on the left side of the room next to the wall. While standing near the table, I could view the doorway and most of the comings and goings in the restaurant. I removed the things I needed from my backpack and sat the bag on the floor next to the wall to the right of my feet. I sat down in my chair, noticing immediately the posting on the wall "Free Wi-Fi." I turned on my iPad and put in one of my earbuds to make it look like I was listening to music while waiting for a waitress to stop by my table. I picked up the menu to check out the different breakfasts and coffees that they offered, and just about the time a waitress caught my motion for her, as a tall, well-dressed stranger walked in making the bell above the door ring and causing the place to go dead silent for a few seconds. The man carried a gold-eagle's-head walking stick and wore a black felt hat, a coat that stopped at his kneecaps, and shiny black expensive-looking Italian shoes.

He walked over to a four-chair table and quickly removed his overcoat placing it and his hat on the seat of the chair next to the one he intended to sit on, then hung his walking stick on the table's edge. He sat down and opened the *Wall Street Journal* that he had carried in beneath his left armpit. The curiosity soon died down, and things returned to normal, with only a few still looking in his direction from time to time while whispering to their companions.

My waitress finally became aware of where she was at and stepped up to take my order with a smile. Once she received the order and departed, I positioned my iPad to take several pictures of the tall gentleman. I took the picture mainly out of curiosity, I suppose, for the man almost demanded unspoken attention and made the hairs on my neck stand up.

Then the bells rang again above the door of the restaurant and two men, looking to be of American Indian descent, walked in and quickly scampered over to the other side of the room from where I was setting. They were dressed like construction workers or boat keepers and seemed to be well shaken up about something. They were staring at the old gentleman, with daggers of hate in their eyes.

I turned up my earbud to see if I could pick up on what they were saying.

"There's no mistake about it, that's him, Joe. So what do we do now?"

"Tuck, we must wait until we get further orders. This thing has become bigger than both of us. We can't let him know we're on to him just yet. I don't believe he came here from New York alone. He's not a man that does his dirty work, for he must appear to be above it all if you know what I mean?" Joe replied.

I could hardly make myself turn my attention back to my breakfast that had finally arrived. The thought of getting a picture of these two crossed my mind, so I dropped my fork and clicked pictures of them. Then the door opened again, and two more men walked in together. They didn't look around much but went directly to the older man's table.

Seeing this, the other two men who had come in and sat across from me by the wall jumped up and hurried out of the restaurant, as though they were afraid of being recognized.

"Something is going on here, but what?" I could only wonder for now, yet I have every intention of finding out. The older man finished up his breakfast and had coffee brought over to his table for his companions. They sat and spoke for a few minutes, oblivious of the two men who had just left while deep in their business talk. I snapped a few pictures of all of them together, then made like I was enjoying my meal as I listened in on what they were saying through my earbuds.

"John," one of the men called the elderly man. "That land belongs by law to the offspring of the thirty men who leased it and put it into a trust, doesn't it?"

"No, I am not sure that's the truth, and I think that I can make a good argument against it. You see, Indians weren't even considered citizens of the United States back then. So how could our government ever lease or put the property in a trust at that time for them? It wasn't until 1969 that our government called Indians citizens, as wild as that may sound. They had always been considered citizens of their tribes, and the Indian Nation, with laws all their own like a foreign government. So that hundred-year land trust could have been the biggest joke ever played on those thirty Indian men when they put down their five hundred dollars each to save that land for future generations. The government never intended to sell that land to anyone, nor did they yet we may find papers of trust just for appearance sake. So if no one shows up at the land trust hearing from the family of those thirty men, we'll be home free without a fight. If they come to insert their right to release or buy it, we'll call their bluff." The older man said as he stood up to put his coat on. He gave a glance in my direction, which I noticed out of the corner of my eye, sending chills running through my body like a speeding bullet.

Had he noticed my interest in him? I wondered, not turning my head to let on that I noticed him.

Once they walked out the door, I hurried and packed up my things to follow them. I wanted to get a look at their car and its license plate. I no sooner grabbed up my bag and turned around than someone ran into me spilling a boiling substance down my back. I lost my balance because of the force of the bump, tumbling over the chair in front of me and crashing to the floor, causing a loud noise. My sweatshirt had quickly soaked up the hot substance holding it against my skin, and I could feel my knees and hands react from the fall. I could only hope that I wasn't severely burnt. Being stunned, I had a tough time getting back to my feet. I noticed a hand extended in my direction and I grabbed onto it. I don't know if I was angrier or embarrassed, seeing that everyone in the restaurant now was looking at me. The waitress came over and did what she could to help, but there was little she could do.

"I am so sorry," said the young man who had helped me up and now stood looking back at me with puppy dog eyes. "Please, let me make it up to you," he added. Before I could answer, he spoke again. "You do live around here in the Village, don't you?" he asked.

"Yes," I replied, picking up my bag from the floor, as I turned to walk away, not answering his request.

He hurried to get in front of me before I could get to the door, almost tripping me up again.

"Let me take you out to dinner tonight at the Pier Restaurant. I hear it's one of the most famous places around here; it speaks very highly of in the tourist magazines. Have you ever been there?" he asked, stepping from in front of me and followed me out the door.

"No! No!" I said, just trying to end it all.

"I promise not to bore you if that's what you're worried about," he added.

"I am not worried about anything. I'm just not comfortable dining with strangers," I answered, to no avail.

"I am sorry, of course, where are my manners?" he whispered, now standing in front of me out in front of the Stain Cup with his hand extended again. "My name is Stu Baker."

"Well, Mr. Baker, thanks, but no thanks. I am much too busy for dinner tonight," I said, getting onto my bike and preparing to ride away.

"You'll have to eat dinner anyway; you might as well eat with someone who wants to eat with you," he called out while running after me like a puppy dog. "If you don't stop, I'll follow you home," he threatened.

Seconds later, I heard a noise and looked behind me. Mr. Baker had stumbled and ended up on the side of a curb in someone's freshly seeded lawn. I turned around and went back to see if I could be of help. All the while remembering the hot coffee that he had spilled down the back of my sweatshirt, which had turned to a wet sticky coldness, and the abrasions on my hands and knees, which were still very uncomfortable. I felt that it was only right to go to him and offer him a hand up.

"Yet had he fallen on purpose?" I wondered as I put my hand out to help him up. We both started laughing, for I was wet and cold, and he covered in wet horsepucky fertilizer.

"Do you believe in karma, and what goes around comes around?" he asked me. "If so, would you reconsider and have dinner with this wounded man?" he asked, grinning ear to ear and smelling like a barn.

"Well, maybe, okay, but it's only one dinner that's all. Are we in agreement?" I replied.

"Sure, sure, anything you say. Unless you change your mind again, sometime soon, I've heard I am an excellent dinner companion," he said, with a mischievous laugh.

"Oh, what have I gotten myself into?" I thought as I got back on my bike and rode away shaking my head in disbelief.

"Wait!" He yelled after me. "Where do you live?"

I turned my bike around and rode up by him again.

"Don't worry, Mr. Baker," I said, trying to stay calm. "I'll meet you at the restaurant at seven tonight—just see that you're not late!" I replied, not slowing down for fear of another one of his replies.

CHAPTER 4

Are You Kidding Me?

I had missed seeing in what direction the men from the restaurant had driven off because of that freak accident, so I wasn't able to get their license plate number or the make of the car; it makes my job a little bit harder but not impossible. So all I had was their pictures and a very short recorded conversation. "That's something," I thought, as I rode my bike back toward Miss Marple's. Once in her yard, I parked my bike next to the bottom steps of her back porch and hurried into the house with hopes of getting right on my computer.

"Sally, is that you, dear?" Miss Marple called out to me from the parlor.

"Yes! Yes, it is," I replied, wishing she hadn't been home.

"Please, can you spare a minute?" Miss Marple asked. "I need to speak to you before you go up to your room," she added, in what seemed to be a somewhat commanding tone.

I set my backpack down on the floor at the bottom of the stairs and moved swiftly into the parlor to see what she wanted.

"Hello, Miss Marple," I said as I entered the parlor. "How are you today?" I asked, only to make conversation.

"Please come over here and have a seat," she said, motioning at me to take the golden Queen Ann chair next to her.

"I am doing well," she replied in answer to my question, then added, "Did you get a chance to go for that early morning bike ride that you spoke of last night?"

"Yes, I did. Miss Marple, there's something that I saw today that almost blew my mind. It's the way the day started," I said without sitting down.

"What do you mean? Please, tell me everything," she said, sounding more than a little bit excited as she moved to the edge of her chair, as not to miss a word.

"It was the sunrise! Have you ever seen an early sunrise?" I asked her, with a renewed enthusiasm as I walked over and looked out the window to the lake.

"No!" she said, whimsically laughing back at me as though it was a silly question. "I am a city girl and have always been a bit of a night owl if you know what I mean," she replied.

"Miss Marple, I am not sure I can truly make you understand, then the splendor of what I saw this morning," I said, turning to look at her.

"Oh my, it was like a giant planet engulfed by flames that fell from heavens and almost touched the earth. The object was huge! It was of the deepest red-orange color that I'd ever seen in my life, with a glow that filled the sky with an unbelievable light. The light reflected off the top of the rippling waves of the water below, like streams of blood flowing inward from the horizon. Then right before my eyes that same object was sucked up and pulled back into the sky from the earth—only leaving a bright blue sky that now surrounded the sun, a look we often take for granted.

Miss Marple, this site sent a fusion of excitement into every cell in my body," I said, only pausing to catch my breath. "Miss Marple, it's a sight I shall never forget," I added.

"Wow! Sally, it seems I've missed out on a lot of things right outside my front door, a gift reserved for the young at heart, and the early morning risers," Miss Marple said with a smile. "So tell me about the rest of your day."

"Oh, the bike ride? Yes, that was a bit of a surprise, too," I replied.

"A surprise? Why, what happened?" Miss Marple inquired.

"Miss Marple, there were at least a hundred riders of all ages, the young children rode with their parents on one side of the road, while the single and faster riders all rode on the other side. I rode in with the faster riders down to the restaurant, then I cut out of the pack and parked my bike in front of the Stain Cup restaurant while the others continued up M119 north.

"Well, what did you think of the Stain Cup? Was it everything that I told it was?" she asked.

"Yes, the food was outstanding, and the coffee was piping hot, full of flavor and aroma, as you might be able to smell even now," I said teasingly.

"Yes, now that you mention it, I do smell a scent of coffee in the air," Miss Marple said, leaning forward again in her chair with the excitement of a mountain cat in sight of its prey. "Is that you I smell, dear?" she inquired.

"Yes! There was a six-foot cluck who wasn't watching where he was going. He ran right into me with a full cup of hot coffee, dumping it all down my back and knocking me to the floor," I said, turning around to show her the back of my wet coffee stained sweatshirt.

"Oh, my dear, are you all right?" she asked, getting to her feet. "You must run right up to your room and get out of those wet clothes," she insisted, with a voice full of compassion.

As I turned to go and do as she had instructed, she added, "I look forward to hearing more about your clucks, for I am sure there is still more to be said," she said, half laughing and requesting me to join her for tea later.

"Miss Marple, he is in no way my clucks," I retorted, then hurried off without giving her an answer about tea.

She probably took the answer to be yes since I didn't say no, I thought, grabbing my backpack off the floor at the bottom of the stairs and my feet hitting every other step on the way up. After entering my room, I quickly dumped my backpack out on the bed. I removed the thumb drive with a photo chip in it from my iPad and ran over to my computer and printer that sat on the desk. I placed it into the side of the machine and entered the program I wanted to run, then I went to shower. Ten minutes later, my photo chip had produced all the pictures that I had taken at the Stain Cup, and the script from the thumb drive was coming off the printer.

The script reminded me that they came from New York and that old man's a lawyer by the named of John. It was a long shot, but I googled lawyers by the name of John in New York City and only came up with five hundred.

"Are you kidding me?" I said aloud. "So what's my next step? Come on, you're a top investigative reporter."

Think! He's a lawyer that's interested in land trusts, so that may have something to do with separating him from some of the others. I googled land and estate lawyers; this brought up only fifty Johns in New York City. Then I asked Google, to show me business pictures of the fifty, and seconds later, they appeared.

"There he is, Sir John Feterly!" I said with excitement. He appears to come from a long line of English snobs, with a pedigree that goes back to the family of the Queen Elizabeth I of England. It also says here that he is a corporate, criminal, and international lawyer to the rich and famous.

"So tell me, Sir John, are you working for yourself here in the harbor or someone else? Why is a big city lawyer from New York interested in this harbor that doesn't even hold three hundred people at most?" I wondered aloud.

"Someone had mentioned at the Stain Cup, a land trust that was due to revert, if not extended within the next few days," I remembered.

So again, I used Google, typing in "land trust" in Emmet County. The screen immediately filled with land conservatories, trusts, and reserves. I clicked on land trust and scrolled down the page to the upcoming date of one that was put in the trust almost a hundred years ago. I clicked on the search key to bring up the story behind it.

It started out telling of thirty men of Indian descent that each put up five hundred dollars on a thousand-acre piece of land along the shoreline of Lake Michigan a hundred years ago. They did so to protect the property for future generations of their tribe. They believed that the laws would change by the time the land trust came due again. Wow, that's a lot of money though even in today's market. I read down the page further and found that if the laws did bend in the Indians favor, then descendants of these thirty men could for a small added price lengthen the trust and thereby prevent anyone from developing or disturbing the property for human consumption. I tried to find the names of the trust holders so I could find out if they had any descendants in the area but to no avail. I wonder where I would go to find out this information, without alerting others to what I was doing. Again, I scrolled down further near the bottom of the page where it said. "All interested parties should contact the Department of the Interior before June 13, 2016."

That's just a week from today, I thought, as my head filled up with so many questions that it started to hurt. *Were there any descendants around here that even knew about the land, and if so, where? Why would men from New York be interested in this piece of property?* I wondered. In the last paragraph of the page, it spoke of an inquiry made on the trust by a New York business firm owned by one Sir John Feterly.

There he is! I like it when a plan comes together, I thought, giving myself a verbal pat on the back.

I must share something about this with Miss Marple, for she has lived in these parts a long time and knows the history of the village.

She did mention wanting to have tea, so I hurried and dressed for my dinner with Mr. Baker, then stopped down on my way out to see Miss Marple in her parlor.

As I stepped into the parlor, Miss Marple's back was to me, and she was walking away to leave by another door.

"Miss Marple, please, may I have a few minutes of your time? I know it's late and you're punctual with dinner, but I must speak to you about something that happened today," I said, sounding a bit anxious.

Miss Marple stopped immediately and turned around to face me with a look of surprise across her face.

"Oh my! Oh my, what have you done to yourself? I feel so sorry for Stu Baker tonight, for he has no idea who he ran into," she said, retaking her chair while trying to catch her breath.

"Why do you say that?" I asked, a bit perplexed.

"How will that mere mortal man ever recognize you? Don't you remember being dressed in a pink sweat pantsuit, tennis shoes, a baseball cap, and a pair of fake black oval glasses? Now you stand here in front of me like someone right out of one of Disney's fairy tales. You look like a princess dressed in a pink chiffon dress that flows down to the tops of your knees with a white satin waistband tied around your tiny waist, then there's your satin covered heels to match. Not to mention that pretty neck of yours draped in pearls and tiny pearl earrings gracing your ears. All of this only adds to adorn the beautiful woman that you already are, with long blond hair and those baby-blue eyes. Yes, Sally, I would have to say—you clean up rather well," she said as we both chuckled.

"Miss Marple, do you think that this is too much for an apology dinner? After all, you must remember it's the Pier Restaurant he's taking me to, not McDonald's," I said.

"Yes, dear, of course, you are right, and I do understand. My only wish now is that I was able to see the look on Stu's face when he sees that it's you. I will be waiting on pins and needles to hear every juicy tidbit of what happens on your date," Miss Marple teased with a soft laugh.

"Miss Marple, this is not a date, not at all," I said sternly and then added quickly, "I will return before dark."

"Sally, Sally, Sally—I think, girl, you do protest too much, for only time will tell us what this night becomes," Miss Marple said as she chucked before leaving.

"Miss Marple, I didn't get a chance to tell you what is most urgent," I said, trying to keep her from leaving.

"Sorry, Sally, but other people are waiting on me in the dining room, so we'll have to pick this up later tonight. Enjoy your dinner with Mr. Baker, dear," she said, leaving me alone in her parlor.

CHAPTER 5

Meeting Cinderella

I left Miss Marple's parlor and headed out to my car with my clutch purse and lightweight summer shawl in hand, while all the time remembering what Miss Marple said about this being a date. That thought soon passed when I entered the parking lot of the Pier Restaurant. I was surprised to see so many people arriving all at the same time; I found a place to park some five rolls back. I stepped out of my car and picked up my shawl and purse before closing and locking the door.

The Pier Restaurant sat on the shoreline of Lake Michigan next to the yacht club; there was no room to doubt whose neighborhood we were dining in; for this was a place of the rich and famous.

I am sure that there are many secrets within the walls of this place, I thought as I approached the double glass front doors of the restaurant where I could see Mr. Baker looking out. When I entered the door, I was surprised that he didn't step forward to welcome me, for he was aware that I had never been here before. Even as other people entered and passed by me, he didn't seem to recognize me and continued watching out the window for my arrival. I opened my purse to take out my lace-trimmed hanky and walked over and purposely bumped into him, dropping my hanky at his feet. He did as any gentleman would do and picked it up and offered it back to me with a smile.

"Well, thank you, Mr. Baker, is our table ready yet?" I asked, smiling back at him.

That's when our eyes met, and we locked on to each other for the first time; for several seconds, Stu stood speechless and just stared at me.

"Wow! Please tell me, Sally, that it's you, or don't wake me from this dream," he said as he moved in closer and gave me a fake kiss on the cheek and pushed the hair over my left ear back to whisper in it. "I believe I've just met my Cinderella." With that, he slid his right arm into my left bent arm and nodded at the waitress to take us into the dining room area. She walked with us past a dozen table, to a table by the window with a marvelous view of Lake Michigan. Stu pulled out my chair and waited for me to sit before taking his seat, all the while smiling like a king, in all his glory.

"Did I tell you how beautiful you are tonight, Sally?" he asked me and then added, "I am led to believe that the lady that I met this morning didn't want to be noticed or stand out in a crowd. I will be very interested in finding out the story behind your sweats and glasses," he said with a smile while handing me one of the menus that the waitress had given him.

I took the menu and opened it as though I was interested in what it had to offer when all the while I was using it to block my face. I was dumbfounded. "How was I going to explain any part of my life to him without lying?" I could only speculate.

"Sally, I didn't get a chance to ask you where you live in the Village," Stu said.

"For the summer, I am living in the home of Miss Marple. She told me that you and your family are good friends of her," I replied in a soft voice.

"Miss Sara Marple?" he asked with surprise.

"Well, yes, is there another?" I responded, with one of Miss Marple's whimsical laughs.

"You're right, there will never be anyone like our Miss Marple. How is it that the two of you know each other?" Stu asked.

For a second, I was given a reprieve, while the waitress stepped up to take our order.

"Please, Stu, would you order for both of us? I am sure I'll enjoy anything you choose," I said with a smile. He did as I asked, as I sat back taking in every minute of his sureness with delight.

"You were telling me, Sally, how it was you came to meet Miss Marple," he said while sitting back in his chair and beaming from ear to ear with curiosity.

"I told her that I wanted to spend my summer here in the village for a little R&R, so she offered me a room in her home. We are both interested in writing and hope to work on something over the next few months," I replied.

"Please, now tell me something about yourself—which Miss Marple wouldn't know," I dared him, while trying to keep the questions off me by putting them back on him. It was one of the first lessons that we were taught in journalism class.

"Well, Sally," he whispered, "Miss Marple doesn't know that I am wearing my brand-new red boxer shorts with big white hearts all over them, just for you," he said, grinning like the cat that swallowed the canary.

I could feel my face turn red with embarrassment and wondered if this was his way of getting back at me for my surprising him in the entryway.

"I guess I deserve that answer from you, Stu. After all, I did dress to look my best just for you. Unfortunately, you won't have a chance to show off your new heart-covered boxers. It almost seems like a waste of money for you, doesn't it?" I asked, smiling back at him.

"I can see that we are going to be good friends after all, for we both have a quick wit about us, Sally," Stu replied with a broad smile.

My, is he ever handsome! I thought. Then I looked around the restaurant only to see that we had become the topic of conversation and glances by the other patrons.

This is something I would have to get used to if I was ever to get an invitation into their homes and to their parties. To think I almost missed out on this dinner by first saying no. "No!" wasn't a word Stu was used to hearing when asking a woman out to dinner. Why else would he have run after me on foot—we know it wasn't because of my appearance, I told myself silently.

The waiter was now at our table uncorking and pouring a taste of wine into Stu's wineglass for him to taste and for his approval; after Stu accepted the bottle, the waiter finished filling our glasses. I picked up my glass of wine and took a sip. It was a full-bodied wine with just a bit of tartness, an excellent wine for prime rib or just for sipping by candlelight.

"Sally," Stu started out saying, just as the waitress arrived at our table with a loaded tray; in seconds, she had dispersed the dishes about the table.

Then she turned and looked directly at Stu and said, as though I wasn't even sitting there, "Is there anything else I can get you, Mr. Baker?" she asked in a flirty voice.

"Stu, darling, could you please ask the waitress to bring me a glass of water with a slice of lemon? It's a drink that helps leave a good clean taste in your mouth," I said, winking at him playfully. He nodded as if to say, *I know where you're going with this.*

"Well, young lady, I believe you heard my lady's request. Would you see to it immediately?" Stu asked before the waitress walked away. Seconds later, she returned with my water and a much-improved attitude.

Stu and I found that we had a lot in common while we ate, and I finished up my meal by drinking from my water glass. Stu put a sizable tip out on the table, then he stood up and helped me slide my chair back, then helped me to my feet; not that I needed his help. But it was nice and an eyeful for the waitress that served us.

"Well, Sally, it pains me to see you go so early, even before the sun has had time to sit. I am fully aware that tonight was only an apology dinner, not a date. I can only hope that you'll allow me the honor of a real date soon," Stu said softly in my ear, and before I could give him my answer, another couple stepped up to him and wanted to talk.

"Hi, Stu, old boy, what are you up to these days?" His friend asked, with his right hand out and his left arm around the waist of the woman next to him.

Stu's hand went out almost automatically to shake that of his friend.

"Darling," Stu said while turning to me. "I would like to introduce you to Dan and Cathy Morhouse. They are visiting here from the great state of New York."

"Dan and Cathy, this is my dear friend Sally Crystal. She is Miss Marple's guest for the summer," he said.

"Well, that's great! You will be bringing her with you on Saturday night to dinner, won't you?" Mrs. Morhouse asked with a smile.

"I am not sure of that yet. I haven't had a chance to ask her. I guess we'll both have to wait to find out what the answer will be," Stu answered as we excused ourselves, as though we were in a hurry to leave. Stu walked me outside where the air had turned chilly. I put my shawl about my shoulders as he walked me to my car.

"This is a nice ride you have Sally, I've always loved the Mustangs. Well, what do you say, Sally, are we on for a dinner date at the Morhouses'?" Stu asked me.

"I'll think about it. What kind of dinner is it, a dress-up or casually dressed?" I asked.

"Oh, it's a backyard grilling affair. We all take a Saturday night throughout the summer. It is up to each of us what kind of dinner or party we have. You'll have to help me figure out what kind of affair we have," Stu replied. An answer that sounded like it had a double meaning.

"You do give a girl a lot to think about, don't you?" I said.

"I'll be calling you then tomorrow, Sally. I can hardly wait for your answer," he said teasingly before walking away; when I drove out of the parking lot, I was on cloud nine. I can hardly believe how our first dinner went; I couldn't have asked for anything better.

CHAPTER 6

Horrifying Darkness

I quickly pulled off my dress and slipped back into my jeans and sweatshirt before tying on my tennis shoes. I scooped up my long blond hair and put it into a ponytail, then grabbing up my iPhone, and made my way downstairs to find Miss Marple. I was full of excitement and could hardly wait to tell her everything about Stu's and my dinner together. It didn't take me long to find her, as she was still on the porch where I left her hours ago.

Had she been here all the while? I wondered. *Who knows? Probably not.*

Miss Marple was a people watcher, and there were many out now walking, biking, boating, and swimming enjoying this hot summer's night. Everyone loved Miss Marple as though she was a part of their family; they smiled and waved when passing—often stopping to chat for a while.

"Oh, there you are Miss Marple," I said, entering the porch. She turned around in her chair so she could see me before saying anything.

"Sally, I see you've had time to change—how did dinner with the prince go?" she asked as we both started laughing. "Did he recognize his Cinderella?"

"No, no, he didn't know at first, but the look on his face was priceless when he finally did," I said, then proceeded to fill her in on everything that had happened, even that out in the parking lot.

"Are you kidding me, Sally? You told him he would have to wait for your answer? Wasn't that a bit risky?" she asked me. "I mean, didn't you just tell me that you enjoyed yourself?"

"He's already called me since I returned here, and we are going to the Morhouses' outdoor barbecue on Saturday.

"Sally, before you went to get dressed for dinner, you said something about your breakfast at the Stain Cup, and you promised to tell me more. I've thought about the concern I heard in your voice—is there reason to worry, Sally? Please tell me what's got you alarmed, or should I say who?" she asked.

"I told you about the sunrise and the bike ride to the restaurant and my running into Stu, but there's more—much more. Miss Marple, while I was sitting at a table in the restaurant, a well-dressed elderly man walked in, then seconds later, a couple of men walked in and sat down with him, and they were packing heat. I could see their guns under their coats, but that's not all. I could hear what they were saying, but I can't make much sense of it. Miss Marple, you've spent a great deal of time over the years here in Black Hawk Harbor. Have you ever heard any stories about a hundred-year land trust and its connection to thirty Indian men or braves?" I paused, waiting for her reply.

"Well, let me see," she said, getting to her feet and walking about the porch trying to collect her thoughts as I waited.

"There was something years ago that I heard. I was never sure if it was real or just a fable. The story was of thirty educated braves that were schooled by our government as an experiment. They were the sons of chiefs, from throughout the Indian Nation, after the War of 1812. These braves were never considered citizens of the United States at that time. They were citizens of the Indian Nation, and their nation was in most parts driven onto reservations against their will.

"The story goes, if I remember right, the braves we speak of were from Black Hawk's tribe. Black Hawk was a great chief at one time, and his people lived along Lake Michigan and down into the Ohio Valley. These braves became men under the watchful eye of the United States government. They didn't have it easy by any meaning of the word. Matter of fact, out of the hundreds that came into the government program, fewer than a hundred lived to tell about it. When they closed out the program, they sent those that were left into the white man's schools—about fifty of them. The others, dead or alive, were never returned to their tribes. Many died in captivity of starvation or illness. The ones that lived were called the strongest and brightest of all the tribes. Thirty of those braves requested the United States government. They wanted to buy a strip of land along Lake Michigan. The government was so proud of how well their experiment had turned wild savages into civilized well-educated men that they considered the men's request. The thirty braves, in white men's clothes each, saved five hundred dollars apiece, and in those days that's a lot of money by anyone's standards. The laws of the United States at the time didn't allow noncitizens own land. So they couldn't buy the land, yet they were granted a hundred-year land trust, with the condition that it be treated as land put into a land conservatory. The land could never be developed by anyone. It had to remain untouched by human hands for the length and terms therein. Then after that—if there were any offspring or descendants of these thirty braves still alive, and our nation's laws were changed to include Indian ownership, they would be given the first rights to it.

"Sally, the land we're talking about is on the other side of the village along Lake Michigan—right over there, as far as your eyes can see and further yet," she said, pointing at the large mass of undeveloped land, with hundreds of miles of mix Hardwood, Pines, and Burch bark. Then she turned around to face me again.

"They say that there are some five hundred acres of prime property out there, and it's well worth in today market in the millions," Miss Marple added before sitting back down.

"Miss Marple, I believe I overheard some dangerous things at the café, concerning that land and those that still hold the trust. Is there any way we could find and warn those men that their lives could be in danger?" I asked, already knowing that these men I saw were up to no good, especially for anyone that stood in their way, for their boss wanted that land.

"Let me call a friend of mine. He will know all the facts. He belongs to one of the local tribes and is a lawyer," she said before leaving the porch.

While I waited for Miss Marple to return, many things crossed my mind. I realized that there were many things I couldn't share with her or her friend. When she read the piece in the paper by Joe Bumgardner that I'd be writing, I had to look surprised by it or blow my cover.

She returned and sat back down; then she informed me that her friend would stop over tomorrow afternoon to talk to us.

Before either of us could say another word the wind outside suddenly died down, and the lake became like glass. The colors of the sky reflected on the water below like a mirror, and everyone gathered at the edge of the water in disbelief. The sunset that was developing before our eyes was so beautiful that words could hardly describe it; for it looked like the window of heaven was opened and the colors were being poured out of it and across the sky. Then came a loud noise from off in the distance, a whining sound that grew louder in pitch as we all looked in the direction of the land preserve.

I looked at Miss Marple, about to ask her what she thought the sound was when a massive swarm of screeching blackbirds filled the sky from a grove of trees to the north several miles away. We both jumped to our feet and hurried out into the yard what a frightening sight was coming in our direction. It sounded like screams out of the pits of hell, as blackbirds seemed to fly in waves by the hundreds right into the glorious sunset and around the lake like they were planning to attack. Their wings stretched out, almost touching each other, blotting out all light and beauty in the sky, flying up from the marsh area known as the land conservatory. The frightening piercing sound of the birds' cry filled the air, sending parents running for cover with their children who were crying and screaming out in fear. You could hear doors and windows shutters slam shut, even though this was the hottest night of the summer and only nine thirty. All the beaches, streets, and boats were quickly emptied here in the harbor as everyone ran for safety.

We walked back in closing all doors and windows on the porch as we entered the entryway of the house. By the time we got into the house, the TV was on in the living room, and the news reporters were already talking about Black Hawk Harbor. No one could ever remember anything like this happening before. The talking heads could only surmise what caused it; it was almost harder listening to them than the birds. I believe it had something to do with that land trust and the strangers among us. The investigator's blood in me was flowing fast and hot, and I was starting to feel a bit closed in if you know what I mean. I wanted to be out there yet even in the dark. There was something or someone causing all this to happen, and I wanted to be the one to uncover it.

"Sally, I've got an idea. Would you please tell everyone in the house to join me in the kitchen?" Miss Marple asked me in passing, as she made her way into the kitchen as though she was in a hurry. I did as I was asked and alerted everyone. I believe tonight is the first time all of us who live in the house were all here at one time. As we entered the kitchen, Miss Marple was standing at the counter with silver dinnerware in her hands.

"Thank you all for coming. I thought it would be nice if we had a late potluck dinner tonight, seeing you're all here. I think it's time we all met each other instead of just passing in the doorways and hall," she said, looking around the room.

"Miss Marple, I don't know if I have anything to bring. Isn't a potluck a food-sharing meal? You know me, Mom—I'm the one that eats your leftovers," Young Kenny McCrery said. He's Miss Marple's nephew, who'd come to stay the summer. He did odd jobs around the house and yard to earn his keep.

"Well, Kenny, do you still have that jug of cranberry grape juice you took upstairs this morning from the pantry?" she asked him with a smile.

"Yes, Mom," he replied.

"Great, it's settled. That's what you will bring," she said, then she turned to the only couple in the room.

"So tell me, what would you two likes to bring?"

"Would bread and butter be enough? You've caught us a little off guard. You see we haven't done any shopping for the week and the cupboard is a little bare," Maxine replied. She and her husband, Toby Falkner, were elusive residents, to say the least. That was the rumor about the house anyway. Maybe this potluck would be more interesting than I first thought.

"Yes, excellent!" Miss Marple said, pleased.

"Now, Mr. Barkley, what say you?" she asked.

"Miss Marple, I picked up a watermelon today at the farmers' market. I could share it—it's a big one," Mr. Barkley replied with a smile.

"Fantastic! So far, so good. So, young lady, what would be your pleasure to share?" she asked while looking directly into my eyes.

"Let me see," I said, smiling back at her. "Let them eat cake!" I replied. "I bought a scrumptious double-layered chocolate cake yesterday, never knowing so many would be helping me eat it.

"Perfect, go run along now and gather up what you're to share, for I've made Swedish meatballs and rice and dinner are ready. I'll start setting the table," she said with a glow on her face. Just about that time, Ralph Barnet, a special friend of Miss Marple, came in the back door.

"Oh, Ralph, it sure is good to see you. Please stay and enjoy our potluck with us," she said while giving him a friendly hug.

"A potluck, Miss Marple—are those your famous meatballs I smell?" he asked, and then added, "Well, Mom, an old sailor like me is no stranger to cleanup, if you'll permit me to make it my part of the potluck, I mean. Sure, I'd love to stay, and it will give us some time to talk," he said in a more serious voice.

By the time we all gathered up our offerings and returned to the kitchen, Ralph and Miss Marple had the table set. Kenny went around it and poured everyone a glass of juice. The Frankers fixed a bread-and-butter plate with cheeses and homemade pickles on the side. Mr. Barkley and Ralph cut up the watermelon into serving piece and plated them before setting the plate on the table. I cut the cake in slices and placed each one on a dessert plate, then set them aside. Miss Marple put the large slow cooker pot in the middle of the long stretched out table, along with a big bowl of steamed rice.

"Okay then, I think we're ready. Would you all come and take a seat? Mr. Barkley, would you please offer a few words of thanks before we eat?" she asked.

"Yes, of course, Miss Marple."

"Dear lord, we thank you for this time to gather together in safety and for the gift of friendship. We ask you to bless this food and bless all those that shared in this meal, in the name of our Lord Jesus. Lord, we also ask you to bring peace back to our harbor tonight, Amen.

"While we eat, I'd like each of you to take a turn telling all of us something about yourselves and what brought you to the harbor this summer," Miss Marple said with a smile. "Let's start with the youngest and go the right around the table," she suggested.

"Most of you already know that I am Miss Marple's nephew. I've come here from England for the past few years during the summer. I keep the lawn, the garden, and the outside of the house looking good, while I enjoy my summer here in the harbor," Kenny said, then proceeded to eat.

"Honey, I'll do this," Maxine said while looking at her husband.

"Toby and I are undercover agents, kinda speaking. We work for a private firm and travel a lot. During the summer when we have the chance to relax, we call this place home." Without another word, Maxine stopped talking, leaving more questions than answers.

Mr. Barkley looked up from his plate and around the table, as though he were trying to collect his thoughts.

"I wish I could tell you that I had an exciting job or knew someone famous—but no such luck. I am a retired science teacher from New York with the great privilege of traveling at will. I first came here to the harbor some four years ago where I met Miss Marple at the card tables. We became close friends and have often traveled to different states and foreign countries together. There is no place like the harbor in the summertime," he said while he smiled over at Miss Marple. I almost believe I saw Miss Marple blushing when Mr. Barkley finished.

"Well, who's next then?" Miss Marple asked.

Ralph took a drink from his glass to clear his throat. He stood up from his chair and walked over to the window, where he stood for a second looking out, then turned around.

"I thank God I am here tonight with all of you. A few years ago, I was out to sea. I'm an old sea dog, and I have fought all kinds of hell therein. I can tell you, none of us has ever seen anything like this. What's going on out there isn't normal. These are not night birds. There is something very wrong in the atmosphere, and the birds are warning us. It's almost like a birds' war party. I fear there is death afoot," he said before returning to his chair to sit down.

Miss Marple and I glance at each other, when he said, "bird's war party and death afoot, for we too felt the same way.

"Sally, would you please do us the honor of telling us something about yourself, for those that haven't met you yet?" Miss Marple asked.

"Yes, of course," I said, standing to my feet. "My mother died when I was very young, and my father raised me. I went to college for journalism, for I enjoyed telling and writing stories. I am also a bit of a snoop—my father would say, I've been that way since birth I believe. Being a small-town snoop hasn't always been a good thing. Many times, a police officer would have to bring me home and often told my father to put a leash on me, for fear that I would get into something dangerous. None of my police buddies back home meant any malice by it. They were like my big brothers. I came here to the harbor to lay back and see if I could stay out of trouble, if you know what I mean, and possibly make some new friends," I said while glancing at everyone like they were the only ones in the room. Then I sat back down to finish up my meal before going up to my room to write out my first installment of the new column.

After saying good night to everyone for the third time, I started up the stairs, thinking no one would be sleeping tonight—I know I wouldn't.

The Night the Birds Cried

Joe Bumgarner

There was an incredible sunset last night in Black Hawk Harbor. Boaters stopped, water skiers fell over themselves, while swimmers hurried to the shoreline to sit and look in awe at the tremendous magnificent sight in the western sky. It was a masterpiece that only God himself could have created. These were heaven's colors, so vibrant and alive that touched the spirit of young and old alike. The sight in the sky was almost beyond words, but the reflection of it in on the still waters of Lake Michigan took my breath away.

That's when it happened! Time will never be able to change the minds, of those that witnessed it: To the north, where hundreds of acres of land were preserved in a trust, thought of as a nature preserve, came an ear-piercing squirreling sound—then waves of blackbirds, hundreds of them, rose to the sky and flew hellishly into the sunset. The birds made a 130-degree turn and headed right for us. We were all frozen in place for a second; then fear filled us all at once, and we scrambled to take cover.

Parents grabbed up their screaming, crying children and ran to their nearby homes. I can still remember the sounds of doors and wooden shutters being slammed shut. Boats sat empty at the pier, and the bikers moved quickly down the street to get away, while cars sped off.

The wings of the blackbirds almost seemed to touch, as they filled up the sky, blocking out any light therein; it became so dark that I could hardly see my hand before my face. These blackbirds were not night fliers; there was nothing ordinary about this. There was something wrong, very wrong, in Black Hawk Harbor. The birds flew in waves, by the thousands all night long, right up until sunrise, and then again, it became quiet and still.

CHAPTER 7

Sleepless Night

I got very little sleep because of the sound of bird wings snapping through the air, like a cracking whip all night long. The noise flowed unabated through the walls of the house. I put in my earplugs and covered my head with pillows to protect my ears from the piercing noise. At six thirty in the morning I got up, and within thirty minutes, the sound ceased.

I pulled on my jeans and a sweatshirt and secured my hair back in a ponytail before tucking it up under my cap and hurried out the door. I moved quickly down the back stairs and was soon mounting my bike and heading for Main Street into the village. It didn't seem like there was another living soul out yet on this beautiful sunny morning, but there was something different—the air was heavy, almost like an unseen force all around me.

The streets of the town were empty, no stores or restaurants were open yet; a ghostlike feeling came over me as I got to the far end of Main Street. I made a left at the stop sign and biked down the hill to the beach area and boat ramp. I stopped, got off my bike, and stepped behind a sizable flowering birch. The two men I was now looking at looked a lot like the Indians I had seen in the Stain Cup. They were running at full speed into the water to a small speedboat. Coming up fast behind them were three men with guns blazing. One of the men stuffed a large envelope into a garbage can on his way to the water to another waiting boat. Once they were all on boats, I moved swiftly to retrieve it from the garbage can; I was hoping it would be useful in some way. It must hold something important, or why would the man have put it there?

Maybe, he hoped to retrieve it later, I thought.

The envelope I now held was substantial and at least an inch thick and sealed and addressed to an investigating agency; the return address on it was a post office box in the village. I slid the envelope up under the back of my sweatshirt, then tucked one end of it under the waistband of my jeans to secure it.

Once back on my bike, I rode like the devil himself was at my heels. When I arrived back at Miss Marple's, I jumped off my bike and parked it near the back door before running in and up to my room. Once in my room, I pulled the envelope out and sat down to catch my breath. For the longest time, I just sat there and stared at the envelope, wondering if I should open it or not—knowing the law about opening another person's mail was the only thing that made me hesitate.

"Should I open it? What if it held something that would help us solve the mystery about the birds and the land trust? It's not like I'm a thief, and they did throw it in the garbage can—I simply took it to preserve the information for a later time. I'll find out who owns that post office box and return it—in a couple of days. I paced back and forth for several minutes before deciding what to do. I carefully pulled the flap of the envelope up, then reach my hand in and pulled out the top sheet of paper. I glanced down at it before reading:

> John, I am writing to you in answer to your request. The land you spoke of when we last met is due to be sold in just a little over a week from now. It's been locked up in a land trust for the past hundred years by a group of Indians.
>
> There may be Indian descendants on hand, and they may be given first rights to it. If there are no descendants, then it will be sold to the highest bidder. In any case, they will want millions for it, and I can't see how Indians will ever be able to afford it.

I have a list of the known descendants and their last known addresses.

John, would you like us to notify those on the list? We could offer them a small fraction of what their potion of the property might be worth; by doing that, they wouldn't have any reason to show up at the sale. I called your Chinese partner and sent them a copy of this letter; they intend to be at the sale. They'll be ready to open up the land and start drilling on the point of the harbor.

Oh no! Chinese, drilling on the point of the harbor? A piece of land that has never been disturbed by human hands. I must speak to someone about this and soon. Oh, God help me! Direct me to someone who can help save this land for future generations and for those who should have care over it, I prayed.

Many were up now in the house, so I decided to see if Miss Marple was one of them. I took the cover letter down with me to show her and get her opinion on what our next step should be. It was good to know that we are kindred spirits and can work together—somewhat.

I found her sitting in her parlor, enjoying her morning tea, in front of an open window.

"What did you think of last night, and the birds?" I asked her as I walked through the door, closing it behind me before I took a seat next to her.

"Child, yesterday afternoon, while I was having tea with the ladies, one of them spoke of some strangers in the harbor. She said her daughter worked in the village inn and witnessed these strangers carrying a concealed weapon—they were ordered to check them in at the desk when signing in. They went up to their room long enough to deposit the luggage and returned to retrieve their guns. She was behind the desk at that time and heard one of the men say that 'death was coming to the harbor.' My friend added that her daughter also spoke of the chill of fear that went through her on hearing these words. So when the birds took to the sky screaming their warning to us throughout the night, it brought back to mind what I had heard at tea. It also reminded me of another time when I listened to what I thought to be a folktale, but I am not so sure now," she said, taking a sip of her tea before continuing.

"It was my first summer here in the harbor some fifty years ago when an elderly gentleman told me something that seemed at the time so unbelievable that I took it with a scoop of salt. He said, 'The night the Indians were gathered up and put on reservations, all the blackbirds along the Great Lakes cried out for a whole week.' Like they did last night." Miss Marple paused again, as though in thought, while she took yet another drink of her tea.

"Miss Marple, I must show you something that I found just this morning while I was out riding my bike." I took the paper out of my pocket and handed it to her. She looked it over, reading slowly, then she looked at me before speaking.

"Where? How did you get this?" she asked, perplexed.

I explained to her the ride and all I had seen and how I had retrieved the papers.

"Miss Marple, what should we do? Should I go to the state police with this?" I asked.

"No, not quite yet. I would like to reach out first to the chief of the tribes in these parts. Remember, our afternoon meeting has already been set up with him. He may know the names of the heirs of that land, and where they are now? We'll see what he wants to do about it first," she replied.

I decided to wait until the meeting before showing any of the other papers; I wanted to hear what the chief had to say.

"Sally, I will call the chief again right now to confirm a lunch meeting. You will join us, won't you?" she asked getting to her feet.

"Yes, yes, of course!" I replied, wholeheartedly, while getting to my feet to return to my room. Noon could not come too soon for me. I had in some ways broken federal law—my stomach was in knots at what might happen.

Once back in my room, I sat down near my desk and reread the papers I still had from the envelope. The more I thought about it, the more I was sure that we were doing the right thing. Our laws and the tribal laws must both be taken into consideration when it comes to anything having to do with their member and land. I took all the papers I had and made two other copies of them, in case we were ordered to turn them all over to the tribe or the police. I believed that it was essential to retain the proof of what I found, should I ever be questioned about them. I took my copies and quickly filed them away. Set the tribal print to the side and put the original back into the envelope and resealed it.

The phone rang.

"Hello," I said on answering it.

"Sally, Mr. Korn here. We received the first installment of your column. Very good! I think we'll do very well with the challenge. This will go into the paper today. I've also seen the other column. It is good but could never hold a candle to yours. 'The night of the birds' in the harbor will stir up our readers for sure. I know it sounds a bit callous of me, seeing that there might be real trouble there. You must remember, Sally, we are first a newspaper, and you are our eyes and ears. Having the news folded into a real story of interest makes it even better, so keep up the decent work. Bye for now," he said before hanging up.

Oh my! I hope I haven't stepped over the line where it comes to ethics and the paper, I thought.

I set my alarm then laid back down to sleep until a knocking at my door woke me up about eleven.

"Sally, Kenny here—Miss Marple wanted me to tell you that the lunch guest was here."

"Okay. Thanks, Kenny, tell her I'll be right down," I replied.

CHAPTER 8

Dead Men at the Water's Edge

Miss Marple and her guest were sitting in her parlor.

"Oh, Sally! Please come in honey," she said while waving her hand directing me to sit near her. "Let me introduce Mike to you. He is a lawyer and the head of Indian affairs in these parts. His grandfather was a well-known chief, right here in Petoskey, Michigan. Please forgive us for not waiting, but I felt it was urgent to get started as soon as possible. He told me that he does know the descendants of the braves who leased the land. Please, Mike, tell Sally what you reviled to me, just moments ago," Miss Marple asked, then she sat back in her chair to listen again.

"Hello, Sally, it's nice to meet you. I am sorry it has to be under these conditions, though. Miss Marple speaks so highly of you. I have found over these many years that she is a good judge of character," he said with a smile while shaking my hand.

"Now, where were we? Oh yes, about the birds last night. In the Indian Nation, we believe profoundly in the spirits of our forefathers being able to connect with us through nature, be it the birds, bears, fish, or even the weather. So when the birds took to the air at night, when they are day fliers, we all knew what it meant. Birds represent the land and the air, where the bear represents financial affairs, and the fish in water when there is plenty or not enough. The great beaver spirit warns us about home and our country or nation's disasters.

"We've been preparing our people to what this land lease means for all of us. It was no fluke for the young braves to do what they did a hundred years ago, and they didn't do it alone. No Indians at that time could have come up with that kind of money on their own.

"There was a large group of well-educated pioneers who also wanted the land preserved. They knew at that time what the laws said on Indian land ownership. They encouraged the United States government to make it a hundred-year lease—that way making it necessary to revisit this issue at another time. They believed that laws would change as men evolved, thereby making it possible for the Indians to keep a piece of their homeland. Those men wrote of their beliefs in the Indian spirit and their connection with the land. We have those letters in our archives and will be showing them at the time of the sale.

"The men who want this land think they're only dealing with those thirty Indian descendants. They will be in for the shock of their lives when they see us as a nation stand up for the land. We own and operate some of the most profitable casinos and can afford to buy the land now." He stopped long enough for me to get a word in.

"Mike, I came by some papers this morning while I was out for a bike ride that you may find interesting," I said while reaching to the back pocket of my jeans. I pulled out a couple of the pages that I had copied and handed them to him and Miss Marple, whose eyes opened wide, almost in disbelief, for we had promised in not so many words to share everything, with each other first.

Mike looked over the pages quietly before reading them out loud:

> John, I was able to reach the Chinese. They wanted me to tell you that they will have armed men at the sale. They have no plans of losing that land to anyone else; if they do, someone will suffer the consequences on the spot. You'd better have all the papers ready to finalize the sale. The Chinese intend to start excavating the land on Harbor Point that very day.

"Chinese, on Indian land in Michigan? I don't think so!" Mike said. "May I take these papers with me?" he asked, looking into my eyes.

"They're yours, to do with as you wish. Just keep my name out of it, okay? That's all I ask."

"Don't worry, Sally, your name will never come up, I promise. Thanks for calling me, Miss Marple: you do understand why I can't stay for lunch now. Within seven days, this will all be over. I can promise you no Chinese will be excavating on our land," Mike said, standing to his feet. No more had he finished speaking than Kenny ran in and told us that two men were found dead at the water's edge.

"Mike, I saw two men running away from men with guns this morning. One of the armed men threw those papers into a garbage can, and I retrieved them. The two men running away got on a small boat and sped away. Then the other men got on a larger speedboat and went out after them. These could be those first two men, now dead."

"Miss Marple, remember the two men I told you ran out of the Stain Cup yesterday? I believe that these two are the same ones. They seemed afraid of the gentleman and his companions. I am also afraid, Mike, that the dead men are also friends of yours," I said.

"Why would you say that Sally?" he asked.

"I believe, I'm not sure, but I think they were Indian," I replied.

Mike's eyes widened with deep concern, then he turned to Miss Marple and without another word gave her a quick hug and ran off. There was a short pause of silence, as though Miss Marple was deep in thought.

"Sally dear, while we wait to hear back from Mike, might I get you to do something for me?" she asked.

"Sure, anything," I replied.

"Good then, please take this postcard over to the post office and retrieve the package that's there. I'll call the postmaster and tell him you are on your way," Miss Marple added before hurrying off to make the call.

I quickly did as I was asked after running up to my room to retrieve the other envelope.

The ride on my bike in the sunshine helped clean the cobwebs out of my brain for a brief time, and the warmth of the sun on my face felt great. As I entered the door of the post office, I noticed Dan Morhouse unlocking one of the mailboxes and retrieving his mail. A lot of the summer people picked up their mail here on a daily base. I first slipped the large envelope into the mail slot provided for it and hurried over to a short line of people that were waiting for their turn to speak to Hank the postmaster at the window.

"Well, if it isn't Sally Crystal. It was good meeting you the other night. Can I tell Sue that you and Stu Baker will be coming to our cookout on Saturday night?" Dan asked me while leaving the post office.

I just nodded in response to his question, as he continued out the door. I felt a bit embarrassed as others looked on. They didn't know me from Adam, but they all knew Stu Baker, the most handsome and richest single man in the harbor. Being last in line gave me plenty of time to introduce myself and meet all the others, some of whom I'll probably see again on Saturday night. I finally got to the window and gave the postcard to Hank. While he went to retrieve the package, I looked around to find out where the mailbox was that coincide with the address on the envelope. I found it and couldn't believe my eyes, for Dan Morhouse had just unlocked it and took his mail out of that same mailbox. It is the address on the large envelope that I'd found, and it was to John, with no last name—just John. That elderly gentleman that I had seen at the restaurant and looked up on the computer by using his photo was John Feterly. Could Dan be in cahoots with that man? They are both from New York, and they're both lawyers, so why not? It didn't make sense. Why would someone who loves this harbor do anything to destroy it, thereby ruining his relationship with all his friends here. Some of these families are close, and they'd been coming here for years.

Hank came back to the window and handed me the package covered with stamps for Miss Marple.

"It's beautiful, isn't it?" I asked, sounding a bit amused by all the stamps.

"Yes, it is—it came from England," he replied.

I had never meant my remark to sound like a question.

"Thanks, Hank, I'll see she gets it right away. Oh, by the way, do we have a John Feterly in the harbor? The only reason I ask is that I thought I saw him the other morning at the Stain Cup. We seem to have a lot of New York lawyers here this year, don't we?" I asked, as though wondering out loud.

"No, Sally, I don't recollect hearing about anyone by that name in these parts, maybe he's visiting friends here. After all, you live with Miss Marple, and I had never heard your name before today. So it is possible, I suppose, that you saw your friend here. Sally, if anyone is to ask—do I know you or not? We are a private community here and don't give out information to others, right? Matter of fact, we don't even give it out to each other very often, if you know what I mean." Then Hank, the friendly mail person, turned and went about his business.

I tied the package into the basket of my bike and started back to Miss Marple. I went down the hill to ride along the edge of the lake in hopes of finding out what the police knew. There were still a lot of people by the water and police tape up everywhere. Why so many police? Had they found something else? I rode closer in hopes of hearing something.

"Sally, what brings you down here today?" I heard a male's voice behind me ask.

"Mr. Korn, I should be asking you that," I replied, now looking into his face.

"Miss Crystal, you do know I am the owner of the local paper, one that's read all over the world."

"Yes, I've heard your name a few times since I've been in this area, but you still didn't answer my question. What brings you to the harbor?"

"Girl, you did hear about the bodies that they found here on the shore? One of the men is dead, and the other hangs on by a thread. What's going on here?" he asked, looking a little perplexed.

I whispered, "Mr. Bumgardner will be writing to you soon. I only ask that you trust me to do my job." I raised my voice a little louder. "You know, newspaper people are not welcome here in our harbor. So it won't hurt your feelings if I ask you to leave now," I said, meaning every word of it.

I couldn't take the chance of him blowing my cover. *What could have he been thinking anyway by coming here? If I am his eyes and ears, what more could he need?* I wondered.

I hurried back to the house and gave Miss Marple her package before running upstairs.

CHAPTER 9

Danger Looming about Us

Once back in my room, I hurried over to the desk and pulled out the chair to sit down in front of my computer. I was out of breath and a little light-headed. Time was running out, and people were showing up dead in the harbor. Our need to know more about the underworld's plan for our small port was paramount to our survival.

I unlocked my file drawer and pulled out the pages that I had copied from the envelope I'd found. More questions were swarming about my brain than an hour ago. I was hopeful that I could see some of the answers in these writings.

The first page I grabbed onto was the letter to John:

"John, here at the New York office need to know how you want us to continue with the list we have on the Indian descendants. Please reply quickly, as our time is running out to eliminate them. It is vital that there are no connections to these men and the land. The laws in the United States have changed, and these men could purchase the land in question outright. There is a lot at stake; our very lives could be at risk if this deal doesn't proceed as planned. Get in contact with us through our other agent there in the harbor and remain incognito. If I don't hear from you in twenty-four hours, I'll remove our problems for good. Our foreign friends from China will meet with you at the 'Harbor Point Inn,' using your code name. Be careful, the room and phones could be bugged, take nothing for granted. In just a few days this will all be over, and we'll be out of there." The letter ended.

"John Feterly is staying at the inn, and Dan Morhouse is a lawyer from New York as well, and it was his address the envelope that I deposited at the post office," I wondered.

I will be feeding more than my face tonight at that cookout, I thought.

I must write Joe Bumgardner's column now and get it out to Mr. Korn.

Land Preserve

Joe Bumgardner

We have gone from "Warring Birds" in the harbor to dead bodies washing up on the shore. That brings us to today's column and the dangers that loom about us. As I told you before, there is a piece of land that was set aside a hundred years ago in a land trust. That trust comes into play in a week, and some men want it, other than those who now hold it. These other people I speak of are ruthless, having no thought for the land or the people that live on or around it.

These men desire that no one be around to protest their take over. They are willing to go so far as to bodily get rid of anyone who would come against them. Yes, this means death to any of the descendants who may plan to carry out their grandfather's wishes for the land by restoring the land trust, thereby preserving the area for all. The Indian Nation doesn't want to own all this land for their personal use; it was the Great Spirit who put it in the minds of a few to protect it. They are long since gone, but we are here—we must show up in numbers to stop any sale of this land.

I have received some reliable information that there are men here from New York in the harbor. These men work for the Chinese underworld who want to destroy the beauty of our land for their gain. I also believe that the birds were the alarm system—used by the spirits to warn us. If you think you were scared the other night, what are you feeling now? Only we can save the harbor!

I hurried and e-mailed my column over to the editor for tomorrow's publication of the *News Review*. Then I quickly put the pages that I had been reading back in my desk drawer and locked it, then ran downstairs to talk to Miss Marple. It was tea time, so if Miss Marple were home, she would be in her Parlor or on the plantation-style porch; I checked out the porch first.

"Oh, Miss Marple, there you are," I said before noticing what she was doing. She had the *News Review* from yesterday pulled apart all around her chair, and she was reading Joe Bumgardner's column out loud. I took a deep breath and blew it out before I got near her.

"*Sally, have you read the column of this new journalist who writes for our paper?* He seems to know a lot about the comings and goings around here. I for one find that a little alarming, for we're a very private community here for a reason. I am going to have to keep my eye on this column and this Mr. Bumgardner. The paper also has another writer doing a sports column, but he has written different columns there before, so I know something of him. His sports column is a bit dry for me, and I labor to read it. Mr. Bumgardner sends chills through my body and makes me question my very surroundings," Miss Marple said while handing me the part of the paper in her hands. I reached out to receive it and proceeded reading it out loud as though reading it for the first time.

"Wow! The way he describes the other night and the birds makes it sounds like he was right here," she said.

"Maybe he was," I said, looking at her. "Miss Marple, you must admit that there are a lot of strangers here in the harbor. I'll listen for his name when I go to the Stain Cup in the morning. Maybe there I can pick up something about him. We are going to the Morhouse cookout on Saturday. Are you going, Miss Marple?"

"Oh yes, it's one of the high points of my summer. I wouldn't miss it. I am so glad that you decided to go with Stu. We will for sure find out something there about the oddities going on around here," Miss Marple said with confidence and a smile.

"Miss Marple, did you hear anything back from your friend Mike with Indian affairs?" I asked.

"Sally, he told me that the sale of the land takes place on Wednesday, and that's all the information has been given to the Indian Nation and the local police departments, for the man found dead on the shoreline here in the harbor was an Indian and a descendant of those on the land trust." Miss Marple paused, with concerned eyes. My phone rang and broke the stillness as its music filled the air. I quickly removed it from my pocket and opened it up to answer it, while stepping aside, so as not to bother Miss Marple with the noise of my conversation.

CHAPTER 10

A Kidnapping in Plain Sight

I quickly moved from the parlor to the white rattan chair on the porch to answer my phone; I could see by the caller ID that it was Stu.

"Stu, I was hoping it was you—it's good hearing your voice," I said, trying to hold back on the uncontrollable excitement now running through my body.

"Sally, it is good hearing your voice, too. It seems like a week since we last spoke, but it's only been a few hours," Stu said, then paused.

"Yes, I know what you mean. I feel the same way," I said, almost giggling like some schoolgirl. "Tonight is the cookout. What time should I be ready?" I asked.

"Sally, I was kind of hoping to start our date a little bit earlier, say noon, if you don't mind. There is a summer luncheon at the yacht club. Would you be so kind as to accompany me to it so that I can introduce you to some of my friends and family before the cookout tonight?" Stu asked.

"That's a bit of short notice, wouldn't you say? After all, Stu, it's already 12:30 a.m., and you want me to be ready by one? I can tell you haven't been around women very much. For it is written that we're the ones that take the longest to get ready for anything. How do people dress for lunch down at the club?" I asked, then paused.

"I am sorry about the shortness of time—we can be a little late. Any summer day wear would be fine, within reason of course," he replied cheerfully.

"All right then, I'll run and get ready—see you in twenty minutes," I replied before hanging up.

I hurried into Miss Marple's parlor to let her know about the call and my lunch date with Stu. She gave me one of her mischievous grins and waved me on my way.

This could be another door opening for me, I thought as I ran upstairs to my room to change. I got out of my jeans and sweatshirt and into a pink polo pullover top and white walking shorts and sandals. I put on a pair of tiny white flowered earrings and a necklace that matched. The necklace did double duty, for it held a small chip that was a camera and voice recorder. I didn't have any idea who I would meet today, but I had to be prepared for whatever happened. You learn that early on in this kind of work; after all, I am an undercover report no matter whose girlfriend I may or may not be.

I pulled my long blond hair back into a low-hanging ponytail and clipped it in place with a gold clasp before putting on my makeup. Miss Marple called up from the bottom of the stairs.

"Sally dear, Stu is here for you," she said with an air of excitement in her voice.

I grabbed my clutch purse off the bed and ran down the stairs, coming to a full stop at the bottom to catch my breath.

Wait a minute! I thought. *No woman should ever show a man that he has that kind of control over her at any time.* So I slowed my pace down.

I approached Miss Marple in the hallway and thanked her before opening the screen door to step out and down the steps. Stu was waiting at the side of his car, looking handsome in his white shoes and slacks and a pink and white-striped tailored yachting shirt, holding my door open for me. I smiled at him and picked up my pace a bit. Once in the car sitting comfortably, Stu closed the door and hurried around to the other side and got in beside me.

"Wow, girl! You look great—if you don't mind me saying," he said, with a grin across his face and sparkles like diamonds in his eyes.

"Thanks, you don't look too bad yourself. I have a feeling that's not the first time you used that line," I said while looking down to buckle up my seat belt.

"You're wrong, Sally. I am not a charmer by trade, if you know what I mean. There have only been two women in my life who have made me feel this way, and neither of them was a family member. I can't explain why you have such a magical pull on me, but I like it," Stu said, starting the car.

"Please forgive me, Stu, I never meant to make it sound that you weren't sincere. It's not often I get complimented for just changing my clothes," I replied, half laughing.

"That's one of the reasons I like you so much. You're quick-witted and a joy to be with," he added.

This time I didn't reply but received his words gracefully as we drove to the club, some four blocks away from Miss Marple's. The cars in the parking lot could almost pay off our national debt—not to mention the yachts in the harbor, and there were a lot of them. These were some of the wealthiest people in the United States or around the world. I can tell you, this small-town girl was feeling a little out of place, for sure.

Stu brought the car to a stop in his own parking space at the club and quickly got out, losing no time getting to my door and opening it. I unbuckled my seat belt and grabbed my clutch off the seat beside me before getting out. Stu opened my door and reached out his hand to help me stand up, then closed the door behind me. It was just a couple of step, and we were at the opened front door to the club—part of me wanted to go in, while the other part of me wanted to run away. I investigated Stu's smiling face and stepped over the threshold; there was no turning back—it was now or never.

Two beautiful young blonds approached us in hopes one of them would be picked by Stu to see us to our table. I don't believe the girls even saw me at his side as they shamelessly fawned over him.

"Sorry, girls, I am taken," he said, looking into my eyes with a smile. "And furthermore, I can still remember where my table is, so no help is needed," he said with authority. The girls could not have misunderstood what he was saying as they stepped aside and let us pass.

We walked from the foyer through an archway that led us into an executive dining room the size of a ballroom. The first thing my eyes saw was the massive window wall at the other end of the room where your eyes could see the full harbor and its pristine blue waters, a really breathtaking sight.

As we walked through, Stu nodded at many we passed by, yet didn't stop until we came to a table where blue-eyed beauty sat. Stu let loose of my hand and made his way over to her. He took her hands and helped her to her feet, glanced into eyes, and gave her a long hug and kiss before speaking a word.

While he was busy with that, I noticed the man to the right of her. He was the elderly gentleman that I had first seen in the Stain Cup, the man named Sir John Feterly, and down at the other end of the table were two of his cronies. They didn't seem very comfortable in these surroundings, nor were they dressed like those around them, making them stand out like sore thumbs. One of the men saw me eyeing them and looked me straight in the eyes. I quickly looked at Stu and grabbed onto his hand again.

"Aunt Kitty, this is a pleasant surprise. I wasn't aware that you were planning to come this year. I thought you had planned to visit Europe instead. Nevertheless, here you are, and I am thrilled to see you. Oh! I am so sorry, where are my manners? Sally, please forgive me," Stu said, looking at me, then turned his eyes back to his Aunt Kitty. "Aunt Kitty, this is my friend Sally Crystal, she lives at Miss Marple's," Stu added. I tried not to let my discomfort show; for now, some people knew more than they should, and this could endanger all my plans as well as Miss Marple's life.

"Sally, this is my Aunt Kitty Karel, she lives in New York," he said, stepping aside so his aunt could shake my hand.

"This is a real honor for me to meet you Mrs. Karel," I said, looking into her face.

"Oh, child! Please call me Kitty, all my friends do," she said, pulling me in with a fake smile and hug—why not, she had never met me before. I am sure I was not the first woman her nephew had introduced to her.

Kitty is a petite woman who freely displayed her wealth about her neck and ears, as well as the diamonds, rubies, and pearl rings on her fingers.

"We'll see the two of you later at the Morhouses' cookout, won't we?" she asked, as though it was an afterthought, as she turned her attention back to those with her. I investigated Stu's face—he would never have been a good poker player, for it showed what he was thinking.

"Why had she flicked us off like that?" I wondered, as Stu and I walked across the room to take our seats at the table set aside for him and his guest. It was near the window with a great harbor view. Stu had become unusually quiet, and I tried not to notice the change in his demeanor. A waitress handed us a special menu for the day, promising to return soon to take our order, then she hurried off to deliver a large tray of food to another table.

"Stu, is there something wrong?" I asked, breaking the silence.

"No, Sally," he replied, turning his face to the right, as though he were watching something out the window.

"What could be on his mind that would cause this kind of a change?" I wondered. I reached my hand over to touch his on the table. He responded by turning his eyes back to me with a smile.

"Sally, I can't put my finger on it, but something tells me that things aren't as they seem over at my aunt's table. There is something very wrong about that situation," Stu said, then paused and glanced in her direction.

"Wrong! What do you mean, Stu?" I asked, in hopes of keeping his attention on us.

"My aunt doesn't seem to be herself. She would have never acted like that. She would have asked us to sit with her instead of blowing us off. Sally, I am worried, for she told me that she just arrived today. I swear she must have a double. I saw someone who looks just like her two days ago here in the village. I almost stopped my car to speak to her, but she wasn't alone. You see those two men at the other end of her table, the rough looking ones?" he asked.

"Yes, I noticed them right away. They seem thrilled to be here," I replied.

"Sally, I must find out more about them. My aunt called that man next to her a friend—but is he?" Stu said more as a question than a statement.

I so wanted to tell him what I knew, but I couldn't. I would surely be risking my cover and our friendship doing so. I would have to sit still and let this play out on its own. Stu pulled his phone out and made a call to the state police department where one of his best friends worked.

"Hello! Stu Baker here—I would like to speak to Bill Sterling, is he there?" Stu asked and then paused while they were getting Bill to the phone.

"Buddy, what's up?" Bill asked. Stu lowered his voice to a whisper: "I need a big favor, and I need it done right away, like ASAP. I need you to go by my aunt Kitty's vacation house and talk to anyone that's there. You know Connie well, don't you? My aunts at the club right now with some questionable characters. Believe me when I tell you things don't look so good. You know me well, Bill, I am not one to overdramatize things, and very seldom do I go off." Stu stopped, as though taking a breath. Stu sat listening to Bill's reply and then hung up his phone and looked over at me with a smile seeming more relaxed.

"There we go, Bill is on it, and we should know soon." He opened his menu, and I followed his cue. I noticed even the simplest salads ran twenty-five dollars or more. The meat dishes started at one hundred dollars if it was a steak burger with a side order of greens and a drink or two. Wow! Lunch here could easily cost you one-seventy-five to two hundred dollars. I always thought that lunch was supposed to be the cheapest meal of the day. I could buy most of the food offered here at a tenth of the price that they pay here. What was the saying? "A fool and his money are soon parted."

"Well, Sally, what will you have, dear?" Stu asked.

"A small salad I think, with a cup of green tea and a wedge of lemon," I replied. "For we'll be eating again in a few hours," I added before he could question my lunch choice.

"Very well then, I, too, shall feast on a house salad and a brew," he said, handing off the menus to the waitress.

It wasn't even five minutes before the waitress was back with our salads and drinks; then she was off again.

"Tell me Stu, who is Kitty Karel? Oh, I know, she's your aunt—but how?"

CHAPTER 11

Stop and Desist

For me to honestly tell you about Kitty, I first must say to you about her husband.

Kurt Karel was one of two sons born to Chris and Martha Karel from New York State. They lived on a small farm barely getting by, before Chris died of the fever. Martha went on to raise Kurt who was eight and his older brother.

Martha ran the farm the best she could and did sewing, cleaning, and other odd jobs to get by. Sundays were set aside for her boys and God. She'd take her boys on long hikes with a picnic lunch up to the top of Lookout Mountain. The hikes sometime took hours, so they had to get a very early start. Once there they would stay for hours watching ships on the Atlantic with binoculars going about their business. It's at these times Martha would drop the seeds of dreams into her son's imagination, hoping that one day they too could be on one of those great ships at sea. She'd tell them stories full of adventure with mind-moving action that kept them hanging onto her every word. Before the day's light was gone, they would start the journey back down the mountain to home.

Both of her boys entered the Navy after high school. Kurt Karel became a young handsome Navy commander, who young ladies swooned over. One summer afternoon Kurt was summoned to the fleet office of Admiral Hudson in Washington, DC. It was there he met Miss Kitty Hudson, the twenty-one-year-old blond-haired beauty and youngest daughter of the admiral, who had just happened to pop in on her father after her lunch for a short visit. Because of her father's work, he wasn't always around for her to see regularly, so she took advantage of every opportunity.

"Commander Karel, I'd like to introduce you to my daughter Kitty," the admiral said as Kitty and Kurt passed in the doorway. "Sorry, dear, but I must get back to work now. I'll see you later at home," he added, kissing her on the forehead.

No sooner had she left than the young commander found out why he was summoned.

"Commander, you will be accompanying me on my last voyage," the admiral said.

"Sir, you're last?" the young commander replied in a puzzled tone.

"Yes, and you will be one of three men tested for a move up in rank; we leave in three days. I will be expecting to see you at my home for dinner tonight. The other two men will also be joining us. Any questions you have for me I will answer at that time," the admiral said then turned his attention promptly to other things. The commander took the cue and showed himself out.

It was that very night at dinner that Kurt and Kitty realized that there was a spark of interest between them. After that night, she wrote to him every day for three weeks while he was out at sea with her father. Heartbreak hit homecoming week when Admiral Hudson had a heart attack and died before making it to shore. Kurt did his best to console Miss Kitty after her father's death, and gradually they fell deeply in love. After they were married, they were informed by Kitty's doctor that she would never be able to have children because of a childhood illness that lifts her with a heart murmur. Kitty didn't believe that she would be strong enough to raise children if something should happen to her husband.

She knew that Kurt had two loves in his life, his wife, and the sea, and she would never ask him to give up either one of them. When possible, she would travel to meet him in each port where he would be able to stop for a few days for R&R. When Kurt made admiral, he gave his wife all the credit for it, and she was thrilled by the honor they shared.

"Sally, Kurt died three years ago, only six months after he retired. These three years have been the hardest years of Kitty's life. I know all of this is true because Admiral Hudson was my grandfather, and my mother was Kitty's older sister. After mom died, Aunt Kitty stepped in and became like a second mother to me. Now I sit here wondering why those men are with her," Stu said, glancing over at her again.

Stu's phone rang before I could say a word.

"Hello. Yes, Bill. What? No, I won't please hurry." Stu took a deep breath, then looked into my eyes.

"Sally, Aunt Kitty's maid—oh, I can hardly believe what I am about to say. My aunt is being held against her will in plain sight. There are men in New York holding her sister's daughter and granddaughter against their will. Those men sitting with her over there need Aunt Kitty to provide them a look of credibility for an upcoming land deal. Her name in these parts is better than gold. If it seems she is standing behind these men, very few will question them. That's what Bill just told me. Sally, what the hell does that mean?" Stu asked me, while looking very confused.

"Stu, there is a piece of land that was put in a hundred-year trust by a handful of Indians. The sale of that land takes place this Wednesday afternoon," I replied.

"Sally, how did you come by that information?" Stu asked.

"Remember the day we met at the Stain Cup?" I asked.

"I sure do," he said, grinning.

"Well, I saw those men in there. They left just before you arrived. I overheard them talking about the land sale. Then the morning after the birds, Miss Marple called the head of Indian affairs, and he confirmed what I had heard. That land is right across the harbor over there," I said, pointing northeast toward the land. "Stu, have you heard about the man they found dead on the harbor shoreline? He was one of the Indians I also saw that morning in the Stain Cup. He and his friend seemed to run out in fear when those men walked into the restaurant and sat with an older gentleman. Stu, these men are not kidding when they threaten death. They mean it," I paused.

"Oh! Here comes Bill now and he isn't wearing his uniform, good. Aunt Kitty knows Bill, so she'll know that we have some idea of her situation that should give her some comfort. What are we to do?" Stu asked. "My aunt is in terrible trouble, and so are her niece's."

"The FBI has been notified and is currently searching for the two missing females. We must play the cards we dealt until we have her relatives tucked away safely, then we'll move in on those that are holding her against her will. I am now going to walk over to her table and talk to her, as a friend. The two of you go about your lunch like everything's all right. I'll call you as soon as any news comes from the FBI," Bill said, getting up to his feet to walk over to Kitty's table. Kitty stood up to give Bill a friendly hug. I think I saw him whisper something in her ear. Whatever he said made her smile over at us and then turned her attention back to him. He didn't sit down after their encounter but hurried off. We soon finished up our lunch and decided not to stay for all the announcements on other club business. We stopped by Kitty's table on our way out so that Stu could hug her again, then he said, "Aunt Kitty, we will be seeing you at the Morhouses' cookout, bring your friends, everyone is welcome," Stu said, giving her a quick peck on the cheek. She smiled in reply.

"Wow!" I whispered to myself as I sat down in the car seat, while Stu hurried around the car to get in his side.

"Sally, I must drop you back off at Miss Marple's. I'll return for you in about four hours. There's something I have to do—it can't wait," Stu said, a bit perplexed.

"That's fine, Stu. I, too, have a few things I'd like to do too before dinner," I replied.

Stu pulled up in front of the house, and before he could open his door to get out, I was already opening my door and got out and without another word, I waved him off. I took the back stairs to my room; I didn't have enough time to sit and talk to Miss Marple right now. I unlocked my door and hurried through it, turning quickly to lock it behind me. I tossed my purse on the bed and went over to my desk and sat down, then unlocked the large drawer to the left and pulled out the manila envelope. I laid it on the deck and powered up my computer. I opened the envelope and pulled out the pages I needed and scanned down to the information I was looking for; then a question came to me. Why would a well-known and world-renowned lawyer jeopardize his reputation to do business with Chinese thugs? I had investigated Feterly's life before but had missed something and was hoping that another look would give up some more clues. I spent the next two hours searching and reading everything I could about him—before computers, this kind of search would not have been possible in such a brief time.

"Did Sir John Feterly think that this was such a small community that no one would notice or care if outsiders came in and got involved in their business?" My phone rang and broke my train of thought.

"Sally, Stu here, Bill just called me. The FBI has been made aware of these men here and this case, they are working on it from the other end and don't want any interference from other law enforcement department. They reassured us that everything is being done to find the missing people." Stu paused.

"That makes since Stu," I added, then stopped myself from saying any more on that subject.

"Stu, I'll tell you what I think we should do seeing that we're all going to be together at the Morhouses tonight anyway. How about we throw your aunt a surprise birthday party? We'll get her closest friends around her and keep her busy for as long as possible. Hopefully, that will give the FBI enough time to find those that are missing and keep Kitty from being with those men alone," I added.

"That sounds great, Sally! I'll get a hold of the Morhouses and let them know what we want to do about giving her a party. I won't tell Dan more than that because I don't want someone saying the wrong thing and getting her killed. Yes, I think I like your idea very much," Stu said before hanging up.

"Wait a minute!" I said out loud to myself when I read what was coming up over my computer screen. Here it is! Sir John Feterly has experience in intelligence as a CIA operative. He worked with them five years ago to capture and imprison a traitor. Could he be working undercover as their operative now?" I could only wonder while looking at the pictures I took of John and the two men with him. Before I gave up the papers, I picked up over to John. I should call Bill so he could have these other men checked out. I knew we're to keep our distance from this case; that didn't mean to ignore it; it was time to put names to faces. Were these men part of the CIA or just thugs? Because of these strangers, two local men, were dead.

"Hello, I am calling to talk to Sergeant Bill," I said to the lady at the other end of the line.

"Who is this?" she asked.

"Oh, I'm sorry, it's Sally Crystal. I met the sergeant today at the yacht club while I was having lunch with Stu Baker. I have a question that I need to run past him," I replied.

"He is out of the office at this time. Could I ask him the question for you?" she asked.

"No. Would you please have Bill contacted me at his earliest convenience?" I said, giving her my number before hanging up.

Then my eyes returned to the computer screen. "What was the name of the traitor, and where is he in prisoned at?" I wondered. There was a short write-up on the court hearing in John's bio. It says here that the prisoner swore Sir John framed him. They both had been CIA operatives, and he had seen something he wasn't supposed to have, so Sir John had to frame him or kill him. No one would listen, even though he had proof that Sir John was a double agent. I made a copy of the news piece and put it with the pictures of John and his cronies. I needed Bill's help for sure; I only hope he doesn't get suspicious of why I am asking. I must take a chance, for Stu's Aunt's life hangs in the balance. The phone rang at the same time Miss Marple called for me from the bottom of the stairs. I poked my head out of my door and told her I would be right down, once I was off the phone.

"Hello," I said to the caller on the other end.

"Sally, Bill here, you called?" he asked.

"Yes, I know we were ordered off the case having to do with Stu's aunt. I've come by some information that I thought you would like to look it over. I found it on my computer, so it's public record. There's a question about Sir John Feterly and the men that were sitting with Stu's aunt and a man that is in prison in New York. Bill, I believe that you will find all of this very interesting. The only problem with all of it is, we've only got a few days to find out who John is. Is he a CIA operative, or a spy for a foreign government?"

"Sally, you've got my attention, where are you?" Bill asked.

"I am at Miss Marple's, where I live. Will you come soon?"

"Yes, I am leaving right now," he said before hanging up.

CHAPTER 12

Party Breakout

I hurried and grabbed the copies I made from the copier and put them in a large manila envelope and sealed it. I picked up my phone and slipped it into my pocket, then made my way downstairs. Before meeting with Miss Marple, I ran out to give the envelope over to Bill who was already waiting on me in the driveway. I quickly ran back inside to Miss Marple, who was in the parlor reading and watching the birds on the feeders.

"Oh, there you are Sally," she said, waiting anxiously to hear any news I might have to share. She motioned for me to sit down with her. "Come tell me about your lunch with Stu. I am sure you found things at the club exciting. It's been a long time since I've been there for lunch," she said, sounding a bit remorseful while pouring us each a cup of hot steaming tea.

I wasted no time in telling her everything that I could, while watching the expressions on her face change like the wind, from excitement and laughter to confusion and total dismay. Her concern for Kitty was almost more than she could bear, and her eyes teared up; they had been friends for years. Once she had gathered in her emotions and was able to speak freely, I explained our birthday party idea with her. Her eyes lit up; she was all for it and could hardly wait to call their other friends; everyone would bring a gift for Kitty. We wanted to make the party believable, as though planned for a long time. She went about her task, and I returned to my room.

I quickly changed out of my day clothes to evening wear and took my ponytail out, letting my long blond hair fall below my shoulders. I also touched up my makeup and changed my jewelry out for something more acceptable for a cookout. The phone rang.

"Yes," I said while I waited for a voice from the other end.

"Sally, Mr. Korn here. We are waiting here in the pressroom for your weekly column. When can we expect it?" he asked.

"I'll e-mail it to you tomorrow afternoon. I am attending a BBQ tonight, and I am sure that it will enrich the outcome of the column," I assured him.

"Great! I can hardly wait. We have received so many calls and new subscriptions because of your column; many have asked us to make it a daily column. But don't worry about that—that was not our agreement," he said before hanging up.

I no longer hung up than my phone rang again. Bill's name came up on my caller ID.

"Hello, Bill," I said.

"My boss, the commissioner, has taken a lot of interest in the information you gave us. I've been ordered to leave immediately for the federal prison in New York State. He wants me to question this so-called traitor and report back to him ASAP. He needs to stop the sale of the property on Wednesday so that we can find the two missing females, for he is now sure they're connected to it. Tell Stu why I am not able to be at the cookout, but don't let anyone else know not even Miss Marple. We can't take the chance of anyone else slipping up and blowing this whole thing out of the water," Bill said sternly.

"I truly understand the importance of all this. I will make sure that no one other than Stu is alerted to our plans," I said before hanging up.

"Oh my god, what a day!" I said out loud to myself, not knowing what to do next. I took the next few minutes to lie across my bed and get still. I would have fallen to sleep if it wasn't for the ring of my phone.

"Hello," I said, then paused.

"Sally, it's Bill again. I forgot to tell you your name never came up between my boss and me. It's best that we keep you out of all of this, for these men are ruthless and would surely come after you. So I suggest we play this all close to the vest. You do understand what I mean?" he asked.

"I agree one hundred percent," I replied.

"Good! Then I'll call you later, once I know more," he assured me.

I sat up on the edge of the bed, trying to digest everything Bill had just told me, when the phone rang again. No longer had I put the phone to my ear; then I heard Stu's sweet voice flow into my ear and fill every sense of my body.

"Sally, are you there?" he asked.

"Yes, yes, of course, you caught me deep in thought. What's up?" I replied.

"I called Dan Morhouse and set up the party idea with him at his cookout. He's clearly in favor of it. I notified most of the people on his guest list. I then went by the bakery and was able to order a large birthday cake, to be delivered in time for the cookout. I am now on my way to pick up Aunt Kitty a dozen roses from us if that's okay with you. You know her birthday is really in December, so she'll know we had something to do with this party idea. Hopefully, she won't question us about it out loud," Stu said, then paused.

"If she thinks you planned it, she'll be comfortable with it. If she is anything like you, she'll go with the flow. I spoke to Miss Marple about the party too and the reason for it. She became a little emotional, then dug her heels in for the ride. She was soon off to notify her and Kitty's friends to inform them so they can all bring Kitty gifts as though it was a longtime planned event," I told him.

"Wow! What a fantastic idea on her part. I for one am looking forward to tonight's event, even more than I was to the cookout itself," Stu added.

"Stu, something's come up, and Bill had to go out of town on business. He won't be back in time for the cookout. He would like you to give your aunt his love," I said cautiously so as not to say too much.

"What could be so important? Well, I know he has many cases to work on, not just ours. After all, the FBI is on the case now. Right?" Stu added.

"Yes, that's right, all the bases are covered, and many people are working together to find the girls and free your aunt," I replied.

"Well, Sally, it's four now, I'll be by at six for you," Stu said.

"That sounds great! I look forward to seeing you then," I said before hanging up.

I returned to the computer and the write-up on John Feterly to find the name of the so-called spy that he helped put away. It wasn't until almost the bottom of the page that I saw his name in tiny print. For someone that was supposed to be so dangerous, you'd think he'd be well-known. I have been in the news business for some time, yet I had never heard of this person before. All of this was on the copy I gave Bill. How did I miss Fineout's name? If he is such a bad guy, I should be able to find him in the CIA or FBI criminal bank. I quickly typed in "federal prison in New York" and entered his name.

"That's weird. No name appeared, it just advised me to look under operatives or field-workers for the government. I did as I was directed, only to get a page up of redacted information. Many of the words had been redacted blacked-out, which was more than puzzling. Bill must have talked to someone up there before he left to see the warden, for a trip like that would have been expensive for his department and moreover unnecessary, if the man wasn't there. Maybe the name here wasn't his real name, if not? What were they trying to hide?"

Again, I'd come against a solid wall with nothing but questions for me to mull over. I hope that Bill had better luck than I had, for time was running out.

I turned my attention to writing up an outline for my column while I waited for Stu to return. It wasn't long before I heard my name being yelled up the stairway by a male's voice.

"Sally, your ride is here for you," Miss Marple's nephew said, then hurried away.

CHAPTER 13

Gunshots in the Boathouse

The road we took out of the harbor led us up to the hill over highway M119 toward New Hart, Michigan, where the Morhouses' estate was. The road was very narrow, only wide enough for two cars to pass each other; it reminded me of the mighty python, for you never knew what to expect around the next curve or over the hill. On one side, you may see plush lawns and estates or deer standing near the roadside, or on the other, high cliffs that were openings to a panoramic view of Lake Michigan; it was the best time of day to take a beautiful ride.

"Stu, this road must become treacherous to drive after dark. Those little posts at the side of the road would never stop a car coming down this hill and around the curve. You do know another way back to the harbor, don't you?" I asked anxiously. He looked at me with a big mischievous grin on his face, and I was almost afraid of what was about to come out of his mouth.

"Sally, darling, if you wish we can get lost together over Hogsback Ridge later tonight. It's a little bit straighter, and there are no cliffs at the side of the road," Stu said, still grinning.

"What aren't you telling me, Stu? And where is this ridge?" I seriously wanted to know if he was playing me.

"I'll show you the road. We passed right by it once we get up to the New Hart Grocery. The road will bring us back to the harbor, the long way around. It's a young road lover like to drive in the moonlight because there's a lot of secluded side roads to pull off on if you get my meaning—one could almost pull up on anything," Stu replied.

"Oh, Stu, are you trying to scare me? Or have you just promised me a drive down lover's lane in the moonlight?" I asked teasingly.

"Sally, if it weren't that I promised to go to the barbecue, I'd gladly show you right now all the side roads and old hang-outs of my youth when we visited the harbor on my summer vacations. Those were the days. We lived wild and free when we were too young to know or understand the problems grown-ups dealt with daily." Stu paused, then slowed down for a small traffic light blinking, right in front of New Hart's Grocery.

"See that hill?" Stu said, pointing across me to the right. "What does that road sign say?" he asked me.

I looked up to see the road sign. "Oh my god, there is a Hogsback Ridge," I said, laughing. "So I must choose the ridge or the cliffs—what is a girl to do?" I asked teasingly. I had a feeling this was going to be a night to remember.

Stu turned off M119 to the left and drove down a wide winding road, to a wrought iron gate that was being guarded by two uniformed men. The gate swung open, and one of the men came over to talk to Stu through his opened window.

"Good evening, Mr. Baker," the boss said. You and your guest are to park by his car, up near the house."

"Thanks, Tony, we'll do that," Stu said, then rolled up his window and drove on.

As we continued up the long tree-lined drive, we could see other cars parked in the nearby mowed field. From there the guests could continue in on foot or catch a ride on a bus provided for them. Once near the house, we saw the sign that Dan had put up, directing Stu where to park. We got out of the car and stood for a few minutes in each other's arms.

"Sally, this night might get a little crazy, and we may get separated in the crowd, but please, just don't leave without me whatever you do," Stu whispered into my ear and then kissed me.

Once I was able to catch my breath, I whispered into his ear, "Stu, you do realize that we are not alone standing here, we are in the middle of a sea of people, and they are watching us like we're on TV." He pulled me in for another hug and kiss—this time it was a longer and more luscious kiss.

"Wow!" I said, trying to catch my breath again. "Stu, I think we'd better join the others before I lose all my strength," I said, half laughing, while Stu stepped to the back of the car and took our lawn chairs out of the trunk.

"Is this a private affair, or can anyone join?" Dan joke while walking up behind Stu. "I am glad you both came a little early. Let's get a cold drink and talk about this party," Dan added while showing us into the backyard through the side gate. The backyard was as big as a football field, with viewing stands and a giant-size pool and tennis courts. The whole yard was surrounded by tall stone walls that had sharp spikes embedded in one-inch spaces all around its upper edge, and cameras were attached to all sides of the house, taking in almost everything.

It wasn't just a home we were entering—it was a fortress. I noticed the bodyguards walking about was dressed for battle, with earbuds in their ears, and the holstered guns on their belts; other than that, they were enjoying themselves like everyone else.

The grills and long folding tables are covered with red checkered tablecloths, which were lined up near the beach and were already being prepared and covered with food. There were four unique styles of dinner guest here tonight—the ones that spread a blanket on the ground for a picnic and those that to sit in large groups of likeminded people at an extended table of some kind. You could also find small four-chair tables of two to four people sitting together; then there were those who put their plates on wicker plate holders and carried them and their drinks to a chair where they would sit alone or with others. I could see one of those long extended tables, and Kitty was sitting on the right side of it in the middle, surrounded by all her closest friends. Two of the men making life hell for her sat one small table away.

Dan led Stu and me to a small table near the wet bar, then he stepped up to the bar and got three spiked lemonades for us.

"Here you go, Sally, try this. Good, yes?" Dan asked as he handed Stu his drink.

"Oh, Dan, that is good, thanks," I replied.

"Stu, what's up with this fake birthday party—we both know that's Kitty was born in December. I knew if you wanted to throw a birthday party, you had a good reason for it." Dan took a sip of his drink and listened to Stu's answer.

Stu explained in detail what was truly going on with his aunt and the men around her and the fact about her nieces. Dan looked completely surprised by it all and thought the party a great idea.

"If it weren't for her nieces, we could take those men out right here," Dan said in a soft-toned voice. "What reason would they have to do such a thing?" I wanted to say something, but I wasn't supposed to know the answer. That's when Stu surprised me.

"Dan, there is a piece of land right across the lake from you near the harbor that goes on sale Wednesday at noon. Those men want it—bad enough to kill for it," Stu replied, then added. "You did hear about the Indian found dead on the beach, less than a week ago, the morning after the birds. Well, it's suspected that those men had something to do with it. There's an FBI investigation going on right now, as we speak. Hopefully, we'll be able to stop the land sale and any to them in the future." Stu sat back in his chair and took another drink while looking over at his aunt.

"Stu, I am the host here, so I'll have to run and take care of some of my duties. I'll talk to both of you later." With that, Dan stood up and hurried off, leaving his half-empty glass on the table. I don't know, but it seemed a bit strange to me—yet Stu paid it no mind.

"Stu, darling, I am going to have to find the ladies' room. Maybe you'd like to visit with your aunt? I will join you over there when I return," I said, getting up from the table. Stu got to his feet as well and hugged me. "Thanks, Sally, for understanding," he said before walking away.

There were some things my nosy personality wanted to know. Dan's reply had a ring of disbelief to it—like he knew more than he was saying. So I decided to do some scouting around, making like I was trying to find a restroom. The maid inside the house directed me to one of the guest bathrooms, which I quickly used, then went out the front door that faced the lake. While walking down the steps from the plantation-style porch, I heard voices of anger coming around the corner of a smaller house just steps from the main house. It appeared to be Dan's boathouse; there was a creek full of water running from the lake under the house. I ran over to see if I could get a peek around the corner to see who was talking. There was a wooded windbreaker near the end of what seemed to be a boathouse with just enough room for me to slip through. Two men were talking; one was John Feterly's bodyguard, and the other was Dan, and Dan was furious.

"What the hell were you people thinking kidnapping that old woman and her nieces? And I've just learned that the FBI has been put on this case since you clowns killed that Indian on the beach. You weren't even bright enough to get rid of the body; you just left him lying there. The three of you have brought unnecessary devastation to this harbor. Come in here. I have something I want you to take back to your boss—the great John Feterly," Dan said, leading the man into the boathouse, along with his bodyguard. I crept over to the slightly open the door to continue recording and taking pictures of what was going on. I lay down on my stomach on the ground to get a better view.

"Wait here, I have to get it off the back shelf," Dan told the two men with him. A few seconds later he returned carrying a gun with a silencer on it; without another word, Dan shot John's man in front of his bodyguard. They quickly rolled back a large rug on the floor and opened a trapdoor in the floor dropping the body into the water below.

I hurried and got out of there before he had time to lock the door back down. I ran back around the front of the house while whipping the dirt off my clothes and put my jewelry back on then slowed down to catch my breath.

I quickly found the chair Stu was saving me at his aunt's table. I took my seat and entered the conversation like I had known Kitty for years; she played along.

Minutes later, Dan was back in sight, talking and laughing with his guest like nothing had happened. John Feterly got up from his table and started gracing at the long table by the grills while looking around for his bodyguard.

I wondered what John was thinking now, now that he was all alone here among all of Kitty's friends. Dan walked up to John Feterly and escorted him over to a couple of chairs near the side of the house. I tried not to stare, yet I didn't want to miss anything. Dan's face was full of anger, and though I couldn't hear them from where I was sitting, I believe John just found out about his friend's fate and what he would have to do to walk away alive. The two men stood up and shook hands, then John got into his car and left. I turned to look at Aunt Kitty to see if she, too, had seen John go; her face was full of questions, one of which, I am sure, was the safety of her nieces and wondering if it was over.

"Stu," I whispered, "please go and talk to Dan, see what he knows about that man who just left. We need to know if Kitty is going home alone or with that man again. She needs to talk to her family members and know they are safe," I said, caressing his arm lovingly while looking into his eyes. He wasted no time in doing as I asked. I remained at Kitty's table and said nothing about what Stu was up doing. Kitty introduced me to many of her friends, one being Sergeant Agatha Williams. She was as hot as a pistol in looks and temperament, and she had already decided to go home with Kitty until her family members were safe. Agatha was built and trained to be a lethal fighting machine.

"Sally, darling, I am so sorry, we haven't even eaten yet, but I must leave. There's a situation going on with one of my clients. So would you like to remain and go home with Miss Marple or leave now?" Stu asked.

"Stu, if you're going into the harbor I would prefer riding with you," I replied. Stu didn't elaborate on what he had to do; as a matter of fact, the subject didn't come up again.

We quickly got into the car and were driving out of the driveway before either of us said another word.

"Did Dan know why that man left so fast?" I asked.

"He told me he didn't even know him and that the man came as a guest of someone else," Stu replied.

"I don't believe him, Stu. For what I observed in their body language, it was not a friendly exchange. Your friend Dan was as mad as hell at a person that he didn't know? I doubt that. Those two men have a history, and it is up to us to find out more about it," I said in a stern voice. "Stu, your aunt's life depends on it."

"Sally, stay out of it. It is dangerous and not something a lady like you should be mixed up in. I do understand your concerns, and I will look further into it as soon as possible," Stu said, looking at me.

"Stu, I am surprised that you would use my being a woman to keep me at arm's length on this matter. I am nobody's fool or a shrinking violet, and I will do whatever I want to. I don't need your or anyone else's approval to follow up on a concern I have," I replied, sounding a little hot under the collar. I hated it when men were condescending toward women as though we were the weaker sex. Why was it necessary for anyone to be the weaker one, when both could work together to make a stronger bond against the problems at hand?

"Sally, I am so sorry, I never meant it to sound like that. Please forgive me, and if you would like to investigate it—please do. I'll be very interested in finding out more on the subject, I am also sorry that this night didn't go as planned. I know we were hoping to take the other way back, but we still have some daylight, and I'm in a hurry. I promise to make this all up to you sometime soon," Stu said while keeping his eyes on the downhill curvy mountain road he was trying to navigate. I had a death grip on the door and closed my eyes when we came close to the edge, which had little or nothing to keep us from going over the side. By the time, he drove up in front of Miss Marple's; I wasn't sure I could even stand up. My whole body felt like I had just come off a mammoth roller coaster.

"I will call you later tonight, Sally," Stu said, leaning over to kiss me goodbye. I returned his kiss and quickly got out and stood on the curve as I watched him drive away and pull out of sight.

Then I heard it again, a thumbing, switching sound, somewhere off in the distance.

CHAPTER 14

Bird's Revenge

No longer concerned why we had to come back from the barbecue, or what was so urgent that Stu would leave me standing on the curb, for I realized everything happens for a reason—good or bad. Right now, other things ran through my mind. That sound off in the distance was making my inquisitive blood run wild, causing the investigating side of me to take control. The harbor was almost empty, everyone was out at the Morhouses', so who or what was making that ungodly noise?

I hurried into the back door and up the stairs to my room. I quickly changed out of my clothes and put on black jeans, black hoodie, and tall black boots that went up to my knees, and I topped off my look with a black knitted hat to cover my long blond hair. Lastly, I put on the darkest skin color makeup I had. It would be dark very soon, and I didn't want to be seen by anyone. I put a large necklace around my neck that was also dark in color that doubled as a camera with a night lens and voice recorder—my tools of the trade. Then I checked the batteries in my flashlight, making sure I had an intense beam, before grabbing up my car key and running to my car.

I drove right down the center of the harbor and followed the noise I heard that led me along the bend around the lake for about five miles till I came to a dead end. The sound was much louder here, and there were no homes this far out. I parked my car and got out, locking it up behind me. I headed to a clearing that held some big vehicles, wider than just a footpath. I slowly made my way into the woods to find a rustic campsite about a half a mile back. I stood behind two large trees, which had a small gap between them, giving me a clear view of everything that was going on. I heard two men talking while they worked at the bottom of an oil rig. The older man had red hair and a stocky build and spoke with a heavy Irish accent. The younger man was of medium build, dark hair, and American descent. The younger man was also very skittish about being on the property and doing what they were doing.

"Tony, why would the boss have us drill on land that is an Indian gravesite. Aren't their laws against this?" the younger man asked.

"Stop bellyaching and do your job. You weren't hired to think, that's above your pay scale, the old man yelled in reply.

"But Tony, there are dead bodies in burial mounds all around here, you moved one to sink this hole. Don't you have any feeling about any of this?"

"Brady, the dead can't talk and if they could, who would they tell?" Tony replied.

No sooner had these words come out of his mouth than what had appeared to be leaves on the trees started moving and before I could blink took flight. Hundreds of blackbirds took to the sky, screeching and chirping loudly across the sky to the left of me, taking the two men by surprise. They just stood in place, as though they were frozen, while the birds flew around overhead and then swooped down like a dive bomber attacking and knocking both to the ground. All the birds ended up on the two men and around the nearby area, screaming out in rage.

I thought, *This would be an appropriate time to get out of here.* So with as little noise as possible, I ran to my car and quickly got in. I had never witnessed such a sight in my life. I was shaking too much to start the car right away. I made some verbal notes on the recorder that was still hanging around my neck before starting up the car and turning it around to drive off. The sound of the birds was gone, as though it never happened. Were they just birds or spirits of the dead?

None of the birds flew out as far as the Morhouses' estate, so those there wouldn't have noticed what just happened here. The first fireworks flash across the sky over the lake; their beautiful colors splashed over my rearview mirror. I hurried and parked the car by the back door near the carriage house and ran up the steps to my room. Once inside, I threw my black hoodie and black knit hat on the bed and kicked off my boots before going into the bathroom to wash the dark makeup off my face. I pulled on my baby-doll PJs. After sitting down in the deck chair, I clicked on the computer and waited for it to warm up. It only took a minute or two, but it seemed like forever. I couldn't wait to find out if the young Indian braves, who were lawyers at the time they signed the lease, made the land permanently uninhabited by the living. I quickly pulled up the website of Emmet County Hall of Records and called up the land lease section to see if there was a provision added to it that made a gravesite possible. All it said is nothing could be built on the land. So what about Indian burial mounds? Would they be moved, for the property to be sold for oil exploitation?

There was one more place I could look, I thought. I went back to the front page of records and pulled up graves and burial sites in Emmet County. I put in the area numbers of the property and waited with high expectation for what I might or might not find—and there it was on the screen, right before my eyes. I jumped out of my chair and danced around the room with excitement. There it was! They had a legal right to place burial mounds throughout the property, and it was signed by the Department of the Interior and the commissioner of Indian affairs, some ten years after the lease was first signed. How smart was that? Those young men were wiser than their white counterparts; they sealed that land's fate forever; what was once taken from them in the past but never again!

After reading both documents that were before me, I ran them through my printer for copies.

"Indian Burial Grounds, Rest in Peace, 2009" was the heading.

An archaeologist investigated cases where Indian burial sites may appear, and if findings were proven right, then stepped to preserve them where they are found are taken.

"It's the respect we have for all no matter how long ago their passing. Even if evidence of a mound is gone, people need to understand that this is a sacred place."

Defining the place of burial that they constitute a particular type of burial place, and be regarded as sacred, in that it acts as a place for pilgrimage of friends and family. A burial site often does not present a unique landscape; some may contain separate areas. Following the war, promises were kept concerning many sites.

I turned my attention to the necklace that I was wearing while I was out. I quickly removed the top crystal of the necklace and opened it up to the video bug and voice recorder. There were two discs, no bigger than a pair of small stud earrings, yet both did outstanding things. The unique computer I owned had a slot for each; I placed them in and downloaded. The picture came out flawless, better than I could have hoped for; after all, I was standing between two trees after dark, with only their camp lantern to see. The transcript of the recorder in written words came out bright and very easy to understand, even though one of the men spoke in broken English. I placed the copies of the documents made and the evidence I found tonight into a giant yellow manila envelope and addressed it to chief of Indian affairs of Northern Michigan. I asked him not to make these things public until the day of the land sale, for it was essential to find out who else wanted that land. I told him that three more men were killed today because of the land grab. Then I closed and sealed the envelope, stamped it, and set it aside.

I hurried and dressed, grabbed up the envelope, and hurried to the post office, although it wasn't open just then. I knew that the express box was the first one opened in the morning for processing, so that mail would go out before noon. Then I hurried back to the house before the harbor residents started flowing back in from the barbecue.

It was Monday, and my piece had to be in the paper that went out on Tuesday, and I hadn't written the first line yet. How could I tell them the truth about what's going on without implicating myself? I pulled up a blank page and got started.

𝔓𝔲𝔷𝔷𝔩𝔢 𝔓𝔦𝔢𝔠𝔢𝔰

Joe Bumgardner

Today is the last Monday of June, and our first yacht club lunch-in of the summer; it was also our club's first business meeting. The club's ballroom was being used instead of the dining room, for so many of us had to be here at one time. We walked into the front door to the foyer where there was a book for us to sign in before entering the double arched doorway into the ballroom. I nodded at many of my friends as I hurried across the room to sit at a table near the glass wall, a favorite place for many because of the glorious view of Lake Michigan and the harbor where so many of our boats were tied up.

Captain Tony Stafford took a seat at my table. He's a man in his sixties and a former FBI research analyst; so when he spoke, I knew it wasn't gossip or heresy. You could take what he said to the bank, for he would've already checked it out.

As a reporter that made a significant difference to me, in my field, you checked and double-checked, for you didn't leave anything to chance, for people's lives could depend on you.

"Joe, you'll never believe what's been going on here right under the noses. Ninety-five percent of our summer residents don't have a clue something wrong. They are so private-minded that only a few share news. I'm telling you, Joe. It's crazy! We had questionable strangers carrying heat, staying at the hotel where a man of Indian descent was found dead on the beach. See those men, setting with Kitty over there?" he asked as he turned so I could get a pleasant view. "Those men are not her friends. You might say she's being kidnaped right in plain sight, and no one can do anything about it. Her nieces are being kept somewhere in New York as hostages until their business is done here," Tony said, taking a breath, then added. "They plan to use her as a pawn to get a piece of property that goes on sale Wednesday. I've been asked by the FBI, to keep a close eye on them, until we can find a way to free her family members.

"Yes, I heard something about the property sale you speak of," Joe replied.

"Joe, the property we speak of is worth millions in today's market," he said before turning his head again. He then looked back at me, like he had just noticed an old friend coming in. "Joe, look over there, it's the captain from the police department—he's not a member here," he said, pulling his pipe out of his pocket and putting it between his lip, but didn't light up; just a prop now, I guess. He used to smoke it but stopped, when his wife died of lung cancer.

Together, we observed the police captain set down at Stu Baker's table. Their faces were translating deep concern; then seconds later, the Captain stood up and walked over to Kitty's table to give her a hug and whispering something into her ear before leaving.

"Did you see how he looked at those three men at Kitty's table? I tell you, Joe, there's something about to take place, and he stopped in to make her aware of it—to let her know that he knew what was going on," Tony said as though he had heard every word.

"Tony, you said something about a dead body on the beach. Was he a local man?" I asked.

"No, he lived somewhere in the county—but he's a member of the tribe's family that leased the property in question that goes on sale Wednesday. Time to free the ladies is running out. If not free before the sale, they may never be." Tony paused before adding, "The man that was found dead, and the terrorizing birds the other night, and those three men there are all puzzle pieces that will soon fall into place. I believe that there are pieces that are yet to be reviled, and someone of some importance in this harbor, which is known well, will also be brought down. I say that because we are a small community here minding our own business, and then fat cats come prowling around. Those things don't just happen by accident, I assure you. In any case, it will be all over come Wednesday." Tony finished his thought as he removed his cold pipe and returned it to his pocket, as the waitress delivered our food.

Good, the column was off to Mr. Korn's desk for review before going to press. It was late, and Stu still hadn't called as he said he would. Everyone was back in the house; I could hear their voices. Miss Marple would have gone right to bed, for staying out this late wasn't her cup of tea. I left my computer on the sleep mode and climbed into and beneath my satin sheets of yellow gold. My bedroom glass door window was still open, for the night was still warm. My mind wouldn't turn off no matter how many sheep I counted. Where was Stu, and what could have been so vital that it could pull him away from me? I knew if I were going to be in his life, these things would surely happen from time to time; we both had careers that were demanding at times. After a half an hour of tossing and turning, I gave up and went back to my computer; if I couldn't sleep, it wouldn't either.

I was happy with the column I had sent out; it almost came together by itself. I only touched on the things others had noticed and tried to leave the rest of the population out of it. The phone rang. It was two in the morning. I hurried to answer it.

"Sally, Bill here, I'm almost home. I landed at the airport near Harbor Springs ten minutes ago. Boy, is my boss ever mad. If he could, he'd go up to that prison himself and kill that son-of-a-bitch warden for leading him on; they could have told him by phone that the trial was phony and was only meant to throw off his partner. They realized shortly before the trial was over that they had the wrong man in prison, yet the cards had to play. They had to catch the double agent red-handed. He wasn't working alone—he had new partners working for him in the shadows. The CIA told me that they were closing in on him in Black Hawk Harbor. They must have strong evidence for espionage, before slapping the cuffs on him. They can't take the chance of losing him again. Well, that's what I was told before I flew back," Bill said.

"Bill, I must talk to you, but not over the phone it must be in a private place. I must confide something to you about myself that can go no further than from my mouth to your ears, for you must know what happened tonight here in Black Hawk Harbor. I promise you that it will be worth your time; it must be soon," I said impatiently.

"Sally, I will stop there right now on my way home. Be out in the back driveway in five minutes, or neither one of us will sleep tonight," Bill said, then hung up.

I hurried and put the clothes back on I had just taken off a short while ago, all but the boots and the dark makeup. I grabbed up some tools of the trade off the dresser and put them in my hoodie's pocket where I could turn the recorder on at will without his knowing. A girl can never be too protected from unexpected outcomes.

Bill's car was sitting in the driveway already when I walked out the back door, with headlights on. Once I stepped down off the last step of the porch, he turned them off. It was a moonlit summer's night and so not that dark out. I opened his front passenger's side door and got into the car by him.

"Sally, tell me what's troubling you? It must be hair bending for you to have me come so late and what did you mean there was something about you I needed to know?" Bill asked as he sat back and turned toward me in his seat, waiting for an answer.

"Bill, what I tell you now is with the understanding that it's said to you in confidence. No one must know where you heard it at or from whom. No, I am not in trouble with the law, far from it. I am an undercover reporter, and I must remain one for the whole summer here in Black Hawk Harbor. Please don't ask me why, because I can't tell you, not yet anyway—maybe someday somewhere down the road. Bill, Stu doesn't even know, and he can't right now. Do you understand what I am asking of you? It's crucial that you do—for there are lives at stake here." I paused to take a breath and then continued.

"I was at the Morhouses' barbecue with Stu tonight, and while he went to speak with a friend of his, I went to find a bathroom. When I was on my way back to see him, I heard angry voices. I pivoted around to go into the direction that the sounds were coming from—it was the reporter's blood in me that drew me to it. I was surprised to see that it was Dan Morhouse who was exchanging angry words with one of the men from Kitty's table from the lunch-in today. Oh, I forgot—you weren't there, but your boss was for about five minutes. Well, back to what I was telling you.

"Dan was furious that the men with her had gone so far as to kidnap her in plain sight while holding her niece's hostage in New York till the outcome of a property sale on Wednesday. He also rebuked them for killing the young Indian man and leaving his body on the beach to be found by police. That's not the worst of it, Bill. I saw and heard all this through a crack in the door of Dan's boathouse when it swung it back open a little. Dan made the man think he had something to take back to his boss. That's when Dan turned and stepped a few steps away out of sight. When he returned, he was carrying a gun with a silencer on it. Bill, I watched him take aim and kill that man in cold blood. Then he and his bodyguard pulled up a grassy-looking rug and unlocked a trapdoor under it in the floor of his boathouse and pushed the body into the water below, splashing when it hit. I hurried and got away at that point before he noticed me watching. I was back with Stu before I saw him again. Shortly after that, we had to leave, as Stu got a call from one of his clients. After he dropped me off at the curb in front of Miss Marple's, and while I watched him drive away, a strange thumping noise came from the land reserve. The investigative reporter's blood in me took over, and I hurried upstairs to change. I dressed much as I am now but in boots and dark makeup.

"I drove out as far as I could down Lake Street until it came to a dead end, then I continued on foot, down a wide path made by heavy equipment. I walked into the dark wooded area with a small flashlight, just bright enough to show me where to step. I heard the voices of two men talking, one with a heavy Irish accent. I found a place behind two trees that had an opening that let me see them. The oldest one had red hair and was the loudest speaking of the two. The other man was timid and fearful of what they were doing there. He questioned the older guy about drilling over an Indian burial mound. The older man just laughed at him and said, 'He knew what he was doing, and the dead can't tell.'

"Bill, it looked like a thousand leaves on the trees took flight, and just like the other night, the birds were out in a terrifying rage. This time they stayed mainly over the land in question, as they climbed to the sky, then dive-bombed those two men, knocking them to the ground and then pecked at them till they were dead. I was sure I could get back to the car without the light if I were careful. I moved quickly, almost falling over a small log before getting to my vehicle. I climbed inside and sit there for a few minutes, trying to digest what I had just witnessed. I started up the car, and it wasn't long before I was back here.

"Bill, those men, or what's left of them, are still in the woods near their pumping equipment. There's a camp light there hooked to a battery. It shouldn't be hard to find—unless the birds destroyed it too." I stopped talking and sat back in the seat. Bill sat still, looking out the front window for the longest time, then turned toward me.

"Sally, do you have any proof of anything? I am sorry for saying it just that way—but I've already been on a goose-chase, and I don't think another one right now would be helpful," Bill asked.

"Yes. Wait right here, and I'll get it for you, but you must keep me out of it," I reminded him.

"I'll do what I can, Sally—that's all I can promise. I am a law enforcement officer. If you didn't do anything wrong, you wouldn't be implicated."

I run up and got one of the copies of both events and put them into a large envelope. Then I hurried back to the car, trying to be a quiet as possible so as not to wake anyone in the house. After getting back in the car, I handed them off to him. He immediately opened the envelope and pulled everything out in front of him on the stirring wheel and with his flashlight looked them over quietly.

"Sally, these pictures and word transcripts speak for themselves. You're one hell of a bloodhound when it comes to this kind of work, girl. If you ever give up being a reporter, you can come and work for me. Your name will not be mentioned in the findings, even if my job depends on it. I'll keep all your secrets," Bill said, slipping all the things I showed him back into the envelope and starting the car.

I opened my door and stepped out and made it up to the steps before he drove away. But before I got up to my room, I was mentally kicking myself in the ass—I'd forgotten to tell him to hold off arresting anyone until Wednesday, for we needed to know all the players that wanted that land and why. It would be better for us all if they were arrested in front of the whole town and not in some private room somewhere.

CHAPTER 15

Unshared Secrets

I woke up with the phone ringing and a jet stream of light coming through the opening in the drapes that fell on the pillow and across my face. I reached over and picked up the phone and with a morning groggy voice answered it.

"Hello, good morning," I said, hoping it was Stu.

"Sally, Mr. Korn here. I can't tell you how excited I am about the irrefutable proof you sent me for your column. I am your biggest fan, and I can hardly wait for your next column to come out. Our sales here at the paper have doubled since Joe Bumgardner started writing for us. Oh, by the way, no one, not even my brother, knows that your name was changed. I mean, they don't know that it's you. Bill, your challenger, thinks that you turned the column down and that we got someone else for the challenge. Matter of fact, he's asked me why you weren't writing it. I never said you weren't, but I never said you were, either. I thought maybe it would take a little of the cockiness out of his attitude if he thought it was a man he was challenging. I mainly called to remind you of our appointment this afternoon, here at the office—and you can pick up your check at the same time. Sally, remember if you run into my brother or Bill, don't let our secret out. Please come before two, for I must leave the office shortly after that. See you, Sally," Mr. Korn said before hanging up.

I quickly returned the phone to its place on the nightstand and jumped out of bed making a beeline for the bathroom to shower and dress. While I was still in the shower, I could hear my phone ringing.

Whoever it was would have to wait until this girl gets her makeup on, I thought as I shampooed my hair. The light on the phone was blinking when I finally stepped out of the bathroom; I pushed down on the button to see what the caller had to say.

"Sally, please meet me in my parlor for breakfast. I have some news to share with you," Miss Marple said.

I dressed for a warm summer's day, in shorts, top, and sandals. I twisted my wet ponytail up into a bun securing it with a hairclip. I grabbed a lightweight sweater from my closet for the morning chill and headed downstairs to see Miss Marple.

No sooner had I entered the parlor than Miss Marple was up pouring tea. She directed me to take a seat in the gold-colored Queen Ann wingback chair, the place she sat most of the time. Then she handed me a small transparent glass plate with a blueberry crumpet and a pad of cream cheese on it and quickly sat down and took up her cup.

"Oh, Sally, I can hardly wait to tell you what I heard and saw last evening," she said, pausing to take a sip and to mess with my head a little. "By the way, where did you and Stu run off to. Neither one of you ate a bite?" she asked, then continued talking, not giving me a chance to answer. "Sally, this morning I have more questions than answers for you," Miss Marple said with excitement, almost gasping for air.

I tried to seem calm, sipping at my tea while sitting back in my chair with my legs crossed at the knees. Inside I was all but screaming. "Hurry up, what news?"

"All right," Miss Marple said after putting her cup down on the table beside her. "Remember those three men that brought Kitty to the barbecue? Well, they were sitting at the table next to ours and making themselves right at home, if you know what I mean? I asked Agatha, Kitty's best friend from New York, to switch places with me at the table so I could overhear what the men were saying. Oh, you never met Agatha. Well, I'll have to tell you more about her later. Anyway, where was I? Oh yes, the men went up to get seconds on the food and enjoyed many mixed drinks—they did and got louder and louder. I think it must've been about an hour after you left when they became aware that one of their friends hadn't returned to their table. They jumped up and went off in different directions to find him, soon returning more puzzled than before at his disappearance. The old man became angry and unpleasantly loud, so much so that Dan Morhouse walked over and sat down with them at their table. I thought he just meant to quiet them down, but what I heard next was confusing."

Miss Marple had me on the edge of my chair. I could hardly wait for the next word out of her mouth. And she continued: "Dan told the guys to quiet down, then asked, 'John, what in the hell have you and your cronies done? Where are those ladies that you put on ice in New York? You know you're going to clean up this mess or die trying. That old lady over there can't live—you know that, don't you? Everybody knows what the three of you look like. You've almost stood in the middle of town and yelled, "Look at us!" Do you think all those people at the club this afternoon are blind? I wash my hands of all of you. Hell, you'll be lucky to get out of the harbor—if you don't get arrested the syndicate will be out for your blood, especially if they lose that land at the sale Wednesday.'" Miss Marple paused, and we both sat in silence for a couple of seconds.

I was trying to process everything that she had just said, and the fact that there was a dead body under the boathouse, something I was keeping to myself for now.

"I told you, I would speak to Agatha. I called her early night before last and told her what was happening here to her best friend; I also told her about the party. She didn't think twice about it—she'd be on the red-eye before breakfast. She arrived at the airport early this morning and had a cab drive her right out to Kitty's house. The man at the front gate had them drive around to the back door near the kitchen when he found out who she was and why she had come. Agatha asked her driver to wait for her, then she got out of his car and went up to the door. The gatekeeper called and let the cook know who was coming to the back door and why, so he was standing at the open the door to welcome her. The cook extended his hand, then stepped to one side to let her walked in. Knowing why she was there, he quickly called Kitty's suite and asked her maid to have Kitty come down to the kitchen ASAP, as something had come by delivery and he needed to know what he was to do with it. The maid went to Kitty's room and whispered near her ear about the delivery. Kitty was a little dumbfounded to what her cook was trying to say. She rose out of her chair and walked into the living room area, where John and his two goons were seated, to inform them she had to go downstairs to the kitchen because of a problem. Sir John ordered one of his goons to follow her, with instructions to kill them both if they tried any funny business."

Once in the kitchen, Ben, the cook took Kitty's arm with his right hand and led her away after he asked the man and her maid to wait a minute and that she'd be right back.

The cook led Kitty over to the storage locker and opened the heavy steel door. Kitty poked her head in to see what was so important to cause such a fuss. That's when she saw Agatha and almost went weak at the knees.

"Dear, remain calm. I'll see you at the barbecue later today. Kitty, I will come back here with you tonight," Agatha promised. Kitty slowly stepped back while the cook closed and locked the door, knowing full well that he would reopen it and let Agatha out once Kitty was gone.

"Thanks, Ben, for alerting me to this situation. I'll see to it after the barbecue is over this afternoon," Kitty said, winking at him before returning to those waiting for her. Ben returned to the locker and let Agatha out; she thanked him for his help and returned to the cab waiting on her. She called and told me she was heading into the harbor, and we could meet at the club. "We spent most of the morning eating and sharing stories," Miss Marple said, remembering aloud the events of yesterday with Sally.

"Wow, you weren't kidding when you said you had news. I have a little of my own—but you must promise not to tell another living soul." I paused. For it was Miss Marple's turn to sit on the edge of her seat. I didn't continue until I got a nod of agreement from her for secrecy.

"First of all, to your question. Stu received a phone call from one of his clients and had to leave immediately. He had asked me if I wanted to stay and come back with you. I told him that I was taught to leave with who brought me. Nevertheless, I wouldn't have come across some important clues if I had stayed."

"Clues, what kind of clues are you talking about?" Miss Marple said, getting to her feet with unbridled excitement. I told her everything about seeing the men and what happened with the birds over on the property that we were hoping to save.

"Oh Lord, we too heard the birds, but we didn't see them. If we had, we would all have run off the beach at the Morhouses'. We were able to stay and enjoy some of the most colorful fireworks I've ever seen," Miss Marple said, then added, "What did you do next, Sally? If I know anything about you, you wouldn't have been able to sit on your hands and do nothing. So what did you do next?" Miss Marple inquired impatiently.

"I hurried back here and went right up to my room to make out a report of all I had seen and to provide proof that what I said was true." I paused, for Miss Marple was looking curiously at me, as though she was trying to figure out what I meant by proof. That was something that I could not reveal even to her, not yet anyway, so I continued: "I sent the report out to the Indian commissioner of Northern Michigan by Express Mail, which hopefully he'll receive today. I also sent a copy of the report to the police department and asked both the commissioner and the police not to arrest anyone until we all get to the sale of the property in question—because we want to hear and see all those who want to buy it—to the point of killing other people." I again paused to get Miss Marple's response.

"Kill, who got killed, Sally?" Miss Marple asked.

"Well, there's that Indian fellow that was found on the beach the other day, and I wouldn't doubt that the man you spoke of who is missing will also show up dead somewhere," I added.

"Sally, do you know something that you haven't told me yet? What would make you think the other man is dead? I don't get it—did I miss something?" Miss Marple asked, sounding quite confused. Before I could answer her, we were interrupted. An old friend of Miss Marple's was entering the house, so we had to table our conversation. I wasn't prepared to tell her anything about the argument at the boathouse or the shooting of the man there. I quickly excused myself and returned to my room. When I entered my cellphone was ringing. I grabbed it up and closed the door behind me.

"Good morning," I said to the caller, hoping it was Stu.

"Please, please, forgive me Sally for running out on you yesterday. Let me try to make it up to you by coming by for you for lunch," Stu said.

"Oh, Stu dear, there is nothing to make up. We both have careers that will often call us away from time to time. I have an appointment at lunchtime that I can't get out of," I replied.

"Then dinner, you must grant me the pleasure of your company at dinner tonight, Sally. It's the least you can do. If you should deny me, I'll surely be crushed. Say yes, and I'll be around to pick you up at five," Stu said.

"Dinner sounds great, Stu. I hope to be back at Miss Marple's by four this afternoon. I can't wait to talk to you then," I replied.

"Good! Then I'll be around for you at five. Till then, darling, all you leave me to do is pine for you," Stu said as though he were acting out a part in a play.

"Oh, Stu, you are a real piece of work—but I like it. Tell me, has that line worked for you often?" I asked laughing.

"Sally, my lovely Sally, how could you say a thing like that? I shell never recover I fear. For you to doubt a word, I say, for there is none other than you for me. Every time I see you, it only makes me want you more," Stu said, then hung up without another word.

After a few seconds of bathing in his delightful words of love, I regained my composure and got off my bed and back on my feet. I still had an hour or so before I had to meet with Mr. Korn. I changed into my tennis shoes and took my hair down out of the bun I had put in it earlier. I grabbed up my hair as if I were going to put it into a ponytail and slipped it through the hole in the back of my baseball cap before putting it on my head. Then I put on my video-recording sunglasses that were able to pick up the conversation up to ten feet away. I stuck a few bucks into my pocket to cover whatever I may want to buy and ran out and got on my bike to take a ride.

CHAPTER 16

A Real Witch among Us

It was only nine in the morning, and I had already talked to my boss, Miss Marple, and Stu. Now I had a couple of hours to ride down to the Stain Cup and see what everyone was talking about today. The harbor was starting to look beautiful, as the decorations for the Fourth of July covered every house and business in the area. Even at this time in the morning, the streets seemed crowded with bikers and walking sightseers and children playing in their yards. I rode down by the beach and noticed the boat owners out on their decks, cleaning their boats with their deckhands. A couple of smaller vessels were out on the water as well, trying for a catch. I drew my bike up in front of the Stain Cup and got off it and put down the kickstand. There were people sitting eating, and music was being piped out from the front of the restaurant. I was hoping there would be an empty table inside as I entered the door. I passed by a couple on my way to a table at the back of the room. I had no idea what I wanted to order until I noticed the order that the waitress was delivering to their table. Once she emptied her tray, she turned and came in my direction.

"Good morning, may I get you something?" the waitress asked.

"Yes, I'll take whatever they're having. It looks good," I said, looking in their direction.

"That would be eggs benedict then, and what would you like to drink?" she asked.

"A tall glass of orange juice would be good," I replied as she quickly scurried off.

I put my sunglasses on the table in front of me and just sat for a while scanning the room. I noticed the lady I had passed seemed upset while talking to her companion. I put my sunglasses on to make sure the auto sound chip in them was working. What I heard next made the hair on the back of my neck stand up.

"Sam, Mom is dying. She called her lawyer late yesterday to revise her will. Damn it, Sam, I wasn't allowed to stay in the room while she spoke to him. She's been throwing a fit lately about how much I have been running up bills in her name. She's right, we have taken advantage of her, but I never thought it would make her change her will. Who else would she leave her wealth to?" she said, perplexed.

"We have to get a look at that will before she dies. I refuse to let her give everything that belongs to us to strangers," her companion replied.

I took my glasses back off before the waitress returned with my order. Once she arrived, I asked her if she knew the couple at the nearby table.

"Those are the Hatfields," she answered.

"The Hatfields! Are you kidding me?" I asked.

"No. That's Sara and Tom Hatfield. Sara's mom is Bonnie Jean Gaither. She's one of the richest people in the harbor. Her late husband was a big-time shipping tycoon. Bonnie has been one of our dearest summer guests for years," the waitress added.

"Yes, I hear that Miss Bonnie isn't doing so well," I replied.

"Oh, then you know she has cancer," the waitress quickly interjected.

"Yes, I just found out today," I replied.

"You are the lady that moved in with Miss Marple, aren't you?" the girl asked me.

"Yes, you're right. I am living there for the summer. Do you live here in the harbor?" I returned with a question. We both should learn as much as we can, I thought.

"I can't talk to you anymore now. I get off in half an hour. Maybe you'll still be here then," she said before running off.

I could only wonder what it was she wanted to say. After all, it wasn't like we knew each other. I returned to eating my breakfast when I noticed John entering the door. I hurried and put my glasses on. The old man wasn't dressed like a million bucks today, nor was he sporting a walking stick. John Feterly and his friends almost came back before stopping at a table a couple of steps in front of me. With their backs to me as though they were watching the door, I listened while I continued eating.

"Boss, where the hell did Mark go, it's like he fell off the face of the earth? I can't believe that he would ever leave town without talking to us first," the man with John said.

"I tend to agree with you; there is something that we don't know going on here. Did you hear what Dan said to us last night? He said that it was us that made this mess—yet he's the one that gave the orders. I think he said if we couldn't clean it up, we were as good as dead," John said.

"Boss, I think we should leave now while it's possible. Dan isn't the nice guy he pretends to be, and he knows people who kill just for the joy of it. If the people around here find out who Morhouse is they would hang him, for he is a cold-blooded, evil man. I am not one that is usually afraid of anyone, but I'd be a fool not to take him seriously. We best go back by Kitty's house and relieve our man there guarding her and that friend of hers, Agatha. We'll take them for a one-way ride," John's companion said.

"All right, I'll first call Jake in New York and tell him to get rid of those women he's holding permanently," John said as he took out his cell phone and dialed. Seconds later, someone answered, "Hello, who is this and where is Jake?" he asked the person on the other end of the phone.

"What do you mean he's tied up and can't get to a phone?" John asked before jumping up from the table.

"What is it, boss? What did that person tell you?" his companion asked.

"Let's get the hell out of here now! Jakes in jail," John said as they made their way out of the door.

I quickly took out my phone and called Bill at the police department to tell him what I had just heard.

"Okay, Sally. I am leaving right now to see Kitty and Agatha to make sure they're all right. I'll bring them both back to the harbor," Bill said.

"Miss Marple would love to have them over. I'll give her a call and let her know you'll be dropping them off soon," I replied.

"Yes, that's a clever idea. By the way Sally, I did hear from the FBI, they told us that they found those two females in New York just a couple of minutes ago. Isn't it amazing how fast we pull everything together here? You and I could make a great undercover team," Bill said, half laughing just before hanging up.

The waitress came over and sat down at my table. She was not the least bit shy if anything she was very open about everything that was going on around here.

"You're the lady that Stu Baker is dating, aren't you?" she asked boldly.

"Yes, I guess you can say that, but we're just friends," I replied.

"I heard the two of you left the barbecue early last night like your house was on fire," she said, grinning like she knew what happened and why. If so, she knew more than me.

"You heard right!" I replied like I cared what she was trying to say.

"You might be interested in the fact that Stu, your boyfriend, and Sara Gaither Hatfield used to be an item around here. Of course, that was before he met his late wife, who died mysteriously of unknown cause after only a few months of marriage. There are whispers that Sara had something to do with her death. She's not someone you want as an enemy. She's a real witch. I think she'd kill her mother for a few dollars and change. I heard Sara say that mom spent the whole night with her lawyer. Sara sounded livid about it and said if her mom dies before the lawyer gets back with the revised papers, she would still inherit the bulk of her wealth!"

All this was very serious, if true—but I must remember that this girl is a quart low and a dollar short. What if she was in cahoots with Sara and telling me a load of crap? I don't know enough about Stu's wife's death to know if there was any truth in what she just told me. The investigator's blood was running fast and hot through my veins right now; if it were true, Sara's mother was in real trouble. The waitress also made it sound like I may have something to fear when it comes to Sara Hatfield.

CHAPTER 17

A Mystery Is Good for the Soul

I noticed Kitty's car in the drive, so I drove in around it to park in the back of the house.

Kitty and Agatha must've had a police escort to get here before me, I thought as I ran up the back steps into the house. My trip to the Stain Cup was well worth it and might have helped to save those two ladies lives, for everyone at Kitty's had seen those men—I am sure, Bill considered that. Once upstairs I hurried over to my computer; sat down and opened it up to my notes so I could enter my trip to the Stain Cup. After doing so, I then sat back in my chair collecting my thoughts on all that had happened this week and the sale tomorrow of the property at the hall: for my column in the paper. I wondered how many would show up at the village hall. Sir John Feterly and his goonies were probably already out of Michigan. Dan Morhouse doesn't think anyone's on to him yet. He could very well still show up and try to buy the property while claiming it is for himself; never mentioning the fact that he is an operative for the Chinese government. I am glad we have the pictures and the soundtrack of that day in the boathouse. Right now, that's all we must stop him with unless the commissioner on Indian affairs shows up that would make it a whole new ball game; even now it's a bit nerve-wracking, just thinking about it. I closed the file after entering a few more notes and shut down the computer. I hurried down to join the girls, or at least poke my head in on my way out to the office.

"Oh, Sally dear, there you are. I was hoping that you would get back in time to visit with Kitty and Miss Agatha. You didn't get a chance to meet Agatha in person yet, did you?" Miss Marple asked.

"Yes, I think we did at the barbecue. It's good to see you again," I said, thrusting my hand out to shake hers, before sitting down on the white wicker couch near Kitty, on the porch.

"Would you like some tea or lemonade Sally?" Miss Marple asked.

"Oh no, thanks anyway—I've just come from the Stain Cup. I heard some good news while I was there from a friend of mine in law enforcement. He told me that your nieces are safe," I said, looking at Kitty.

"Yes, we too just received the news. Hopefully, the nightmare is finally over," Kitty replied. "It was the kind of news that put smiles on all of our faces," she replied, then added, "A couple of good things did come out of all of this, I got an extra special birthday without a year number attached to it and all my friends, and I got to meet the love of my nephew's life," Kitty said, turning slightly to look at me with a smile.

"Oh, thank you, Kitty, but Stu and I are only friends. We've only known each other for a brief time," I said, flashing a smile back at her.

"I do have a question. You ladies might be able to help me. Do either of you know Sara Hatfield?"

"Oh yes! Do we ever know Sara? Who in these parts doesn't?" Miss Marple exclaimed.

"I for one didn't until today," I replied. "I was told to watch my back around her, some say she's a witch," I added, then paused to see if one of the ladies would tell me more.

"Stu and Sara dated for three years, and everyone thought they would marry one day. Then something happened—Stu never told me why, but they just broke up. A few months later Stu met and fell in love with the girl that he would later make his wife. They made a lovely couple and were so much in love. They hated it when he had to leave and go out to work. It was just three months after their wedding when his wife became ill, and within a few weeks she died. The doctors to this day aren't sure, but they think it was some unknown poison that killed her. Most around these parts do believe that Sara had something to do with it, but there was no proof of that. They refer to her in whispers as the witch. Stu went into the depths of grief and then to the pinnacle of anger; everyone was sure that Sara's life was in danger. Instead, Stu drowned himself in his work, barely sleeping at all until he came here this summer. I am not sure what it is about you, Sally that has brought him back to life and gave him joy again, but we all thank God for sending you here," Kitty said and took a sip of her lemonade.

"Wow, what I heard wasn't just gossip, after all. It was a warning," I said, looking at Miss Marple, then continued, "I believe Sara has just met her match," I said, getting to my feet. "I am sorry, but I must leave—I have an appointment in Petoskey, and I can't be late—I'll see you all later." I got to my feet and hurried upstairs to get my purse before going out to my car.

I almost felt like a chameleon, stepping back and forth between different lives and stories. That is the life of reporters. On any given day, they may be expected to keep a lot of crucial facts separated on many ongoing stories. Now, I must put my mind on the challenge in front of me.

The parking lot near the newspaper office was full, so I had to park across the street at the post office.

It'll be okay, I thought. *I will only be in the news office a few minutes.*

I got out of my air-conditioned car into the noonday sun; the temperature was well into the nineties. I hurried across the street and entered the cool lobby of the newspaper office.

"Hello, Sally!" a voice rang out from behind the counter.

"Good afternoon, Joan, how's your summer going?" I asked her, making small talk.

"Summer? I don't know. I am here till dark every day. It's that new column by Joe Bumgardner. We can't seem to print enough papers to keep the public happy. Tell me, what I can do for you, Sally?" she asked in a hurried voice.

"I am here for an appointment with Doug Korn. Could you call him and let him know I've arrived?" I asked.

"Sure, right away," she said. While she was making the call, Jake Bates stepped out of the pressroom into the lobby.

"Sally, what is it that brings you back here? Oh yes, if I remember it right, you're a freelance writer. How's business these days? By the way, I thought we were in a challenge against each other. I can understand why you dropped out. After all, you're not as experienced as I am so it would have been an unfair challenge," he said smugly, then he added, before giving me a chance to respond: "By the way, have you ever heard of a reporter by the name of Joe Bumgardner? I've tried to find his name in the trade papers and publishing houses, and there is nothing written on any of his work—is he even an American?" he asked.

"I am sure I can't tell you, although I've read the column and find it very interesting. Didn't you? Maybe this time you've bitten off more than you can chew Jake," I replied, trying not to smile.

I suppose he thought I was going to help him. The only way I wanted to help him was with my foot square up his ass, I thought. *It will do my heart good to see the look on his face at the end of this challenge.*

"Sally, Mr. Korn will see you now—just go on back, you know the way," Joan said.

As I approached his office door, he stepped out into the hallway to greet me.

"Sally girl, it's good to see you—please come in," he said with his hand on my back, directing me through the doorway of his office and to a chair that sat near his desk. He walked around his desk and sat down, then opened a drawer on the right side of the desk and handed me a pay envelope.

"Joan told me that Jake was trying to give you a tough time out in the lobby, and you gave back better than you got. Joan is one of the few people that knows who Joe Bumgardner is, so she got a big kick out of it, and so do I," he said, then laughed while handing me my check.

"I couldn't be happier with your work, Sally. The property sale that you spoke of in your column takes place tomorrow. Every newspaper and television station will be there to cover it, and it's only because of your column that they even know about it. Your column has made a significant impact on this community and county. So tell me, what clues are you keeping that could change the outcome of this sale?" Mr. Korn asked, then paused to let me get a word in.

"You're right, there will be some surprises. Will you be there?" I asked.

"Yes, I wouldn't miss it. Look here, Sally, I am your boss—you can let me in on some of your secrets," Mr. Korn said, trying to compel me to surrender some of the many facts.

"You know, being a newsman yourself, you know a reporter is a very secretive character who doesn't share well. See this check you just handed me? I'd have to burn it and leave this business if I was so weak that such a suggestion could make me give up my story before it's time. Besides, a good mystery is good for the soul. Oh, look at the time! I am sorry, but I must run—stay well, Mr. Korn," I said while getting to my feet to make my way out his office.

I hurried out of the building and over to my car. Once inside, I took a few seconds to open my pay envelope. To my surprise, Mr. Korn had added an extra hundred dollars to it.

Wow, this will come in handy, I thought. I put my key into the ignition and started my car, and as I prepared to pull out of the parking lot onto the street, Jake Bates drove by in front of my convertible. He wasn't one to miss an opportunity to spread his charm with a big grin on his face and a good long-armed wave. I was free to laugh out loud now and did while waving back. He thought he's all that and a bottle of wine. We'd see who's whining in the end.

I now needed to call and talk to Officer Bill, I thought, so I told my phone to dial him for me. I loved my phone; it's like having a secretary without the payroll.

"Bill, is that you?" I asked the person on the other end.

"Yes, of course, who else would answer my phone?" he replied.

"You're right," I said, then laughed. "Bill, have you uncovered any other clues?" I asked.

"Yes, Sally, we have just found a body that washed up on the beach near the state park in Petoskey, Michigan. The body is bloated badly by water, but there is no doubt he was shot. They have to dry him out before they'll be able to identify him," Bill said, then added, "I think we both know who it is, for it would have been easy for Morhouse to pull the body out of his boathouse into deep water and leave it and for the body to wash up somewhere else. Sally, I sent all the auto texts and photos to the FBI. They plan to be at the sale, and that is where they'll arrest him. They also picked up John Feterly and his crony at the airport and planned to have them at the sale, too. I have to run, Sally. There are no boring days around here," Bill said before hanging up.

The drive back to the harbor was delightful. I took off my sun hat, allowing my hair to fly in the breeze. Then something white dropped on me from the five seagulls flying over. I looked up at them, scolding them with a shaking finger, though I am sure they neither heard me nor cared. Once back at the house, I hurried upstairs to shower and wash my hair. I quickly changed for the rest of the day and ran downstairs to find Miss Marple. The ladies were still on the porch just finishing up their lunches at the bridge table.

"Oh, you're back, Sally. Would you like to join us?" Miss Marple asked.

"Yes, I'd love to, but I know nothing about the bridge," I replied.

"It is good to come into the game as a person who's never played before and learn it right the first time. You would be surprised at how some people play this game. At the club, we instructed our inexperienced players to learn the game by the stated manufacturer's rules; that way we all play the same way," Miss Marple said.

"Sally, I would be honored if you would be my partner for your first time," requested Kitty.

I took a chair at the table across from Miss Marple; while Kitty and Agatha sat across from each other as partners. For the next three hours, we snacked, laughed ourselves silly, and played bridge. It was one of the most enjoyable afternoons that I had ever had; time flew by, and before I knew it Stu was walking up the porch steps to the front door.

"Oh, I see now what the prominent ladies of the harbor do with their time in the afternoon without a good man around," Stu said laughing, and we joined in laughing.

He walked over to his Aunt and Miss Marple and gave them both kisses on the cheek before approaching me.

"How are you, beautiful?" he said, as he put his hands in mine and helped me to my feet. Then without another word, he wrapped his strong, protecting arms around me and our eyes met locking onto each other. Then he kissed me, and Angel's harps of heaven played. It was good that he was holding on tight, for my knees went weak as he folded me ever so gently into him. I had never totally wanted a man like this before. If it had not been that there were others in the room, I am not sure how far this might all have gone; neither one of us wanted to let go.

"Wow, you two—should we call paramedic?" Miss Marple said, laughing.

"There's no way either of you can deny your love for each other now. That kiss kinda sealed it, I'd say. What about you girls, do you agree?" Kitty asked.

"I sure do, it even took my breath away, and I was standing several feet away from the two of you," Agatha said, half laughing.

I wasn't sure what they thought they saw, but if the heat radiating from my face was any clue, then my embarrassment was well-founded.

"Well, darling, are we ready to go?" Stu asked while looking into my eyes.

"Go! Where are the two of you off to?" Kitty asked.

"I am taking my lady to the Pier Restaurant, where we can sit on their deck to eat and enjoy the view of the harbor. Perhaps, even catch the sun while it's setting."

"Stu, I am ready. I need to grab a sweater in case the air turns cool over the water," I replied and hurried upstairs while he visited for a few more minutes.

As we left the porch, everyone was grinning from ear to ear. Me too, for the excitement, was almost more than I could bear. Stu and I walked hand in hand to his car, he opened the door, and I slid in while he ran around and got into the other side. The car pulled away from the curb, and before we knew it, we were sitting in front of the restaurant. Stu wasted no time in helping me out and into the restaurant.

"Hello, Mr. Baker," one of the young waitresses said.

"Good evening, is our table ready?" Stu asked.

"Yes, sir. Right this way, please," she said, directing us to our seats out on the deck. With his hand in mine, we walked through the restaurant and out of a set of glass doors to the large deck patio. Sun umbrellas covered their tables, and our table had a candle and flowers on it. Stu pulled out my chair for me, and he sat down beside me. Then he asked the waitress for a special bottle of wine. We were both amazed at the beauty of the lake—it looked like dark cobalt glass with the sun reflecting off it.

"Sally, thank you for your understanding about my job," Stu said, taking my hand in his and very passionately laying out his feelings before me. "Sally, you can't know how hard it was for me to leave you last night. If it hadn't been an emergency, I would have had my client wait till today."

"Stu, this is lovely. You called and made reservations, even had flowers put on our table. You make me feel so special."

We spent the next hour and a half eating, drinking, and dancing. Then Stu's phone rang while we were dancing close together.

"I am sorry, Sally, but I have to take this call," Stu said, pulling out his phone and stepping away from me. I return to my seat, realizing that he might leave any second now. I understood our night was coming to its end. I couldn't be upset about anything, for we'd had a perfect night in every way. I finished up my dessert while waiting on Stu.

"Sally, something horrible has happened—I must go immediately. I know the sun is about to set, but I can't wait. I'll take you back to Miss Marple's," Stu said, offering me a hand to help me.

"No, Stu, I think I'll stay right here for a little while longer, then I'll walk back to the house. Thank you for a lovely night—go now and do what you must," I said, giving him a kiss goodbye as he leaned over me. Then I sat and watched him disappear around the corner. The sky was full of bright colors beyond belief, so vibrant that they seemed almost touchable. As I was drinking in the beauty of it all, something happened, or should I say, someone? The sight of her almost knocked me for a loop.

CHAPTER 18

A Scary Place to Be

"I'm sorry, are you alone?" a voice from behind me said. As I turned to see who it was, I almost fell off my chair.

"Yes, for now," I replied.

She walked around my table and sat down, as though I had invited her.

"You're the lady Stu Baker is seeing, aren't you?" Sara Hatfield asked, trying to sound like a dear old friend.

"Yes, we are a friend. Why would that concern you?" I asked bluntly.

"Stu's an old friend mine, and you might say we have a history," she said, trying to feel me out.

"Yes, I am aware of who you are, Sara. Stu hasn't told me yet, why he broke it off with you after all those years. He's been too busy these days, and you're the last... Maybe, you would like to fill me in on it seems you're in the sharing mood," I replied.

Sara's eyes stayed on me, as her face turned red with anger showing a twisted distortion.

"So you know my name. I haven't yet heard yours or where you're from?" she inquired in a sharp tone.

"Sara, my name isn't important to you, seeing you and Stu are only friends. I am a guest at Miss Marple's for the summer and only met Stu a couple of weeks ago myself, and where I am from is none of your business, nor is where you live mine. So if you'll excuse me, I will be leaving now," I said while getting up to my feet. She deliberately stepped in front of me, as though she was silently daring me to say more before I walked away.

"You're so called friend spent the other night with me at my mom's house," she said with a wicked laugh.

"Yes, I know, your mother is one of his many clients. Oh, I am sorry. Did you think I didn't know?" I said, picking up my clutch purse from the table beside me as walked away, leaving her to stew in her mind. *A terrifying place to be I'm sure*, I thought, almost laughing out loud.

I was glad that the encounter was over; it had to happen sooner or later. I walked back to Miss Marple's under a full lover's moon. My mind now was on the earlier events of the evening when Stu and I truly connected at Miss Marple's. Alone with my thoughts in the moonlight was a lonely place to be.

It only took me ten minutes to walk back to Miss Marple's; she was still up when I walked in the house which was a bit surprising for she was still one to turn in early and get up late.

"Sally, is that you?" she asked as I walked through the door.

"Yes, it is," I replied as I entered her parlor. She was sitting alone with the phone in her hand when I took a seat across from her.

"Sally, I've just gotten some sad news. Bonnie Gaither has been found dead in her daughter's home. Her daughter is Sara Hatfield."

"Did they say if it was because of her illness or something else?" I asked.

"What do you mean—something else?" Miss Marple asked perplexed, after hanging up the phone.

"While I was at the Stain Cup this morning, I overheard Sara and her husband talking. They were sitting just a table away from me and were talking so loudly, I couldn't help but hear every word. They were furious about her mother revising her will. They were concerned that if the new will that Stu was making up for her got to her in time to sign it before she died could strip them of everything. And there's something else that you might find interesting. While Stu and I were having dinner, he received a call and had to leave immediately, just like the other night. I remained at the restaurant and finished up my meal. Sara Hatfield showed up and sat down at my table like she was invited, without even asking. She then implied that she and Stu spent the other night together at her home. When I informed her that I was aware that Stu was at her home spending time with her mother, let's say she was not amused. Miss Marple, do you think that she could have had something to do with her mother's death?" I asked, genuinely concerned.

"Oh, my dear, where did you say Stu went?" Miss Marple asked.

"His last words before he departed were 'Something horrible has happened, my client needs me.' Miss Marple, if your information is right, and I see no reason why it shouldn't be, I can only surmise that he's at or with Bonnie—alive or dead," I added. "Please forgive me, but it's late for both of us, and we have a big day tomorrow at the land sale," I said as I stood to my feet to leave her.

"Sleep well," Miss Marple said.

Once in bed, all I could do was wonder where Stu was. Did he go to see Bonnie before coming to see me and had she signed her revised will before she died? If Stu hadn't got to her first, and her will lay unsigned, then was it possible this wasn't a natural death? I could now feel the overwhelming concern and pain Stu was going through for Bonnie, his dear friend.

"Stu's a good lawyer, and he will get to the bottom of all of this, so Sara better hope she had nothing to do with her mother's death," I said to myself before surrendering to sleep hours later.

The morning of June 28, I woke up to a pale light floating in through the opening in my drapes and creeping over my bed. I looked over at my clock on the dresser to notice the time. I shot out of bed like a bullet. It was already eight, and the land sale would take place in just four hours from now. I hurried into the bathroom and showered, then prepared for the day. I was so excited about the sale and its outcome that the need to eat didn't occur to me. I sat down at my computer to read over my notes of the events ahead and felt a lot like a child on Christmas morning. This questionable land box could bring beautiful things to this area or be a Pandora's box, for the land may not belong to the Indians since the hundred-year lease was over.

The fact that there are burial sites on it legally, the state may keep it as a land preserve, for how could they sell it to any private landowner? Nevertheless, there would be some bad guys going to jail before it was all said and done. Stu and I had talked a little about the land and sale, but I wasn't sure he knew it was today. His plate was full now, and I wasn't going to call him. I'll meet with Bill and the commissioner at the center to get some firsthand news for my column.

I went about tidying up my room and making up my bed; time seemed to be crawling along. The phone rang, and I jumped to pick it up.

It could be Stu, I thought.

"Hello, Sally, your favorite cop here. Could you get to the community center early? There are going to be a lot of people showing up for sale, and we'll want to have the seats right up front. The Indian commissioner called me; he's bringing about a dozen tribal members with him. The young man found dead on the shoreline was part of their tribe; he was also an offspring of those that leased the land a hundred years ago.

"Sally, thanks for the research you've done in finding the amendment added to the land lease," Bill said, as though today was going to be a history lesson for all those concerned.

"I'll be there by eleven. Oh, by the way, have you heard anything from Stu today?" I asked.

"No, why?" he asked. I explained everything that had happened in the past twenty-four hours.

"Sally, girl, you seem to be in the center of all the action around here. If something unlawfully happened to Bonnie, we'll get to the bottom of it. I've got a few phone calls to make, so I'll see you later at the center," Bill said before hanging up.

I quickly picked up my purse off the bed and headed downstairs.

"Sally, is that you?" Miss Marple asked as my foot hit the last step on the stairs.

"Yes, it is. Where are you?" I asked, passing by her parlor on my way to the porch.

"I'm in the kitchen," she replied.

I walked in laughing. "This is the last place I would have looked for you, this time of the day you're usually out and about by now. Aren't you feeling well?" I asked, a bit concerned.

"Oh yes, I feel great! The only thing that could make me feel better is for you to tell me that you've heard from Stu," she said, smiling mischievously.

"No, not a word since last night at the restaurant. I am afraid Bonnie's revised will didn't get signed in time. He could be somewhere blaming himself if that's the case," I replied.

"Sally, let's not presume anything; it's better to let time take care of such things. He has a large practice here and many clients, anything or nothing at all would be wrong. Do you understand what I am saying?" Miss Marple asked, then added, "It's better not to borrow trouble." She picked up her tea tray and headed out of the kitchen. I followed her, as we entered the porch and she sat the plate down on the table, we both filled our cups and took a seat.

"Are you and the girls planning to be at the land sale today?" I asked her.

"Oh yes!" she said with excitement in her voice. "We wouldn't miss it. I am sure it will be the most exciting happening of the summer. There won't be any standing room at the Center, and the parking lots will be full as well. That Joe Bumgardner made sure that everyone in the county was aware of the history of the land, and it's important to the local Indian tribes. You better get there early if you have any hopes of getting inside the building," Miss Marple added.

"I am meeting Officer Bill and the Indian commissioner there at eleven this morning. So please forgive me if I have to drink up fast and run," I said.

CHAPTER 19

Questionable Death

I pulled my car into the parking lot behind the community center and went into the building through the back door. Television reporters were set up across the back of the room from several nearby news outlets.

"Sally," Stu said, walking up behind me.

"Oh, you're here. Good!" I said, turning to hug him.

"Stu, would you and Sally sit here in the front row next to me?" Bill asked.

"Sure," Stu replied as he took my hand and moved us over to where Bill was sitting.

I looked around and noticed how fast the place was filling up and the many faces that were now turning toward their seats on the platform in front of us.

From left to right: United States Attorney from Washington, the commissioner on Indian affairs of Northern Michigan, Emmet County attorney, Emmet County records secretary, Sir John Feterly, and Dan Morhouse, who was acting as an attorney for the Chinese businessman, who thought he was here to take possession of the land in question. The businessman from China tried to bail both John and Dan out of jail was arrested for the kidnapping of three females, and the death of two men who had been drilling without a permit on a land preserve, one Indian and thugs killed on Morhouses' property.

"Bill, who are those men over there?" I asked, nodding in the direction of six men dressed in black suits and ties around the platform.

"Sally, those men are FBI agents. They have every intention of taking John and Dan back into custody before all this is over here today. Just look around you, did you ever think that so many people would show up for this? This building only holds three hundred, and it is packed, with hundreds outside standing or sitting on folding chairs that they brought with them and who will be listening to all these proceedings by the overhead speakers," Bill replied.

The Emmet County secretary of records stepped up to the mic, and everything went quiet.

"We are opening this land trust disposition on June 28, 2017, here in Black Hawk Harbor in the State of Michigan. I will now turn these proceedings over to the commissioner of Indian affairs," she said.

The commissioner stepped forward with a folder full of papers in his hands.

"Thank you all for coming out today and making this an important part of your day. We are here to decide what will be done with a large piece of land that had been leased one hundred years ago by seven educated Indian braves, with the full agreement of the Office of Interior and the head of the United States government at the time. These braves worked hard and saved to preserve the land for future generations so it couldn't be sold for development as some here today wish to do. Ten years after it was first leased, an addendum was added to it that would make it possible to use the land as a burial site for tribal members, with the understanding that the land itself had to remain intact. By adding this to the land agreement, the young braves pretty much secured any future uses of parts of the land as it is now deemed sacred land. We have laid out all the evidence and historical papers on the tables before you to examine and we will listen to anyone here today who wants to add their opinions to these proceedings," the commissioner said stepping back from the mic.

"Yes, I do have something to say," Dan Morhouse said, standing to his feet; we waited as he made way to the mic.

"If you knew all of this, why then was the land posted for today's sale? My client came here today expecting to pay for the land in question an amount that would serve all these people in your county. We were given the amount of thirty million dollars with the understanding that we would be able to drill on the property and later build there. Now you stand here and tell us none of this will ever be possible and that this land will forever be tied up, by a trick pulled off on all of us by some well-meaning Indians. Is that really what you're saying?" Dan asked as he looked pompously into the cameras pointed at him now from the back of the room, pausing just long enough to catch his breath he continued: "Are you people so dumb that you don't understand what this kind of money could do for all of you? Why should the wishes of a few people override those of many? All that land out there is being used for nothing more but a graveyard for Indians and only Indians! Doesn't that make you mad? What right do they have over the rest of you to that land? Today and only today you have a chance to change these facts. Who among you will join me to break this lease once and for all?" Dan asked.

The next thing I heard was the voices of hundreds of angry people, inside and outside the building.

"End the lease that land belongs to all of us. Tricked by the dead," were just some of the things being yelled out. Other things were not printable.

The United States attorney from the Office of Interior stepped forward and took the mic and platform.

"My name is Rob Silver. The president of the United States is aware of this case and asked me to come here today to share with you what he thinks should happen to this land. I know it all seems straightforward to most of us and if it were as Mr. Morhouse said I would be angry too. Something has been left out in the explanation of this land and these potential buyers.

"A few nights ago, just before dark, two men met their death on the property in question. They were attacked by large blackbirds while drilling over an Indian burial mound. We've since found out that they were working for Dan Morhouse and his Chinese partners, those men right over there." Rob paused and pointed at the men.

"We have talked to them and Dan about their actions. I think it is essential for you to know what we found. These men intended to bring big digging rigs and pumps, with the plan of drilling for oil or natural gas under our Great Lake shoreline and then ship their findings to the China marketplace in New York. In other words, they want to rape your land and pollute your waters to make a profit for their country. That is one of the reasons why they did not get a drilling permit when they applied for one. It has only been in the last few days that news came to us of all that has been happening out there on the land. You'll all remember the night of the birds a week or so ago. We now believe it was at that time these men set up their operations and the birds tried to warn us. It is in the best interest of all us to keep that land and our waterways safe from those who wish to do us harm.

"These men have kidnaped three people and killed a young Indian man to gain ownership of that land, so who do you think they were trying to serve? Truly, it wasn't any of you. The money they brought here to purchase the land with is blood money, but in the end, the highest cost will be paid for by all of you," Mr. Silver said before taking his seat.

Three men came in the center from the boat docks carrying ropes from the boat docks, for a hanging party. Then the FBI agents who had been standing around the platform stepped forward and recuffed John, Dan, and the Chinese businessmen. Before another word was spoken, three CIA agents stepped up.

"Remove, the cuffs," a man said while showing his badge to the other officers. "These men have foreign diplomat immunity and cannot be held, and two of them have dual citizenship, and we're here doing business for their other country," the CIA officer said. The men were quickly removed to waiting cars and hurried away with sirens blaring.

We were all left a little dumbfounded, yet it was clear that the land would remain as it was—or would it?

Mr. Silver stepped back up to the mic. "Please, may I have your attention, for this meeting is far from over? What happens to those men isn't what's important to most of you—it's the land. There is no longer a lease on this land. It to be kept as a national preserve and used in some areas as nonmotorizing park land. There will be camping, walking and bike areas, also, a portion on the west side for a beach and marina. Then a section of about one hundred acres that has burial mounds on it will be kept and maintained as an ancient burial site. There will also be a five-hundred-acre partial set apart untouched by any development. The men and their families buried there are the ones who put through proper planning, not trickery—they set this property aside for all of you and your children's children. Anyone wanting to show their respect is welcome to come and do so.

"We will move quickly this year to set up the camping, and the biking and walking pathways for all of you. The portion of land on the west side that will be for the marina and beach won't come about for a year or two. There are some in Congress who want to see first that the land will be respected by all that use it, before putting more taxpayers' money into it, so, it is truly in all of your hands how all this comes about," Mr. Silver said before stepping away from the mic.

The commissioner of Indian affairs retook the mic before closing out the meeting.

"As an Indian, and not just as the commissioner I would like to thank Congress and our President for moving so quickly on all of our behalves where it comes to the burial sites of our past loved ones. We believe all burial sites are protected by the Great Spirit; before closing this meeting, I would like to find out how many of you agree to this meets outcome; by your I's, and nays," he said.

The yelling started again from inside and outside the building, it could be heard from miles away, and everyone seemed to be happy with the outcome.

"With that said, we'll offer up a closing prayer for this meeting, and we'll all come together next year right here to see where things stand." The commissioner added, "God, thank you for your direction on these matters, and for bringing us all together here today. Take us now safely to our homes wherever that may be. Amen."

Wow! Who would have guessed to the outcome of this meeting? It seems like a higher power or spirit has always been in control of this land, I thought as Stu and I stood up and slowly made our way outside and over to our cars. We could see that we weren't going anywhere at least not by driving for a while.

"Sally, what do you say we walk over to the restaurant for a bite of lunch, and maybe by the time we get done, things here will be thinned out?" Stu said.

"Yes, I like that," I replied. We hurried across the street then quickly removed our shoes to walk across the sandy beach to the restaurant.

"Wait a minute, you two, Officer Bill Sterling yelled out while running to catch up with us. He left on his shoes and asked if he could join us; as we walked, Bill imparted some of his thoughts.

"Everything with the land lease done, but there is still an unanswered question that concerns me, and it should concern you too," he said, making the hair on the back of my neck stand up.

"Let's talk about it over lunch. I can hardly wait to hear what has got you so concerned," Stu said. Once at the restaurant, Stu and I put back on our shoes before entering it.

By the time we walked in, Bill had found us a table out on the deck at the back of the restaurant near the shoreline. We quickly got settled in and ordered our lunch, and while we waited on our waitress to serve us, Bill spoke his mind.

"No one considered what almost happened here today. It's not just happening here but all around our country. Foreign enemies are buying up our lands and removing its resources or bringing other people from their countries to lay hold to it as part of their country—much like we see our embassies in foreign lands. These enemies see all the lands they buy in the United States as belonging to their country. If we don't wake up to what's going on, there will no longer be a country for us to call ours. There is another matter," Bill said then paused. Stu and I waited for him to gather his thoughts.

"Remember the trip I took to the New York, to see a prisoner that had been there, then moved before my arrival? That matter is still open. His whereabouts is still in question and my boss is still on his high horse over it. The trip cost our department over two thousand dollars, and we are on a very tight budget with the city. He's ordered to write a report giving a good reason for the trip. He'll lose his job. I believe I had a hand in the decision for him sending me there. How can I now sit back and do nothing?" Bill asked.

This was truly a mind-boggling situation, I thought and wasn't sure what the next step should be; both subjects that Bill brought up are worth checking out. I refrained from putting in my two cents until I could research it further. I promised Bill that I would investigate both matters and get back with him as soon as possible. He stayed just long enough to eat his sandwich then got up and returned to work, but Stu and I remained.

"Sally, I owe you an explanation for leaving you again last night at dinner," Stu said.

Before he could say another word, we were interrupted.

"Stu, darling, it's so good to see you enjoying yourself. Who is this, another one of your summer flings? Does she know you're not the committing kind, darling? I suppose she's already told you that she and I spoke the other night at the Pier Restaurant, the night you ran out on her. You're running out on her brought back old feelings and memories when you used to do that to me. My love for you was stronger than my knowledge about playboys, for it took me three years before I became aware that you weren't going to love me forever. I was nothing but a trophy for you, to use on your arm when you needed me around our rich friends, then you put me on the shelf," Sara Hatfield said.

"Sara, like always, you are more drama than anything. It is true, we did date for three years, and we would have gotten married if you hadn't gotten pregnant by a friend of mine. Then you hid your affair with him and got an abortion, as though you'd just gone to the dentist. The only life that ever meant anything to you is yours. I can tell you one thing for sure. Sally would have never kept secrets from me, and yes, I was made aware that you had words with Sally last night after I left. So tell us now what we can do for you?" Stu said a bit teed off.

"The will, Stu! When are you going to read Mom's will?" Sara asked, as though she was in a hurry.

"Not until the report comes back from the lab, and the doctor knows the true time of death, so it may be a week or two before we know for sure. Why, are you in a hurry to leave town to parts unknown? I'll give you some free advice, Sara. If you had anything to do with her death, you'd be better off in China—if you get my meaning."

"Everyone knows Mom was dying of cancer. She received large doses of morphine for pain. How dare you sit there and accuse me of hurting my mother? You are her lawyer up until her will is read, but I will always be her daughter." Stu listened to every word she had to say somewhat in disbelief.

"Sara, we both know that you understood she had her will revised. You also heard her tell her nurse that she would not take any more morphine until the new will was signed, no matter how great the pain. Her nurse was with her until five o'clock last night, only leaving long enough to get dinner and change clothes. When the nurse returned, your mother was dead," Stu replied, then added, "Sara, we'll all know more in a few days, so I'll call you later. Please excuse us.

"Sally, be careful, for bad things have been known to happen to people around him," Sara said in a threatening tone as she walked away.

Stu's face stiffened up in anger, and if looks could kill, Sara would be meeting her maker right now.

"Darling, don't let that woman bother you. She has no power unless she can get to you and make you angry. She not worth it," I said, looking out the front window. The harbor had pretty-well emptied of all the onlookers, and things were almost back to normal; so, we tried making it back to our cars.

"Sally, Sara said she spoke to you last night. Were you planning on sharing that with me?" Stu asked.

"Stu, I am a big girl and very capable of taking care of myself without running to someone to fight my battles for me. If you think for one minute that our relationship can only work by my acting like a whining, spoiled child, then maybe we should part company right here. For I am not going to come to you and complain every time someone speaks cross to me—that would be ridiculous," I said firmly.

"Sally, you should have been a lawyer, you argue your case very well and in very few words," Stu said, now smiling again.

I reached down into my cloth shoulder bag and withdrew my car key then unlocked my car door. Before I slid into the car seat, Stu and I kissed and promised to call each other later. He was headed back to his office, and I needed to get back to Miss Marple's, I had a column to get out and research to do on the prisoner move in upper New York.

It was now three o'clock, and it seemed like everyone was out of the house when I returned. I hurried up to my room and got seated in front of my computer and pulled up my files on the prison in New York: Archive 1608, James Anderson, CIA agent, imprisoned for life for spying. Primary testimony against him came from his partner Sir John Feterly. James Anderson has always said that he was set up and was innocent. His fingerprints were found throughout the dead man's premises and on the weapon in question. He was also seen in a heated argument with the dead man earlier about the information that was found in red folder that evening. The warden of the New York prison number is 915-723-7676. Before calling him, I thought I should first find out what information had been put on the CIA website today about John Feterly. Using the private website address I brought up the site and left a question, one could retrieve answers from here but no direct access. The problem was as follows:

"What about James Anderson? You know the man that John Feterly framed and now sits in a New York federal prison." Then I hurried off the site and took up my cell phone and dialed the prison then waited for the phone to be answered.

"Hello, Warden Reed's office, how may I direct your call? The operator asked.

"My name is Sally Crystal, and I would like to speak to Warden Reed," I replied

"Please hold, and I'll see if he's in," the operator said.

"Hello, this is Warden Reed, do I know you, Miss Crystal?" The male's voice asked from the other end.

"No, sir, not yet. It's come to my attention that a prisoner that you once held is now somewhere else. How would I go about finding out where he is now?" I asked.

"Miss Crystal, it is not our policy to give out confidential information. Why do you think I should speak to you on this matter?"

"Warden Reed, I have come across additional information about James Anderson, which lead us to believe that the prisoner you have is innocent and that the person who testified against him was a spy. This information has just come forward in the last few hours," I replied.

"You said the prisoner's name is James Anderson?" the warden asked.

"Yes, James Anderson, he was a CIA agent and received a life sentence. My information tells me he was there with you up until a week ago," I said.

"Miss Crystal, your information was almost right. James Anderson came to us three years ago and has always said he wasn't guilty of the charges against him. I have gotten to know James quite well, and I for one believe him, but I am only a warden. A law officer came from Michigan in hopes of seeing him a few days ago. Between the time he first called and told me he was on his way up to visit with James to the time he got here I received a call from Washington to stop all visits. No reasons were given. So I had to make up a reason why the officer couldn't see him, I lied and told him Mr. Anderson had been moved. Miss Crystal, James Anderson is still here and if you think you can help him with this additional information, please come up and visit us soon," the warden urged.

"Thank you for the invitation, and I will be there tomorrow," I said before even speaking to Bill about it.

"Tomorrow, good, I'll let James know of your upcoming visit, I know he will be thrilled. With that, I will say goodbye for now," the warden said before hanging up.

I quickly called Bill to tell him about our trip—this one I would pay for.

"Hello," Bill said, answering his phone.

"Bill, do you have any personal time coming to you that you might use for time off?" I asked.

"Yes. Why do you ask?" he replied.

"Bill, I've got us a date with the warden in the New York federal prison and a prisoner named James Anderson for tomorrow. If you come with me, I'll foot the bill—but it must be tomorrow. Are you game?" I asked with excitement.

"Yes, yes, I am. I will get us a round trip flight, for it is law business related. So I'll call you back on the time of our flight in a few minutes," he said as he quickly hung up.

I promptly put my thoughts back on the column at hand, to make sure it would be in the paper first thing tomorrow. I named the column this week "Doing the Peoples Business," trying to help those reading it get the full picture of what happened at the land meeting and what Bill had said about foreign countries buying up American property. I also shared the passing of their dear friend Bonnie this week, she was a real community organizer and participant.

CHAPTER 20

Foreign Diplomat Immunity Clause

Bill and I met at the airport parking lot at 6:45 a.m. in Harbor Springs and boarded a small jet to fly directly to an airport close to the Upper New York federal prison. Once we landed in New York, we were met by a local police officer who had met Bill the last time he was here. The officer drove us from the airport to prison. Once at the prison the officer walked us in to meet with the warden. The warden's office door was standing open, and he was sitting at his desk waiting on us. The officer introduced us, then excused himself before we sat down with the warden.

"Sally Crystal, you're the one that called me yesterday and asked for this meeting. You also said something about having news that might clear James Anderson of being a foreign spy. Did I understand you right?" the warden asked.

"Yes, Warden Reed, all of that is true. I do believe that news has recently surfaced that could clear James Anderson of being a spy against our country. First, it is imperative for all here to agree that it is Bill who the official person bringing you this information, for my name is never to be used in connection with anything discussed here today. I am an undercover reporter and must remain in the background to do my work. I hope you both understand." The warden and Bill both nodded in agreement.

"There will be another person joining us along with Mr. Anderson," the warden informed us.

No sooner had he finished speaking than an officer with James Anderson and his lawyer came through the door, and the warden quickly stood to his feet to welcome them.

"Please come in, James. I would like to introduce Sally Crystal and Bill Sterling to you," the warden said as we too stood to our feet to shake their hands. The warden walked around behind James's lawyer and closed the door before they all took their seats.

I walked across the office to look out an open window before turning around to look at James.

"James, have we ever met or spoken to each other before?" I asked.

"I have no idea who you are or what you think you know about me," he replied, looking at his lawyer a bit perplexed.

"Your old partner John Feterly has been caught up in an illegal con game where he was involved in a land invasion scheme that ended up in the death of four men and the kidnapping of a lady and her daughter and grandchild in New York. We were convinced with all the proof we had against them that they surely had met their fate and would be spending the rest of their lives in prison. We were soon made aware of something that boggles the mind. We were told that because of a little-known law called the foreign diplomat immunity clause. He was freed as a citizen of China. The CIA led John and his goonies away and said they wouldn't have to stand trial for the things that they did in the United States. I believe that in doing this, John Feterly gave his secrets away and opened a can of worms that would be his undoing. For it was because of his so-called citizenship that the CIA was led to revisit your case again almost immediately. They found additional information that proved John framed you in giving China vital information about the United States. He held dual citizenship, as many spies do. But after your conviction and without our office knowing, he tried to drop his dual citizenship, to only being a citizen of China.

"However, he forgot to make out papers giving him permission to be a foreign operative in the United States and thereby canceled out the changes he thought he'd made about the dual citizenship. Of course, it wasn't you but he who informed China of our plans with other foreign countries to stop their progress across the Korean peninsula. Bill and the warden will find if they go on the CIA network that your case has already been reopened. John Feterly has always been a spy as we knew but not the other side," I said, sitting down feeling that I had done all I could.

"Let's get to work, Warden, and get James out of here before sundown. I have some friends in the CIA who would like to brand John Feterly as a foreign spy for life," Bill said excitedly.

No sooner had Bill finished talking than my phone rang. I excused myself and stepped outside the office before I noticed on the caller ID that it was Stu.

"Hello, Stu. What's up?" I said nonchalantly.

"What say, I come over to Miss Marple's and pick you up for a late breakfast or early lunch?" Stu asked; before I could answer him, he added, "I guess what I am really trying to say is that I miss you." He paused, giving me a chance to answer.

"Stu, darling, I am in a meeting at this time but should be free and home again by six. We could do dinner if you like?" I replied.

"A meeting that takes all day? I can hardly wait to hear more about that one. So we're on for dinner. Is that right?" he asked.

"Yes, and I can hardly wait," I said in a teasing voice, then hung up before he could reply. I quickly pocketed my cell phone in the inner pocket of my red blazer and reentered the warden's office.

"Sally, we just hung up from talking to the top brass in the CIA. It seems that John Feterly and Dan Morhouse were not released to go out of the country after all. They did not get immunity as we were first informed. It's because they do hold dual citizenship that they can't claim immunity. Foreign diplomat immunity only applies if you don't hold citizenship to ours. The head of the CIA is planning to hold a special meeting on James's case in two hours, and he promised that a decision will be made before the end of the day," Bill told me.

"That is all good news. Bill, how much longer do you think we'll be here? I must get back as soon as possible I just talked to Stu, and he doesn't know I am here, and he is planning to pick me up for dinner at six," I said.

"I guess we're done here then—that is, after the warden signs this paper proving I was here on law enforcement business," Bill replied.

"Thanks to you and Bill, I may soon be out of here for good, there is no way that I can show how much that means to me. If you ever need me to help you in any way, Sally, please, feel free to call on me. You'll be able to get word to me through the CIA," James said.

James was left alone in the warden's office with his lawyer while the warden walked with us out into the lobby of his office. The officer who drove us there was waiting patiently to drive us back to the airport. We thanked the officer for helping us, then we boarded the plane.

The pilot promised that we would be landing at the Black Hawk Harbor airport by one. We were both tired and spoke very little during the flight back. I for one had too much on my mind, about what was going on back in Black Hawk Harbor.

Sara Hatfield and Stu will soon become entrenched in legal quicksand, concerning the illness of and death of her mother, while questions and rumors still connected her with Stu's wife's death. God help us all if any of this is true. A person with nothing to lose is dangerous, I thought as I leaned back in my seat and closed my eyes. Once the plane landed and the door opened, we deplaned quickly to the view of a beautiful summer's day. Bill walked with me over to my car and thanked me for going with him, then turned to go his car.

"By the way, Bill," I called out to get his attention again, "I never asked you who I needed to know to get another plane ride like that. I know the department couldn't afford it," I added, always thinking like the reporter that I am. He just smiled and wished me a good day without offering me any further explanation.

Another mystery afoot, I thought, laughing to myself, as I headed home.

My entering Miss Marple's didn't go on noticed.

"Sally, is that you, dear? Please, come in and join me for a fresh cup of hot tea and tell me what you've been up to," Miss Marple said. It sounded more like a command than an invitation, so I turned from the bottom of the stairs and joined her in the parlor. I took a seat in the white wicker high-backed armchair while she handed me a full cup of tea on a saucer and a cinnamon bun, then she returned to her chair and her tea. For the next few minutes, she spoke excitedly about what she had done today as she filled me in on the races.

"I have just returned from the yacht club where we discussed the upcoming sailboat races. I can't believe the races start in just one more day. They are truly a sign that summer is here. On every Monday there will be a race that is open to all comers, and that's the only day that anyone and everyone can race. Half of the racers from Monday will sail on Wednesday evening, then the best three out of those will race on Saturday. The first and second runners-up will receive a trophy, and the winner will receive five thousand dollars and a trophy. On the last week of the races only the winners of the previous nine races can sail on Saturday night just before sundown the winner will receive the big prize of fifty thousand dollars and a Golden Sailboat Trophy. The racers start their run from Traverse City, Michigan, through Charlevoix, Petoskey, and into Black Hawk Harbor. We'll be able to see all the racers as they come into the harbor while sitting right here on the front porch," Miss Marple said, pausing only long enough to take a sip of her tea.

"Sally, maybe you won't be here with me," she added with a smile and twinkle in her eyes.

"What are you talking about, of course, I'll be here with you, where else would I be?" I asked.

"Oh, I thought you'd be with Stu, he'll be running his boat in the races. He's been so busy, I am sure he just forgot to tell you. Do you know how to sail, my dear?" she asked me while looking at me over the glasses that sat on the end of her nose.

"Yes, I do know how to sail. My father and I were avid weekend sailors. He loved sailing just before sunset, those were some of my favorite times with him," I replied.

"Good, then you'll make a great first mate for Stu," she said with a wide smile as she set her cup and saucer down on the table next to her chair, then leaned back in her chair while looking at me in silence, as though waiting for me to say something.

I sat quietly drinking my tea as though I didn't notice her prying eyes.

"Well, don't you have anything to tell me?" she asked, sounding disappointed.

"What is it you would like to know?" I asked her.

"Where did you get off to so early this morning?" she asked.

"Officer Bill and I had to take care of a legal matter having to do with John Feterly. You remember him, the older gentleman mixed up in that land grab. They had thought because of his dual citizenship that he would get off scot-free but not so. The fact is, because he was a citizen in our country, too, he was stopped in his tracks and will be placed in federal prison as a spy. If he were only a citizen of China, he would have gone free," I told her. Her eyes lit up as though she just received a big scoop, something she could share with her card group this afternoon. "Remember, Miss Marple, you didn't hear it from me," I said.

"Wow, how exciting! Oh, look at the time, I really must run, the girls will be waiting on me again," she said, jumping out of her chair and running out of my sight before I could turn my head. I sat and finished my tea while laughing at how predictable she was. I tarried for a moment longer watching the sailboats out on the water and thought about what Miss Marple had said about the races, before I hurried upstairs to write out my next installment to the paper. I would include some of her comments along with Bonnie's Gaither death. Bonnie was well-known by the community because of her hands-on work with them during the summer months while she was here. I would also mention the arrest of John Feterly and his cronies; many would be glad to read that. I stood up and put the teapot and cups back on the tray and returned them to the kitchen before going up to my room. Within an hour, I had run off my column and sent it over to the paper in time for printing; then turned off my computer.

"Hello," I said, waiting for the caller's voice.

CHAPTER 21

An Unpredictable First Mate

It was almost six o'clock, and I was ready for my date with Stu, so I decided to take a seat out on the deck while I waited. It was a beautiful early summer's night, and the air was filled with a sweet aroma that drifted up from the flower beds below. The boat harbor was busy this time of night, for the wind had cooled down enough to enjoy a quick sail before sundown. I leaned back in my chair relaxing and mindfully recounted the movements of the day: a quick trip to New York to meet with Mr. Anderson an encounter with Miss Marple before she ran off to join the girls at the club, then the write-up for Joe Bumgardner's column for tonight's paper. The best part of the day was yet to come, having dinner with Stu still filled me with excitement. I knew he'd ask me questions that I couldn't fully answer the way I wanted to, and he would hold back on things he was working on. We both understood our professions and took our jobs seriously, which sometimes meant we had to be secretive. I was not sure that Stu thought at all about my work, as he believed I was taking a little R&R. I often wondered how he would take it when he realized who I really was. Would it bring us closer together or drive us apart?

A horn tooted and drew my attention to the red BMW convertible sitting in front of the house. I jumped up and waved down at Stu before running into my bedroom to grab my black handbag off the bed. I hurried out the door and down the front steps of the house to meet Stu at the passenger side of the car where he stood with the door open. Stu gave me a quick kiss before bending down and removing the *News Review* paper from my seat, so I could sit down. He handed me the paper, then closed the door and ran around to get in. I glanced down and read the headline while he buckled up.

"I see they already have the news on Bonnie's death. She seems to have been loved by many people around these parts, even though she didn't live here all year," I said.

"Yes, she was personally involved with the children's clubs of all the nearby counties. I have been her personal lawyer for many years and was often moved by her generosity. Many children around here don't have it so easy, and it tugged at her heart to see them suffer. She did everything in her power to help change laws and raise money to help those that couldn't help themselves. Many of the first kids she helped are parents now and have become volunteers themselves, to help others because she helped them. She will be genuinely missed by all."

"Sally, there's something else. This writer Joe Bumgardner, I haven't been able to locate him. He writes like he is one of our neighbors. Everything I've read of his has happened right here in the harbor," Stu said.

"Yes, I read the piece he wrote on the land grab and the history of the land trust. It was fascinating and brought out a lot of people on the day of the sale. It also surprised the men who thought they had the land almost in their hands," I replied.

"You're right, the column has helped out in some cases, but my aunt's name appeared in it when she was kidnaped, without her knowledge or permission. And why just to sell some papers? You can't think that's right?" Stu asked, looking at me.

"I read that piece, too, and her last name was never mentioned. But it did make the reader understand how important this land business was. It wasn't so much that it was happening in Black Hawk Harbor but why it was happening.

"There are a lot of people in these parts still today related to those braves who paid so much of their money to save that land for future generations. Therefore, there are many today who are connected to the story. In the same way, many were concerned about your aunt's safety and the arrest of the men involved. I haven't yet read anything in his column that would bring dishonor to any of the good people in the harbor. To your point of the papermaking money, how else would people be informed or a paper stay in business?" I responded.

"Wow, Sally, did I hit a nerve or something?" Stu asked, looking over at me.

"No, not really. But you are aware that I, too, am a reporter, when not on R&R. I believe it is an honest trade, and sometimes it's tough to get the news out without making someone upset about how I must do it. So please don't form unfair opinions before knowing all the facts, that's all I ask. I see that he writes on the sailboat races starting tomorrow. Miss Marple just told me today that you will be in the race. Is that true?" I asked as Stu pulled into the restaurant parking lot.

"Yes, I intend to share all of that with you over dinner," Stu said as he turned off the car and stepped out. I waited for him to open my door before moving.

"Stu, please don't get me wrong, I am not trying to be nosey. I am sure you will share everything you can when you can. We're both very busy people, and often get tied up in our daily affairs," I said while getting up to my feet with Stu's hand in mine. Then his arms enfolded me as our lips found each other's and for a short time, we were the only two people on earth. As we regained our senses, we took each other's hand and walked into the restaurant while talking small talk and nodding at those we knew as we passed by. We were quickly shown to our seats and handed our menus by the waitress before picking up on the conversation we were having in the car.

"Sally, I do recall you told me that you and your father used to sail often while you were with him. I was planning to ask you to race with me as my first mate, but something came up. I hope you will understand and don't form an unfair opinion of me when I tell you that you won't be my first mate on the first race, Sara will," Stu said as I listened in disbelief. I sat quietly waiting for the next shoe to drop as I looked into his eyes.

"Sally, you know I have some testing done on Bonnie's body to find out how she died. Those tests won't be back until next Friday by the earliest, and I had to find a way to keep Sara here in the harbor. She used to sail with me all the time, so I asked her to be my first mate for the first race. It'll just be this one time, I promise you, for I'll know the outcome of the test by Saturday," he said.

"Stu, I can't say I am happy about this, but thank you for telling me. I do understand and hope you win," I said trying not to show my disappointment—these were memories we were supposed to be making. "Miss Marple and I will be watching for you to come into the harbor from her porch," I promised.

The waitress returned and took our order before Stu, and I continued our conversation.

"Sally, when I talked to you by phone earlier, you said you were in a meeting that might take all day. How did that go?" Stu asked.

"I was with your friend Officer Bill, on some local business, and we were done by one this afternoon." Giving me time to visit for a while with Miss Marple, before she went off to play cards with the girls," I replied.

"Oh, there you are, darling. I was sure I would find you here with your friend.

Did you tell her that we are racing together tomorrow? It's too bad that you're afraid of the water, dear, for sailing is a very romantic way to spend time with your lover. With the waves and the wind, it is impossible for two people not to fall in each other's arms.

I am looking forward to being with Stu alone out on the water again," Sara said.

It was all I could do to keep quiet, only moments ago he told me she was going with him. I wasn't expecting to see her here tonight, but why not? This was where she and I always saw each other.

"Sally, please excuse us, I need to speak to Sara before she goes home," Stu said. I just nodded in agreement. I was afraid if I opened my mouth more than kindness would come out.

"Sara, darling, that was no way for you to treat my friend. Remember, you're a married woman, so go home to your husband and let me enjoy what remains of my night with my friend.

Tomorrow will soon be here, and we have a race to win. I'll see you early in the morning for our flight to Traverse City, where we will board the sailboat," Stu said as he watched Sara walk away before returning to Sally.

Sara did as she was told. Believing that she would soon win Stu back, she informed her husband of their upcoming divorce.

"Sally, I am so sorry about that crazy woman, but it's not all her fault. You see, I had to make her believe she still meant something to me to get her to stay and do the race. Yet I never thought she would talk like that to you. Just a week, dear, we'll know if she caused her mother's death," Stu said, taking my hand in his.

"Stu, you're missing something aren't you?" I asked.

"What do you mean?" he replied.

"What if you're wrong and she didn't do what you think she did, and you've led her on this way. What will you tell her if she ends up without her husband because she thinks you want her back? If you truly think she could have killed her own mother for wealth, what would she do for love? What has she done for love in the past? Miss Marple told me that many think she had a hand in your wife's death. Do you think she could have caused her death too?" I asked.

"Sally, you make some good points. I never thought she was innocent of either death but was never able to prove it. If I can't prove Sara killed her mother and she thinks I crossed her, my very life could be in danger," Stu said, perplexed.

"No, Stu, you're wrong. She goes after those you care about and love," I said, very concerned.

Stu was dealing with a very sick person, one that wasn't about to give him up and he was playing right into her hand, and he couldn't even see it, I thought. Our waitress delivered our meal, and we ate almost in silence, afraid of what was coming next.

"Sally, I really believe things will turn out okay, just keep the faith, baby, you are the only lady I want in my life," he said with a smile, and I believed him. We finished our dinner, then went for a long walk on the beach and enjoyed a beautiful sunset together before returning home.

"Sally, my sailboat is in Traverse City where the beginning of the race will take place, so Sara and I will fly there early. I'll try to call before the race starts. Please meet me at the end of the race down by the shore," Stu said while kissing me good night. "Stu, Sara will still be with you then. It would be better if you called me once you get home," I replied before leaving him to go into the house.

CHAPTER 22

Silence Runs Deep

"Sally! What are you doing here? Why aren't you out there on the lake sailing with Stu?" Miss Marple asked as I entered the porch.

"Stu asked someone else to be his first mate for today," I replied.

"Who? Tell me who he thinks will serve him better than you?"

"Sara Hatfield went with him early this morning by helicopter to Traverse City, Michigan, where the race starts."

Miss Marple jumped up from her chair and moved quickly to the edge of the porch, where she grabbed hold of the railing and looked out on the harbor.

"Sara! Is that man out of his mind? If there were ever two people that should never be alone together, it's those two. I can see no good that could come from this," she cried out in fear. I walked over and put my arm around her shoulder to console her.

"Miss Marple, it's not what you're thinking. He must keep Sara from leaving until the tests come back on her mother's death. He believes that she and her husband had something to do with it. He promised me last night that I would be in the next race with him," I said, with silent reservations of my own. We walked back to the seating area and sat down.

"Sally, as he thought about what he'll do if the test comes back inconclusive like his wives did? If he's letting Sara think he still cares for her…it won't be good for the two of you."

"Miss Marple, I am not his fiancé or his wife, just a friend. He's a full-grown, educated man and he'll have to live with his decision whatever comes of it," I said while pouring us a cup of hot tea.

"You mean you're not worried about him out there on the water with her, knowing what you know? I can't believe that!"

"Yes, of course, I have some concerns about it, but they're surrounded by other boats and sailors, they're not alone if you know what I mean."

"Sally, there is something else you should know," Miss Marple said, then paused to take a sip of her tea before continuing. "One of the girls from my club called me this morning early. She told me that she saw Sara's husband packing up his car last night, he drove off at ten. What do you think that means?"

"He could have just headed home early. Sara has her own car and probably plans to meet him there after the race," I replied.

"I hope you're right, we will soon see in a few hours, won't we?" she uttered, almost under her breath. I saw no reason to give her a reply. I finished up my tea and put my cup back on the tea cart before excusing myself. I just needed some fresh air to clear my head. What I said to Miss Marple was the truth. I was just a concerned friend of Stu's, nothing more. I couldn't allow myself to think of us in any other way.

I took my bike out of my storage area and mounted it for a ride through the village. The village streets and sidewalks were full of visitors and cars packed in like sardines. Riding my bike around those walking became an overwhelming challenge. I found I made better time on my feet pushing the bike, and it was safer too. I passed a couple of ladies talking at the side of the road and caught a few words of what they were saying.

"Poor Sara Hatfield. Did you hear what happened to her last night, Julie? That husband of hers left in the dark of the night while yelling from his car that he wanted a divorce; her mother hasn't even been dead a week and now this," her friend said.

No! That can't be true, I thought as I hurried back to the house. Without saying a word to Miss Marple, I went directly to my room.

I grabbed a bottle of apple juice out of the icebox and went out to sit on the deck.

Oh, Stu, what have you gotten yourself into? I thought while looking over the water at the horizon. I felt so helpless; I to could see no good coming from this. It would still be hours before they would arrive back in the harbor. After about thirty minutes, I returned inside and started up my computer to work on my column for the week. *I'd get as much done as possible then finish it up once the boats came in this afternoon*, I thought. For the rest of the day, I tried to read and nap and went for a walk around the block. I couldn't shake the distress my spirit was going through. As the daytime hours grew shorter the fear, I was feeling got stronger.

"Sally, are you up there?" Miss Marple called from the bottom of the stairs. I hurried to my door to give her a reply.

"Yes, yes, I am here. Have you heard anything yet?" I asked.

"No, dear, please come down and join me for a bite to eat and we'll wait on them together.

"I'll be right down, I'll just grab a sweater," I replied.

When I entered the porch, she had already poured me a cup of fresh hot tea and left it on the tray for me to retrieve.

"Dear, please have a sandwich or some cake with your tea," she said softly with a smile.

"Not just now, maybe later, thanks."

"Sally, please take my extra pair of binoculars, you'll need them to see which boats are coming in."

"Yes, thanks," I responded as I took them in my hands, and we turned our attention on the harbor from the porch.

"Sally, hurry! I can see the first sailboat coming around the bend," Miss Marple said excitedly. I ran over to the edge of the porch to see if I could catch Stu coming in. It was a pink sail, not Stu's. His was white with the number 21 on it. An hour went by, and many of the boats came in but not Stu's. I stepped away from Miss Marple to call my favorite officer and told him of my fears and why. He promised to call out to the police boats already on the water covering the race, and he would call me back as soon as he heard anything.

I quickly returned to Miss Marple and enlightened her of the call I made.

"Thanks, Sally, it helps to know that someone is aware of our concerns," she said, sounding more than a little perplexed.

It was a bit unnerving waiting around here, but we couldn't go down by the docks or anywhere else as there wasn't enough space in the streets to even walk, let alone drive a car. I paced back and forth across the porch floor as we continued seeing boats come in. Two hours after the arrival of the first boats my phone rang. Again, I stepped away from Miss Marple before answering it.

"Hell," I said.

"Sally, we've got a problem. Stu's boat has been found pulled up and hidden in the tall weeds by the shoreline near Crow's Landing, just on the other side of the bend from you. Stu and Sara have both been found, and they have lost a lot of blood. Sally, I am not sure if either of them will make it. They've been taken to the hospital in Petoskey by ambulance. I will be around to give you and Miss Marple a police escort to the hospital, or you'll not get there until late tomorrow because of the heavy traffic. I should be there in an hour," he said before hanging up.

"Sally, was that Bill? What did he say?"

"Miss Marple, please come sit down. I am afraid it's not good news. Stu and Sara have been found on his boat, but they've been shot and have lost a lot of blood. Bill is coming to give us a police escort to the hospital in about an hour."

"Oh, Sally. Oh, Sally, how am I going to tell Kitty about this? She loves Stu like a son," she whispered.

"I am sorry, but she'll need to know now; they're not sure he'll make it through the night. I have to go up to my room for a few minutes if you don't mind," I said before leaving her.

This was a hell of a time to find out that I had done the one thing I promised myself I wouldn't do, I thought as I entered my room and threw myself on the bed and the flood gates opened; I couldn't hold the tears back any longer. I had fallen in love with Stu and never realized it. Now I may never be able to tell him. I got back up off the bed and went into the bathroom to wash my face and pull myself together. Bill would soon be here. I was going to add the race to my column, but I don't even know who won. I didn't feel very much like writing anyhow.

"Sally, are you ready, dear? Bill is here," Miss Marple said from the landing on the stairs.

"Yes, here I am Miss Marple," I said, running down the stairs. We hurried out the door and got into my car and followed Bill's police car out of the village with his siren on. There was a police car behind us as well. We traveled as fast as the roads would allow, as people moved aside to let us pass. A ride that would have taken a good twenty-five minutes only took fifteen. We pulled into the emergency area of the hospital and parked, then got out of our cars and walked quickly into the hospital and onto the elevator. Bill had been here and knew where Stu and Sara had been taken to.

"Let's sit over here and wait for the doctor. He has Stu in surgery," Bill said, opening the door to the waiting room.

"Bill, would you please tell us all you know about Stu and Sara?"

"Sally, Stu was shot twice, once in the right arm and in the upper chest. When he fell, he struck his head on the rudder arm of the boat. Sara took a bullet to her upper left leg near the groin area. They both lost a great deal of blood and were unconscious when the police pulled up to Crow's Landing. The boat was gone over with a fine-tooth comb and no gun was found. They pulled the boat out of the water and divers are searching around the area for a gun or any other evidence. We really don't know if it happened there or someplace else yet," Bill said. No sooner had Bill finished talking than Kitty and Agatha walked in the waiting room.

"What have you found out about my Stu?" Kitty asked Miss Marple.

"Oh, Kitty," Miss Marple said as she reached out to hug her, dear friend. The ladies stood for a few seconds, crying in each other's arms before turning and looking at us.

"Oh my!" Kitty said while looking at me. "How this must be tearing at your heart, we must try to console each other for now," she added, hugging me; it was all I could do to hold back my tears.

"Doctor," Kitty said, hurrying over to the elevator as he was stepping off. "Please tell me how my Stu is," she said, almost pleading.

"Come, let's sit down with the others, and I'll tell you as much as I can for now." Once in the waiting room, he reached out his hand an introduced himself to the others.

"Please, understand it will be some time before we can be sure of anything. Stu Baker was grazed by a bullet in his right upper arm. By the looks of it, he probably tried to take the gun away from the shooter, because the second shot to his chest was made when the gun was up close to him. The lady that was brought in with him was shot in the leg with the same gun. Would any of you know if either of them owned a gun?" the doctor asked.

"Stu never spoke of owning a gun, yet I can't be sure he didn't," I said.

"Who would you to Stu?" the doctor asked.

"I am a good friend of his," I replied.

"Officer, may I speak to you in private?" the doctor asked in a cautious tone.

"What do you think that's all about? Now, I wonder what he's not telling us," Kitty said with fear in her eyes.

CHAPTER 23

Reconciled Differences

"There he is," Kitty said as Bill stepped off the elevator. We quickly got to our feet and walked in his direction in hopes of learning more about Stu and Sara's condition.

"The doctor said that you can go in and see Stu for a few minutes. He is not conscious and has just been taken to his room from surgery. They may have to go back into surgery if complications arise. The doctor is concerned about the way Stu was wounded and thinks that whoever did it may return to finish him off. Therefore, he has written in his report that Stu died. They have put Stu in a room under someone else's name and wouldn't want someone to follow one of you here and locate him. So only the police or FBI will be allowed to see him, and a guard has been posted outside his door until we have more information on who might have done this. What we want you to do is have a closed-casket funeral for him and make everyone believe he's in it. Sara will soon be informed of his death. We hope by doing it this way she gives up more evidence knowing or unknowingly, for she was the only other person on that boat as far as we know now. It will take time for the police to unravel and put this matter to rest. I will keep you all informed daily of Stu's condition and make sure he understands the reason for your absence. I will take letters to him from any of you as soon as he is up to reading them," Bill said as he led us to the room where Stu was.

Stu's head was wrapped tight, and we could only make out his face. He was in a hospital gown and covered all the way up under his arms with a sheet and blanket. They had two machines to keep track of his breathing and temperature connected to him and bags of clear fluid and blood hanging from them. His skin looked pale gray in appearance, almost as my fathers did as he lay in his casket. A cold chill shot through me and for the first time I found my entire body growing weak, I hurried to sit down as sweat covered my face.

"Are you all right, Sally?" Miss Marple asked.

"I don't know, this has never happened to me before," I replied. The nurse in the room advised me to put my head down between my knees for a minute to help the blood flow. She told us that this was normal when someone has been shocked by something they've heard or seen. I was surprised that it happened to me, for I've heard and seen things as a reporter that I couldn't even put in print because of how grossly ugly they were. Yet this was different.

My mind and heart were fighting between love and disbelief. Was my heart winning a losing the battle? Only time would tell. I got back to my feet and whispered to the girls. I would meet them in my car after they visited with Sara as I needed some fresh air. I went down to the parking garage and slid into my car seat, rolled down the window, and pushed the button on the left side of my seat to recline so I could rest. No sooner had I got comfortable than my phone rang.

"Hello," I said just above a whispered.

"Is this my favorite reporter? You don't sound like yourself," Mr. Korn said.

"Please forgive me, I am exhausted. I am at the hospital where I just lost a friend today."

"Oh, I'm sorry to hear it. Who was it?" the boss asked.

"It was Stu Baker. He's a lawyer here in Black Hawk Harbor and sailed the boat with twenty-one on its mast in the race today. He and his first mate Sara Hatfield were found shot and left unconscious on the boat that had been hidden or drifted into some tall weeds at Crow's Landing, just around the bend, almost at the end of the race at Black Hawk Harbor. Stu was shot in the right arm and upper chest areas and fell back, striking his head on something; they say he died of his wounds. Sara Hatfield was shot in the left leg near the groin area and will recover," I replied.

"Sally, I'll add this to the column you sent me earlier and get it in the morning paper. Again, I am sorry about your loss. Goodbye for now," he said.

It almost felt wrong giving him all that information at this time, feeling the way, I did and knowing the hospital would put it out for publication in the morning. "How will my friends feel tomorrow when they read it's in Joe Bumgardner's column?" I wondered. When the ladies finally came out to the car, it was just past eleven o'clock. Kitty got into the front seat, and Miss Marple and Agatha climbed into the back.

"Sally, you wouldn't mind driving us home, would you?" Kitty asked with a smile.

"It would be my honor," I replied.

It was late, and they were all tired, so it was quiet all the way to Kitty's. Once I dropped Kitty and Agatha off, Miss Marple got into the front with me. A minute down the road she turned and looked at me.

"Sally, Sara told us that she and Stu reconciled and that she and her husband are getting a divorce. That goes along with what I heard at the club today from her neighbor. Who said, 'She had heard Sara's husband yelling in front of his house that he intended to get a divorce before he drove away.' We weren't going to tell her anything about Stu until she asked what room he was in. We didn't want her to be alone when she found out, so we told her that he had died of his wounds. We tried to console her, but we couldn't and had to call a nurse in to help. Once we explained the problem to her, Sara was given a shot to sedate her. If she didn't shoot Stu, who did?" Miss Marple asked before turning to lean back in her seat. It wasn't a question either of us could answer, and we remained quiet for the rest of the ride home. We walked into the house at midnight, and Miss Marple went right to her room without a word and me to mine. I threw my handbag on the dresser and went into the bathroom to prepare for bed. Moments later, I was lying in bed staring up at the ceiling, my mind going a mile a minute.

Somehow, I had to find a way to pull myself out of this picture with Stu and Sara. I can't do justice as a reporter if I can't be objective. If what Sara said is true, I will soon be nothing but a memory to Stu anyhow. I turned over and closed my eyes in hopes that my mind would let me sleep.

I woke up to my phone ringing and someone knocking at the door a few hours later. I jumped up and grabbed the phone on my way to the door.

"Yes," I said in the phone while opening the door as I waved young Kenny in and to a chair to wait a while I finished up my call.

"Yes, Bill, I am still here, had to answer my door. What's up?" I asked.

"Sally, the Hatfields own a gun like the one that was used in the attempted murder. Stu's office called my office and told us that the Hatfields are under investigation in Sara's mother's death. They are only waiting on conclusive evidence to come back on some tests that were done."

"Yes, I was aware of all of that. Stu shared it with me when he informed me that Sara would be his first mate on this leg of the race, saying he needed to keep an eye on her. I am afraid that he overplayed his hand and made her believe that he was still in love with her. It is believed in the village that her husband left her the night before the race. Some heard him yell that he was getting a divorce. So what are we going to do now?" I asked.

"Sally, we have to allow Sara to believe what she does until we have all the evidence."

"I understand, Bill. Many have already convicted Sara, of Stu's late wife's death in the court of public opinion, but what if she isn't guilty? You're right, we can only go on facts. I'll be talking to you soon then. Bye for now," I said as I hung up.

"Kenny, what can I do for you?" I asked.

"Miss Marple is already up and wants to see you as soon as possible," he replied, getting to his feet.

"Please, tell her I'll be down in ten minutes." He nodded in agreement, then turned and walked away.

CHAPTER 24

Only the Facts

"Oh, Sally! There you are. I hope we didn't wake you. Lucy just called me from the Stain Cup, where she and her husband are having breakfast," Miss Marple said, pausing to pour us each a cup of tea. After giving me a cup, she sat down and looked at me a bit perplexed.

"Sally, this is serious! Sara's husband is back in the village and down at the Stain Cup. Right now! He told many of our neighbors there that the police got a hold of him at his home in Ohio and informed him that his wife had been shot and he should hurry back. He said he drove all night, and after arriving, the police told him that Stu Baker had also been shot and killed. Then they asked if he knew of anyone who'd want his wife and Mr. Baker dead? He seemed surprised that they would call him to find out if he was really at home in Ohio and believes they're going to try to blame it all on him. He said he left for home the night before the race and was already in Ohio before the races even started. He was boasting of how wise he'd been for leaving when I did, or they would be locking him up and throwing away the key. So if he's telling the truth, who did it?" Miss Marple asked, taking a sip of her tea.

"This is all very interesting, but it proves nothing. There are many ways to have someone killed without doing it yourself. Remember, Sara's mother died leaving a 'will,' and Sara and her husband stood to inherit everything if it hadn't been changed. With Sara out of the way, dead or in prison for killing her lover, her husband would end up filthy rich. Just because he said he was in Ohio doesn't mean he was. The police will make some calls there and try to find someone that might have seen him on the day of the race. Or he could have paid someone to do it, offering them a great payoff once it was over. Don't be moved by anything but facts. I think I am going to call Bill and ask him if I can buy him lunch. There's a chance he'll let something slip if I ask the right questions and I may come back knowing more than we do now. There's a mystery afoot, and we are the two that can solve it, Miss Marple," I told her before hurrying back up to my room. On my way to the stairs that led to my room, Kenny ran into me coming through the side door.

"I am so sorry, Sally," he said, bending over to pick up the pages of the *News Review* newspaper that had slipped from his hands.

"No problem, Kenny, please let me help you with those," I said, handing him a few pages I picked up.

"Sally, have you ever read Joe Bumgardner's column?" Kenny asked.

"Yes, I have," I replied.

"It's great, isn't it? To tell the truth, I've never been much of a news hound, if you know what I mean. But Joe Bumgardner had my attention the first time I read his column, and all my friends in this area feel the same way. We are all puzzled about how he seems to know so much about our village, and so is my aunt. I can hardly wait to read what he has to say today, and I am on my way in to share it with Aunt Marple," he said with excitement as we parted. I hurried up to my room to call Bill for a lunch date.

"Hello, Bill. Sally here, are you busy?... Yes, I am aware Sara's husband is back. I am calling to see if you would let me buy you lunch?" I said. "Yes! That's great! Then I'll see you at the Pier Restaurant at noon," I replied.

Hours later: "There you are, Sally, I almost thought I'd been stood up," Bill said, then added, "I humbly say, it's not every day a good-looking young lady asks me out to lunch." He was half laughing as he took taking a seat at my table on the deck of the restaurant.

"Bill, would you mind if we moved inside? I thought I'd like sitting out here while the sailboats are in the harbor, but it only saddens me knowing Stu is in the hospital."

"Sure, Sally, that would be just fine with me," Bill replied. We moved quickly to another table inside and gave our order to the waitress before we got comfortable and started talking.

"Sally, I just came from checking in on Stu. His condition hasn't changed since last night. I believe that's good news since the doctor said the next seventy-two hours would be crucial to his recovery. They tell me at the hospital that Sara seems to be taking his loss hard. She is either a good actress or really one of the victims in all of this, but until we know for sure, we can't take any chances," Bill added.

"I understand the police got a hold of Sara's husband and asked him to come back to the harbor. Miss Marple's friend called her early this morning from the Stain Cup and informed her he was in there. She said he sounded proud of himself for leaving the area when he did two nights ago," I told Bill.

"Sally, I am not free to discuss this case with you in its entirety, but I can tell you that just because he says he wasn't here at the time of the race doesn't make it so. I've been a law officer for decades and have seen how people who think they're clever try to outthink the law usually ends up residing in a state or federal housing unit. We must not only look at the Hatfields, though, for Stu has other clients who might have reason to harm him as well," Bill added.

"I am a big girl, Bill, and I, too, have been around awhile. I can only surmise that you're trying to ease my mind, but that's not going to do it. I'll tell you why. Sara told Miss Marple, Kitty, and Agatha, last night that she and Stu had reconciled, and she'd asked her husband for a divorce before he left for their Ohio home."

"Well, that would make sense, seeing Stu asked Sara to be his first mate," Bill replied.

"No, Bill, you don't understand. Stu told me earlier at dinner the night before the race that the only reason he was taking her instead of me was to keep an eye on her until the tests come back having to do with her mother's death, and furthermore, he promised I would be with him in the next race. Why would he have done that if he was thinking about reconciling with her? Her husband packed his car and left their summer house at ten o'clock the night before the race, yelling that he was getting a divorce. It's almost like he was staging it for his neighbors," I said while accepting my order from the waitress. We started our meal and didn't say a word for a few minutes until Bill broke the silence.

"Sally, thanks for that information, it's helpful and gives the puzzle another piece that we didn't have before. When I can share things with you, I will, for I know how much Stu means to you and you to him. I would be glad to take him word from you once he's well enough to read it. You can be sure of one thing—once he is awake, he'll tell us who shot him," Bill said endearingly.

Bill and I finished up, and I got into my car to drive back to the house. The visit with Bill did offer up much additional information. As I passed the house to pull into the driveway, I noticed the ladies sitting on the front porch. I hurried out of the car and up to my room to put my handbag on the dresser; then I turned and closed my bedroom door behind me before going back downstairs in hopes of talking to the ladies.

"Yes, I thought I saw you drive in. Come sit down with us and have a glass of lemonade," Miss Marple said, then added, "Agatha, Kitty and I went to talk to Stu's secretary, I think you'll be interested in what we found out. She informed us that Stu didn't have any clients that would hold a grudge—he normally handles corporate law cases, not criminal. Furthermore, she doesn't believe for a minute that he reconciled with Sara. He had held her in contempt for years ever since she aborted the child without talking to him first about it. Stu had told his secretary that the only lady in his life was you. So what do you think about that?" Miss Marple said with a smile.

"Words cannot express how I feel about that information, it gives me something to hope for," I replied, smiling back at her while she handed me a tall glass of lemonade.

"There's something else you should know," Kitty said, looking at me. "After the funeral services Saturday at noon, Tony Grant will tow Stu's sailboat behind his up around the bend into the harbor with the winner's flag flying from its mask. Stu had been so far ahead of all the other boats in the race that everyone believes that he would have won if he could have. You should also know that Sara is going to be released from the hospital on Saturday before the funeral service; the service will take place at the little brown church in the harbor. I think we'll all see a good show from Sara if her husband isn't by her side. Yet if he does show up and believes she shot Stu or she believes he shot him, they just may try to make us believe they're back together, each fearing the other." We all went quiet for a few minutes as we drank our lemonade and looked out on the water.

"I am not sure what the others were thinking about, but me, I wanted to grab onto Sara and shake the hell out of her, then ask her why she lied to the ladies last night about her and Stu. If either she or her husband shot Stu, I'll find out, and they won't leave this harbor until I do," I promised myself.

"That's not all we found out today," Agatha said, breaking the silence. "Miss Marple brought her morning newspaper to the club. Can you believe it, Joe Bumgardner had the shooting in his column already? Some of the men down at the club seem to think he's a cop, for how else would he know so much about the harbor and the people here? Nevertheless, he is good, and everyone I've spoken to wouldn't miss his column. Some say they purchased a subscription for an entire year, just to read his column, and so did I. He reports the news and gives details you wouldn't find anyplace else."

"I didn't get a chance to read the paper, did you bring it back with you?" I asked Miss Marple.

"I sure did, I've saved all of them. I guess it's the amateur sleuth in me, for I see them all like puzzle pieces of a summer's mystery," she replied with a mischievous smile on her face, as though she knew my secret.

"Great! Then I'll get to read it after all," I replied just as my phone rang. I excused myself and went up to my room. I no sooner answered it and slipped it to my ear than I heard: "Sally, Mr. Korn, the newsroom is going crazy here. It's something that we've never seen before. The phones are ringing off the hook for new and renewing subscriptions, not only for this area but to the homes of all our summer visitors throughout the United States and parts beyond.

Boy! Is my brother and Jake Bates ever mad. They want to know who Joe Bumgardner is—of course, I didn't tell them. We've had to hire more people, not only for the office but newspaper boys and girls too, and it's all because of you." He paused to catch his breath and to give me a chance to respond.

"Mr. Korn, I am e-mailing you my column for this upcoming week, you might want to print a few lines of it off today. I promise you'll understand what I mean when you read it. It has to do with the place and time of Stu's funeral and what the winner of the race yesterday, intends to do after the funeral. I'll be in touch later, I must hurry back downstairs to our guest," I said before hanging up.

"Sally, where did you go?" Kitty asked when I reentered the porch.

"Oh, I had to take a phone call, sorry," I replied as I took my seat. "Did I miss anything?" I asked.

"Yes, we were just talking about going to the club at five for dinner. There will be a comedy floor show. Would you join us?" Agatha asked.

"Yes, I'd' love to, thanks for asking me," I replied. We continued the porch talking for another hour before we went our separate ways to prepare for dinner. This could be an eventful night or just a night out with the girls. Either way, I was looking forward to it.

CHAPTER 25

A Deadly Threat

"Hi, Miss Marple, it's so good to see you and your ladies tonight. I don't think I've ever seen you here at the club this late. Please follow me and I'll help you get seated," stated Betty Ann, our hostess. Betty Ann and Miss Marple were friends and had been for years. Once we were seated, our first-wait person came over and took our drink order, and as he turned to walk away, Kitty was surprised by someone she saw coming through the dining room doors.

"Oh my god, I don't believe my eyes, Sally, tell me who that couple is." I turned quickly to get a look at who she was speaking of as the other girls gasped in surprise.

"I don't believe it," I said, turning back to face Miss Marple. "It's Sara Hatfield in a wheelchair, being pushed by her husband Sam," I said, just above a whisper.

"Well, that was fast wasn't it?" Miss Marple said, sounding disappointed. Not because Sara was with her husband, though we were all confused by it. It was the act she gave at the hospital after hearing about Stu's death.

"It…but had she been sincere at the time?" I wondered. We continued laughing and talking about everything from men to the funky fashions being worn these days. Once our food order came, some twenty minutes after we got our drinks, we turned our attention to eating while our food was hot. It was about ten minutes later when I noticed Sara's husband roll her chair over to the washroom doors. I waited until I saw her roll herself in, then I excused myself from the table to join her. There were a few questions I had to ask that only she could answer.

"Sara, I thought that was you. I saw you come in with your husband. I see you're out of the hospital, how are you doing?" I asked.

"You're a trip, Sally. You want me to believe you care how I feel when I know that it's me that you wish had died. Why did you really come in here to talk to me? We don't have anything in common, let's admit it. Stu was our lightning rod, and now he's gone, and you'll have to move on and find some other rich man to drive your claws into," she said, sounding heartless, which didn't surprise me in the least.

"Sara, be careful, for you're like a zit on the tip of the nose that others can't help but see. You are the only one suspected in Stu's murder," I said.

"Are you kidding? In case you can't see, I am sitting in a wheelchair since I, too, was shot. Unless you're naive enough to think, I shot myself before throwing away the gun. How simple-minded you'd have to be to think that. After all, it wouldn't take much for divers to find a gun under the water near the boat. Who would be that stupid?" she asked.

"Well, Sara, I see you've thought of almost everything."

"Oh, what are you talking about now?"

"You forgot about me. I am like a bloodhound that gets onto the scent of her wounded prey and won't give up until it's caged," I replied before walking away to rejoin the others at our table.

"Sally, you didn't really need to go to the washroom, did you?" Agatha asked with a smile.

"No, I wanted to tell Sara that all eyes are on her and she should know she is the only suspect in Stu's murder and whoever is with her. Of course, I meant her husband. Sometimes, it takes a dose of fear by mouth to trip up even the best-laid plans of an enemy. This story is far from over, and the ending will be a total surprise," I said. We all chuckled, as Sara and her husband walked passed us on their way to the door. Once they were out, I hurried over to the doors and followed at a safe distance behind them, so they couldn't see me. With my phone in my hand, I was planning to try and get anything they said as they got into their car.

"I don't care what that woman told you in the washroom, Sara. If you say anything about the shooting, you'll end up dead, too, or arrested for murder," Sara's husband said as he closed her car door. Wow! I could hardly believe what I heard and hurried back into the club to let the girls know. "Was she a part of this horrible plan, or was she now just one of his victims?" I wondered.

"You're not going to believe what I just heard, listen to this," I said as they leaned into my phone to hear the recording.

"Sally, call Bill, to tell him what was heard, and that you have it on your phone. If her husband is threatening her and holding her against her will, then Bill has to help her," Kitty said, then added, "That's a form of kidnapping, too." I did what Kitty said and called Bill immediately and told him what I'd heard and had on my phone. He told me to stay where I was and that he would be there in ten minutes. The floor show was beginning, and the girls seemed relaxed and enjoying it, so I slipped away from our table and out to the front of the building to wait for Bill. As he pulled up in front of me and turned down his window, I walked up to his car and turned on the phone before handing it to him.

"Sally, I am sorry, but your phone is going to become evidence. I'll tell you what I'll do for you because I know you have special things on your phone that you want to keep secret, we all do. Go home and clean off everything you want to keep private, then I'll be by to pick it up. You'll have to buy another one as this one won't be returned to you. It will be kept as evidence for years to come," he said.

"It'll take me a couple of hours to do what you ask, Bill. Since I drove the girls here and we are watching a floor show before leaving," I said.

"That's fine, call me when I can come by for it," Bill replied, then rolled up his window before leaving. I walked back into the club and retook my seat to enjoy the rest of the show with the girls before leaving the club to take them home. It was about nine fifty when Miss Marple and I walked into her house. I went upstairs and cleaned my phone of confidential information, then called Bill, who came by and picked it up. I ran back up to my room and removed my dinner clothes, then I dressed in black sweats and shoes of the same color. I put on my darkest makeup and pulled my long hair back and twisted it before sticking it up under my ball cap. I grabbed an amplifying recorder that I could attach to the outside corner of a window to hear what was being said inside the room. I also picked out a night camera to use that didn't need a flash and a hot seat of the kind used at a football game that I may need for sitting outside on the ground close to the window for a while. I wasn't sure I'd get anything, but I had to try for Stu's sake. I quietly creeped down the staircase and out the back door. I rode my bike two miles around the lake to the Hatfields and hid it in some bushes. I saw a light on in the house, so I got in between the hedges and the house next to the window in question, and I attached the recorder to the corner of the window with its suction cup edges and then plugged my earbuds in to listen.

"Frank. Hey, man, thanks for staying at my home and using the ID I left you to pay for everything, from turning on the lights and water to the food order. Oh, the flowers I sent, you did put them in water, then place them in the middle of the dining room table so my wife would be surprised that I was home and got her flowers too? I'll send you a large bonus if all goes well." Hatfield promised whoever he was talking to on the other end of the phone. When I peeked in the window, I saw Sara walking with a limp into the bedroom.

"Honey, who was that you were talking to?" She asked.

"Oh, no one, just a wrong number. Sara, darling, I think we should think about going home to Ohio tomorrow, summer's over for us here," Sam said.

"Sam, that's impossible for two reasons. My mother's funeral will be held here before her body is shipped to her hometown, where there will be another funeral for her friends. Her sister will have to take care of her services there. I must stay here or go into protective custody until they catch the person that killed Stu and wounded me. I had to sign an agreement to this before they would release me from the hospital," Sara replied.

"That's crazy! Who made you sign this paper?" Sam asked.

"A state police officer and an officer from the FBI. They told me my life was in danger, and the shooter may come back to finish his job. I laughed at them and said that no one wanted me dead. Someone hit me by mistake, thinking I was that little bombshell that he's been hanging with. No one knew that I was going to be on that boat with him other than you, and you were in Ohio, but they didn't agree with me. If I leave now, I will be picked up and put in protective custody," Sara said.

"They can't do that! I'm not only your husband but your lawyer too, not that you should need one. After all, you're a victim of the shooter. They can notify our police department to keep an eye on you. Besides, it was probably an unsatisfied client of Stu's, and you were just in the way. As far as your mother's funeral goes, she has a lot of friends here that could handle it, and the funeral director here can have the casket put on a plane to send it home to us, and we'll take care of it there. Don't you think that sounds a lot better? I am aware that Stu did some tests to prove or disprove how your mother died, but we already know it was cancer and nothing else, right?" Sam paused for her to reply.

"Of course, it was her illness. Everyone knew how sick she was and that she could die at any time," she replied in a soft tone.

"Okay, it's settled, we're calling the police in the morning and heading home," he said. Sam walked over to the window and lifted it up halfway; it almost took my breath away as I sat next to the outside of the house. Thank God, he didn't see the recorder in the corner of the window.

"Baby, I'll do anything you say once you okay it with the police, I don't want to end up in jail," Sara said.

Some soft music was turned on in the room as the lights went out. I wasn't interested in what might come next, so I took my recorder off the window, picked up my hot-seat pad, and climbed out of the bushes; then I took my bike out of it's hiding place near the driveway and arriving home twenty minutes later. I put my backpack on the bed and went into the bathroom to prepare for bed.

After preparing for bed, I unpacked my backpack and downloaded the recorder into my computer; this would give me a printed copy of what was said. It was late, and I couldn't do anything with it now, so I filed it for later and climbed into bed.

Sam Hatfield is a lawyer that will open another door for me to look into, I'll be able to find out more about him in the public law files review, I thought as I drifted off to sleep.

CHAPTER 26

Inconclusive Evidence

It was now Friday morning, and the tests Stu had asked for on the death of Sara's mother would be back. The outcome of these tests may determine what steps are taken on the request of the Hatfields to go home or Sara's arrest. If she is found innocent of any wrongdoing, the law may have compassion for her after looking at the death of her mother and her personal condition and give her the green light to leave. I couldn't get what the police told Sara about the shooter the fact that he may not believe he's finished his job yet off my mind. Had Sara been shot by mistake, or was she shot to make the killing look good and the questions directed toward someone else? The police would know by now if there was any gun powder residue on her hands, so the chances of her doing it didn't seem realistic. It could have been someone not on Stu's sailboat, using a high-power rifle from the shoreline or another passing sailboat that ran alongside them. I now found myself feeling sorry for Sara, with the loss of her mother, her injuries, knowing someone may still be out there to kill her; then there's the death of her friend, or at least she thinks he's dead. All these things happening at the same time could be more than one can bear.

First things first, I must get over to Stu's office and find out what the tests had to say, that is if Stu's secretary, Amanda, will tell me. I first wanted to look up Sam Hatfield's file in the law review records. Call it woman's intuition or the skeptic blood that flows in my veins, but I thought I would find a missing piece to the puzzle there. His file was substantial up until he married Sara, at which time he seems to have stopped his practice, his last client recorded is his mother-in-law. Before going to law school, he served eight years in the Army Sniper's Division, out of Fort Brag, Texas.

"Wow! Look at that!" I said out loud while sitting in my room. Sure, many have served our country as professional snipers, and it doesn't mean he's guilty of anything, but I decided to run off a copy of the file anyway and called Bill and asked him to meet me at Stu's law office in an hour. I dressed for the day and went downstairs to find Miss Marple; she'd be having tea in her parlor.

"Good morning, Miss Marple," I said as I entered the room. She looked up over her glasses from the book she was reading and smiled.

"Sally, please come in, pour yourself some tea and have a seat. Forgive me for being a nosy old lady, but I couldn't help noticing you leaving on your bike just before dark last night, dressed in black and wearing a dark baseball cap. I couldn't relax for one minute until I see you return. I know it's none of my business what you do, and I do try to respect all those that live here." She paused while looking at me with questioning eyes.

"Miss Marple, I do not see you as a nosy old lady but more as my partner sleuth because we seem to be like-minded. Yes, you're right, I did go out last night on my bike. I rode over to the Hatfields to see if I could find out more about their future. I found out that Sam is a lawyer himself and once served in that capacity for his late mother-in-law. I have no idea at this time why she changed lawyers and hired Stu. Yet it seems a bit strange that he would suddenly stop his law practice after marrying Sara some three years ago. Now he plans to serve as his wife's lawyer, if she should need one, or as her spokesperson. He is planning to take his wife and leave for home before Stu's or her mother's funeral today after the tests come back that Stu ordered to prove her mother only died of cancer," I said sipping from the cup of steaming hot tea in my hand, knowing full well that I couldn't tell her any more about Sam—for a good reporter never says everything they know until it's necessary.

We sat in silence for the next few minutes while she processed everything I had just told her.

"Sally, I won't ask you how you got close enough to them to hear all of this, and I do believe you. What makes them think for one minute that the law won't make them remain here until they find out who shot and killed Stu?" she asked, as though Stu was really dead.

"Sam believes that the law in Ohio can work with the law here, making it possible for Sara to go home where he believes she'll be safer from anyone wanting to harm her again," I replied.

"Well, what do you think about it?" she asked me as she put her teacup to her lips.

"It's hard to say, not knowing who our shooter might be. I am not sure, nor is anyone else, as to where her husband was at the time of the shooting. Until they can prove without a doubt that he was in Ohio, he is still a suspect on my list. With that said, Miss Marple, I have a date to make with our favorite cop, so I'll see you at eleven o'clock at the church for Stu's funeral." I placed my teacup and saucer back on her tray and made my way out to my car.

It was a beautiful day with a soft warm summer's breeze from the south. I decided to drive with the car top down and let the breeze blow through my hair. I pulled up to the curb in front of the Stain Cup Restaurant just as Bill was stepping out of his police vehicle across the road. I hurried out of my car and met him at the door, so we could walk in together. Bill is single and almost old enough to be my father; he seemed to step a bit more pridefully, with a younger woman by his side. The looks we got when we walked in said it all, while he just smiled back at them and nodded as we found a table and sat down. The waitress wasted no time getting to us.

"Sally, I didn't know you knew our favorite office," she said with a grin.

"Yes, I met Bill shortly after I moved here for the summer, we have a lot in common. Wouldn't you agree on Bill?" I asked, passing her inquiry over to him.

"I'd love to play this gotcha game with the two of you women, but I am on my break and must eat and go. So I'll have two eggs over easy, bacon, toast, and a cup of coffee," he said.

"Yes, I'll have the same thing," I said to the waitress. She hurried off as I reached into my shoulder bag and pulled out the file.

"Bill, the reason I called you this morning was to share this with you. I wasn't sure if you had come by it already or not, and I couldn't speak about it over the phone," I said, handing it off to him. "You should also know that Sam Hatfield intends to take his wife back home to Ohio today," I said, then sat back to give him time to look over the file and respond to what I had just told him. The waitress delivered our coffee before Bill looked up from his reading.

"Sally, you have some talent coming up with important pieces of our puzzle, I am not sure how you do it. We haven't found any gun yet, but we know one was a sniper's special the other a handgun. I'd say a derringer," he replied.

"That's odd, a derringer is a small handgun and is made to shoot one shot. Tell me, was the bulletin Sara's leg from a derringer?" I asked.

"Yes, it was," he replied.

"If I were asked for my educated guess, I'd say Sara shot herself in the leg, and somehow Sam did the rest. Here's another thought, I'll just throw it out there you can do whatever you want with it. Sam is a gold digger and only married Sara to get his hands on her mother's millions. I will be looking at him, too, if the tests on Sara come back inconclusive in her mother's death. I am not sure which one of these two is trying to outdo the other, for Sara is still in love with Stu and her husband knows it. When she told the ladies the night of the shooting that she and Stu had reconciled, she meant it. After witnessing Stu being shot, I think she had to go ahead with her husband's plan and shoot herself. Of course, I have no proof of any of this, just an educated guess," I said as I accepted my plate of food from the waitress. Bill received his plate too, and we ate in silence for a few minutes.

"Sally, I am not sure right now how the FBI will handle Sam's request to take his wife home today. They may agree to it in hopes of setting up a sting, after getting permission from a local judge in Ohio to bug their house in hopes of finding out what they know or did. The fact that they intend to leave before both funerals is very questionable," Bill acknowledged. "By the way, Sally, the doctor said you may visit Stu tonight after eight. Stu is awake and has been asking for you. There's something he says he needs to tell you," Bill said while taking a swallow of his coffee.

"How long has Stu been able to talk, and does he remember anything of the shooting?" I asked.

"He's been awake and talking since midnight. No! He can't remember any of it, not even the beginning of the race. The doctor said it's because he fell and hit his head on something hard, yet it's possible that he could regain his memory at any time. So you can see how important a sting could be in the Hartsfield's home," Bill concluded as he got to his feet and looked over the breakfast bill lying on the table next to him. He took out a twenty dollars and put it on the table, as I watched.

"That's cheap, compared to the dinner check you paid for at the Pier the other night," he said with a smile as he walked away.

I remained to finish my meal and think about everything I had just heard about Stu's condition. *At least, he still remembers who I am*, I thought, with a spark of hope as I wondered what it was that he wanted to tell me.

I made sure the waitress got the money for the bill and her tip before leaving the restaurant. I hurried over to Stu's office to find out about the test and ran into the Hatfields coming out of the door of his office.

"Sally, sorry about Stu," Sara said, almost in tears and fear across her face. "Sam and I are heading home now to Ohio," she added.

"Oh, you're not staying for your mom's funeral?" I asked.

"No, we'll have a funeral for her in our hometown, that's the way she would have wanted it. The one here is for the summer people and is being put on by her bridge club," she replied, hurrying away. I stood outside the office door until they drove off and then I entered.

"Hello, Amanda. I met the Hatfields on my way in. They say that they're heading home tonight to Ohio. I take it that the tests came back and cleared her of any wrongdoing?" I said.

"No, not exactly," she replied.

"How is it then that they can leave town?" I asked.

"Sally, I don't ask why. When the FBI tells me not to release finding but to tell Sara she's free to go, well, I do as I'm told. I don't have Stu here to tell me otherwise. They must know something and want to follow their hunches a little longer. It takes a lot of bait to trap a wolf if you know what I mean. If those two had anything to do with her mother's death and the shooting, they'd want an airtight case against them," she replied.

"That sound reasonable to me. I'll see you at the funeral in an hour if you want you can sit with us," I said as I turned to leave.

I hurried back to my room to type up my column and get it sent over to the paper to be published in the evening paper. While dressing for the funeral, I wondered why we were going through with it, seeing as Sara and her husband had already left the village. Who was it we were trying to fool now? Did anyone think that there was someone else who would have shot these two people? Who else would have had a reason?" I asked myself. I grabbed my sweater off the bed and a hanky for my pocket before running downstairs to meet up with the other girls. They would go in Miss Marple's car, while I drove mine since they would be going on to another funeral before they returned home.

Our seats had been saved for us at the church. There was a closed casket in the front of the church that had been donated by the county morgue, thanks to Officer Bill. The local greenhouse and friends had sent flowers that filled the church with color and summer fragrances. Every seat was filled, and many stood along the walls and in the entryway. The minister stepped forward and offered a prayer and then asked if there was anyone who wanted to say something about Stu. Several men stood up in front of their seats and provided stories and some of their memories of Stu. I was almost ashamed of the fact that this was all a ploy, knowing that these men had opened their hearts believing Stu was dead. I couldn't bring myself to stand up and say anything; all I could do was weep in my hanky.

"My nephew was my dearest friend. He often protected those that most would think were beneath them. He had everything to live for, yet someone thought they had the right to end his life. If you're here and watching this, for what you have done, I want you to know there's a place in hell for people like you. I will not waste a second of my life hating you, for you're not worth it," Miss Kitty said, then she sat back down. The minister spoke on what the Bible said on life and death. Thirty minutes later it was over, and the church started emptying out, all but the two of us remained seated. When we were sure we were alone, we stood up and hugged each other; we had pulled it off. If the person behind it all was here today—though I doubt it—he would have believed Stu was dead. I traveled back to Miss Marple's while the other girls went on to Sara's mother's funeral.

While driving back to the house, I longed to be with Stu. My heart ached for him, and what he's been through, I had to wait until eight o'clock tonight before I could go to his side. I also had to remember that he had no memory of what happened; I am sure he will be asking me questions about why he is there.

This visit may not be so easy, I thought. I puttered around most of the day; it was hard keeping my mind on any one thing. I had heard the ladies come in an hour ago but remained in my room; there was nothing I could add to today's events right now. At seven I took a seat out on my balcony for a few minutes trying to collect my thoughts before leaving for the hospital. I was so excited that he could remember me. Bill said, "Stu said that he had something to tell me." These past few days were some of the roughest in my life.

I picked up my sweater off the bed and my purse and keys from the dresser on my way out the door. As my foot graced the bottom step of the stairs, I heard Miss Marple call out.

"Sally dear, could you please come in here a minute?" she asked.

I took a deep breath and did as she asked. I entered her parlor where the three of the ladies were having tea while they visited.

"Miss Marple, how can I be of help?" I asked.

"Sally, are you feeling all right? We haven't seen you since Stu's funeral services." Miss Marple asked, a bit concerned.

"We all knew it was a fake funeral, so why would she be so concerned for me?" I wondered.

"Sally, we heard today that the Hatfields left the village; they didn't even stay for Sara's mother's funeral. What kind of daughter wouldn't stay for that? They seemed to be in a hurry to get out of here," she said. Was she really concerned about her friend's daughter, or was she on a fishing exposition?

"Miss Marple, I did see Sara before they left. She told me that the bridge group was taking care of the funeral here and that she had to go and take care of the one in their hometown in Ohio. She seems to have her hands full with all that's happened," I replied.

"Yes, yes, you're right. We see you're heading out, is everything all right?" Miss Marple asked. All the ladies lowered their cups to hear my reply.

"Everything is fine, and it's a nice night for a ride, wouldn't you agree?" I said as I turned and left the room on my way to the car. It had gotten a little cooler out, so I put up the top of my convertible before getting in. I decided to stop by the greenhouse on my way to the hospital to pick up flowers for Stu. Minutes later, I was on his floor in the hospital passing the nurses' station. I slowly opened his door a crack not wanting to wake him. I heard him talking on the phone—it stopped me in my tracks when I heard what he said.

CHAPTER 27

Not All Desires Can Be Had

"Sara, darling, stop crying. What's wrong?... Yes, of course, I love you... He did what?"

"How did she know Stu was still alive? Who told her how to get in touch with him and what did he mean that he loved her? All these questions slammed against the walls of my brain. Had he wanted me to come so he could tell me that he still loved her?" I wondered as I turned and walked over to the nurse's station after gently closing the door so as not to interrupt them.

"Please, see that Mr. Baker gets these flowers. I would deliver them myself, but he is on the phone. Just tell him that there from Sara, would you?" It was all I could do to keep myself together as I entered the elevator and pushed the button that would return me to the garage; as the elevator went down, other people stopped it and got on, also taking it to the garage. Once in my car, I unloaded on myself. "You stupid, stupid fool." I cried as tears streamed down my face uncontrollably. For the next twenty minutes, I was too weak to move. How could I ever have believed he would want me to be part of his world. *I am a writer, not just a writer but a reporter. The first thing we learn is not to get involved in the story or with those being reported on. My objectivity has been marred by my feeling for Stu*, I thought as I pulled out of the hospital parking lot and drove back to the village and down to the shoreline. I planned to sit in my car until I could walk into the house without being questioned about Stu; that was the last thing I wanted to do.

Back in Stu's room: "Sara, I'll always love you, but I am in love with Sally, and I intend to ask her to be my wife when she comes in tonight," he said before hanging up.

Hours came and went, but Sally never went through the door of his room. The nurse brought in the beautiful flowers from Sara, but Stu's heart ached for Sally. He couldn't reason in his mind where she was. At ten o'clock he called Bill to see if his message had been delivered to Sally.

"Yes, Stu, I did tell her, and she was so excited about seeing you," he said, "The wait would be hard for her since she wanted to come straightaway," Bill said.

"Well, she never came. Why do you think that is, Bill?" Stu asked.

"I'll call her if you'd like and find out why," Bill replied.

"No, don't do that. This must be between us, one way or the other. Thanks for all your help, Bill," Stu said before hanging up.

As Stu's world seemed to be crumbling inside the hospital; hers did as well it wasn't Stu's fault that she fell in love with him, it was her own. Only time and work could ease the pain. Once back at Miss Marple's she went straight up to her room to close out this chapter of her life.

The phone started ringing as she turns the key in her door.

"Hello."

"Sally, Mr. Korn here. I just read the last column you sent in, while I was approving it for publication. Sally, I fear that you are getting to close to your subjects and losing your objectivity. Don't get me wrong, your column is still fascinating too read, but there seems to be something missing, if you know what I mean. There are four weeks before the challenge is over, and we decide on a new member of our staff. Do you think that you'll be able to end your summer columns in the way it was started?" he asked.

Oh, what a time for him to call and ask me about the column. Of course, he's right, and I must keep my head in the game and do what I came here to do, I thought.

"Yes, everything is going fine here. I promise I won't let you down," I replied.

"Good, then I'll let you go, for now, sleep well," he said as he hung up.

"Sleep well? How was I to do that?" I said aloud to myself.

I spent most of the night sitting out on my balcony, dozing occasionally but never really sleeping. I thought about what I heard Stu say repeatedly.

"Sara, why are you crying? He did what? Of course, I love you."

Who did what? Had her husband Sam hurt her in some way? Was she calling Stu, thinking that he could come and protect her? Or was it another way for her not to take any responsibility for her actions in the shooting, putting it all on her husband. He had married her for her money, that was obvious. Had she done all this to get Stu back and frame her husband for the shooting, so she wouldn't have to share her inheritance?

This would be something that my readers would like to know, for her mother had been a beloved friend of many of them. Solving this mystery would either free Stu's of Sara or turn him entirely against me when he found out that I was Joe Bumgardner.

I hurried and dressed and headed down to my car, only to be stopped at the bottom of the stairs by Miss Marple who was up hours earlier than normal.

"Sally, I need to have a word with you," she said seriously as she led me back to her parlor and closed the door behind us.

"Please, have a seat," she said, sitting down in her chair. "Sally, there is something that you should know that I found out at Sara's mother's funeral yesterday. Amanda, Stu's secretary, sat with us. She was very talkative, more than I remembered her ever being in the past. Sally, Amanda told us that Sara and her husband had been cleared of her mother's death. There's more, she said that she told Sam and Sara that Stu was still alive and what room he was in—in the hospital.

"I can tell you that I, Kitty, and Jane could have been knocked over by a feather and the anger that rose up from my deepest parts made me want to kill her. How could she have thought it was all right to tell them that? Doesn't she understand that they're under suspicion?" she asked, then sat back in her chair perplexed.

"You must call Bill and tell him all of this, only he can protect Stu now," I said, getting to my feet.

"Sally, wait, I don't understand. Why wouldn't you go to him now and tell him yourself? Weren't you with him last night?" she asked.

"Yes, I stopped by his room, but he was busy talking on the phone with Sara. He was comforting her, and I didn't want to interrupt them, for what I overheard sounded quite serious," I said as I departed. There was nothing left to say. She is a very clever lady and would put the pieces together by herself.

Now I knew how Sara found out—I wanted to know why Amanda shared that information. What was it she hoped to gain? I dialed her office at nine and asked her to lunch; to my surprise, she accepted immediately. We would lunch at noon at the Pier, on my dime. If this was the only way to get to the bottom of the shooting, then I would consider it a cheap lunch. I had three hours to use up before lunch, and I didn't want to be sitting at Miss Marple's, so I went around by Sara and Sam's house knowing full well that they were not there. I had bent up a book of matches and left it under the window, so it couldn't be closed all the way. I took a pair of plastic gloves out of my glovebox and stuffed them in my pants pocket before parking my car a block away from the Hatfields' backyard and the window in question. Once I arrived, I slipped on my gloves then opened the window and climbed into the master bedroom. I took off my shoes to not leave footprints throughout the house then went to work. I went into the kitchen and noticed they hadn't put out their garbage in their hurry to leave. You'd be surprised what I've found in the past when going through other people's trash.

I found a large clean garbage bag in the cupboard and laid it on the floor, then I emptied the garbage out on the bag. I sat down on the floor next to it and methodically went through every piece of it. I found receipts from gas stations, flower shops, and eateries in Ohio. I also came across a round-trip airplane ticket that was dated the day of the shooting and a pair of men's gloves with the fingertips cut off. There were empty shotgun cartridges, six of them in all. I jumped up and ran through the house looking into all the closets in hopes of finding a rifle or a scope, a box of ammo, and maybe a small derringer. I emptied every closet and went through all the shoes and hat boxes. When I was returning things back to their places in his closet, I came across a movable wall panel in the back corner of the closet. It concealed a safe and a steel gun case with combination locks on them making me unable to get into them. After taking pictures of everything I put all of it back as it was before—yes, even the garbage. I gave Bill a call and asked him if they had searched the Hatfields' home since they left town. He seemed quieter than usual and surprised by my question.

"No, why do you ask?"

"Well, Bill, we still have to find out who shot Stu and Sara. He might have kept somethings in his home of interest, so this would be the best time to search for it. Don't you agree?" I asked. There was a long moment of silence before he replied.

"Sally, that is a clever idea. Would you like to accompany me to their home after I get a judge to sign a search warrant?" he asked.

"Are you kidding? You'll let me go with you?" I asked.

"Sally, you understand I am not sure about this, but something tells me that you already know what I'll find. Not every day do I get a call from a member of our community telling me to search for someone else's house," he said.

"Bill, you know it's not like that at all. There are a lot of reasons to expect these people of wrongdoing in this case. There are more questions than answers that just a possibility we haven't investigated. Sam was a sniper in the service, you read that in the file I gave you, didn't you? It just seems a logical place to look, that's all. I am not trying to tell you how to do your job. I just called to ask if anyone had looked into it yet," I said. "So I ask you again, were you serious when you asked me to come along?"

"No, of course not. But I can't keep you from stopping over once I get there—say about four this afternoon?" he replied.

"Gotcha," I said, then hung up. I put on my shoes back on and climbed back out of the window I came in through; I lowered the window completely before removing my gloves. I walked back to my car and drove to the Stain Cup for a cup of coffee and to waste some time and pick up on additional information.

As I walked into the Stain Cup at ten, I was hopeful that something new might be said or done to add excitement to my day. I found my seat on the right side of the restaurant at a table for two. I hadn't brought any of my tools of the trade with me, for this had not been a planned stop.

"Sally, it's good to see you," the young waitress said as she stopped by to take my order. This was the girl I labeled as the village gossip.

"Good morning, it's good to see you again as well," I replied.

"What can I bring you, Sally?" she asked.

"A cup of coffee and an order of rye toast, please," I said, and she moved away quickly.

As I sat and waited, I scanned the room. It was an elderly crowd who came here religiously. A couple of men sat at the table behind me, drinking their coffee and sharing the morning paper.

"Peter, have you been reading the columns of the two new writers at the paper? The editors of the paper introduced them in the at the beginning of the summer. One is a sports writer and a damn good one, too. He doesn't just write about the game but speaks of the players as if they were his extended family members. He is a man who enjoys his job and what he's reporting on. The other man writes a lot about our village, yet I can't find anyone who's ever met him. He's much like an eavesdropper that hides in the bushes and listens outside of a bedroom window for gossip. He seems to be as elusive as an Irish elf. What is he afraid of?" one of the men asked.

"Jack, I think the reporter you speak of is a great one, and he's helped us a lot. Just look at what we've been through this summer. It's been one like we've never known before. First, there was the night of the birds and the land they were protecting. He enlightened us about a piece of land that was sold to a small group of Indians and why. Then there was the land swindle and the spies from China that were trying to gain ownership of the Indians' land. We found out all the things they did and the people who died in the village because of it. He was the one who brought us all together by using his column and the village hall to have the ownership of the land in question placed in the right hands. He writes about the sailboat race and the shooting and promised that we would know the truth about it. If anyone, he can solve this mystery, and he'll forever have me as a reader. I don't care if I never know who he is. Sometimes it's faster getting information if no one knows who's looking," Peter replied.

My waitress returned with my order. "Sally, please hang around a few minutes. I'll be done here in ten minutes. I want to talk to you about something," she said before hurrying away.

As I ate my toast and drank my coffee, I thought about what the two men behind me said. In a way, they had both been right about their view of me, and that didn't sit well with me. It was then and there that I decided to promise everyone who reads my column that they would be able to meet me at the end of the summer if they so choose to.

The waitress did as she had promised and returned to sit down at my table as the men behind me walked away.

"Sally, there's something that happened yesterday. I don't know what to make of it, but it's about Sara Hatfield before she and her husband left. She came in as soon as we opened and sat over there just before sunrise, about five thirty. She was wearing sunglasses, and I noticed bruises on her arm. As soon as she saw me looking at them, she pulled her sweater sleeve down. I asked her if I could do something to help her. She shook her head no and just sat here for a good hour before getting up and leaving. She never ordered anything, just sat there. It was quite eerie if you know what I mean. If something horrible happens to her and I didn't say anything... Oh, Sally, do you understand what I am telling you?"

"Yes, I do, and I'll tell Officer Bill what you have told me, I promise," I said in hopes that it would give her some comfort. She got up and went about her business while I had another cup of coffee and remained at the restaurant until eleven.

Miss Marple would be going to the club for lunch and her bridge game now, so I could return to the house without having to talk to anyone about last night. I needed to dress in something that looked a bit classier than blue jeans and a sweatshirt to have a serious lunch with Amanda. This is a woman that's been around the wealthy most of her life, and she doesn't let it go unnoticed by the way she carries herself, her rich-looking appearance, and her speech and mannerisms. You might say, she oozes of her standing in society, some refers to her as a rich snob.

I was sitting in my car outside of the restaurant in the parking lot when Amanda pulled in; I quickly got out of it and met her at the door so we could walk in together. We were ushered to a table by the windows overlooking the cove.

"Thank you for letting me buy you lunch today, Amanda," I said when we sat down.

"Nonsense, I'll be paying for my own lunch. Sally, I, too, wanted to have some time with you, so your request for lunch came at the right time. Yesterday morning, when you stopped by my office to find out about the tests having to do with Sara's mother, I was a bit flip with you. For that I am sorry, but I was also relieved. Sara has been a friend of mine ever since she and Stu dated. I never wanted to believe, nor do I know that she would ever hurt anyone, not Stu's late wife or her mother. That's not to say those women weren't hurt by someone else, for I believe they were. The tests that came back didn't clear anyone of it. The report just said it was inconclusive. All that means is that there is not enough evidence to pursue this person. Yet for me, it did clear Sara," Amanda added.

The waiter came back and took our lunch order before we continued our conversation.

"Amanda, this morning while I had my breakfast at the Stain Cup, the waitress told me that she spoke to Sara yesterday morning about five thirty. It was still dark out when she walked in with glasses on, and she had bruises on her arm. When the waitress appeared to notice them, Sara pulled her sweater sleeve down. The waitress said, she asked if she could help her. Sara just shook her head no and sat there without ordering anything for at least an hour. When she stopped in to see you, did you notice anything?" I asked.

"She was wearing long sleeves, but it was cool out and expected at that time of day. She was also wearing sunglasses, but that wasn't uncommon either. I remember the bright smile that crossed her face when she read the tests report," Amanda said as the waiter placed her plate in front of her.

There wouldn't be a better time for me to pop this question than now.

"Amanda, I believe that you are a brilliant woman. That's why I was thrown for a loop when I heard that you told Sara about Stu still being alive and his room number at the hospital while knowing full well why they wanted to keep it a secret. I must believe that you have a good reason for it, though Kitty and Miss Marple and I are clueless to what that reason could be," I said. She almost choked on the first bite of her salad. Once she regained her composure and straightened the napkin on her lap, she looked up at me.

"Sally, as I told you, I don't believe Sara could hurt anyone, and she was suffering so thinking Stu was dead. She's like my sister—can't you understand that and have some compassion for her? She had just lost her dear mother, been shot and then led to believe her beloved Stu was dead. Really! You think I was wrong as her friend to want to relieve some of her pain? If that's the case, what good is a friend in one's time of grieving?" she replied as she looked out the window. There was a brief pause in our conversation as we both ate our lunch. She had made some good points, but there was something she wasn't saying that I couldn't quite put my finger on. As the waiter came and removed our dishes and offered us dessert, we both said no in unison. We remained at the table and enjoyed our iced tea as we continued.

"Amanda, how long have you worked for Stu?" I asked.

"I've worked at his side for over five years, here and back home in New York. He would never think of coming here without me. I helped him through his breakup with Sara and the death of his beautiful wife. I nursed him back from a deep depression he fell into after her death. I've been his constant companion through it all," she replied. Her words sent chills up my spine. It was as if I was talking to a woman in love with her boss.

Could it be that we are looking at the wrong women in all of this? Could she have had something to do with removing these women from Stu's life, thinking if she couldn't have him, no one else would? I wondered. *But how would she involve Sam in her plans, if his gun did the shooting? These two people didn't really show much liking for each other*, I thought to myself.

"Sally, I really must run, for there is much to do with Stu out of the office. I must run to the hospital and take him some files he needs. Can I give him your love?" she asked with a smile.

"No, that won't be necessary. Thanks anyhow," I replied. Minutes later, she was gone, and I held our lunch check in my hand; two plates of salad and iced tea for each of us came to fifty-five dollars plus tip. I had a new outlook on Amanda, and yet some questions had to be addressed to make this puzzle all come together.

CHAPTER 28

Running Out of Time

    I drove by Sara's house at four and noticed two police cars parked in front of the house. I turned my car around at the corner and drove back to the house and pulled into the driveway. I got out and hurried up the steps to the opened front door.

"Bill, are you here?" I called out from the doorway.

"Oh, Sally, what a surprise it is to see you here," he said with a smile.

"What if anything, have you found?" I whispered.

"My men are going through the garbage as we speak, and I have one in the bedroom and closets," he replied.

"Boss, look what we've found in the garbage," the officers in the kitchen yelled out. No soon had we entered the kitchen to see what was found then the officer in the master bedroom yelled out. My mind was more at ease now, knowing that they had found all the things I had seen before.

"Sally, how did you know I'd find something here?" Bill asked in a stern voice.

"Bill, give me a break. You're too good of a cop not to have thought about doing this without my help or suggestion. There are a few things that I found out today that may add to the puzzle that you're trying to put together." I explained my visit to the Stain Cup and my lunch with Amanda, which also put him in a state of perplexity and the look on his face said it all.

"Well, I must run, see you later," I said, running out the door and down the steps to my car. I pulled out of the driveway, waving goodbye to him, as he stood watching me drive away.

Amanda at the hospital: "Stu dear, I've brought you the files that are on this month's calendar; are you sure you're up to all of this?" she asked.

"Yes, I might as well be, there's nothing else for me to do here," he replied.

"Have you had any visitors yet?" she asked.

"Sara called me last night—thanks for giving her my number. She was crying, Sam has become very physical with her it seems. She sent me these lovely flowers," Stu said, pointing at the flowers on the windowsill.

"She did what!" Amanda said as she walked over and inspected the flowers. She noticed a gift card that had been shoved down into the middle of the vase and took it out and read it. "Oh no, she didn't," she said out loud. "Look at this, where did you get the idea that they were sent to you by Sara?" she asked, handing the gift card to Stu. Stu took it and read it aloud. "To my dearest Stu, my love blooms like these flowers for you. Love, Sally."

"Amanda, you are an angel, what would I ever do without you. Sally must have come by last night and heard me talking to Sara and thought that we were back together," Stu said.

"Amanda, have you heard how long they intend to keep me here in the hospital?"

"No, why hasn't your doctor been in yet today?"

"No, I haven't seen any doctor, and all the nurses will tell me is that they don't know since the doctor hasn't left any orders for them yet for my release," Stu replied.

"Stu, you've had serious surgery, it was touch and go for a while. We all believed that you might not make it," Amanda informed him.

"Be honest with me, Amanda, not to say that you haven't been, just tell me what happened to me. Why am I here?" he asked.

"Wow! Are you serious? You really don't remember? You and Sara were about to win the first sailboat race of the season when you and Sara were shot."

"Why was Sara with me and not Sally? I don't understand," he asked, rubbing his head as though he were trying to rub memories to the front of his thoughts.

"Stu, take it easy, everything will come back to you in time—just relax. You've already found out that Sally did come by last night. I had a delightful lunch with her today. I was puzzled why she didn't want me to give you her love, but now I know why. Unfortunate she believes that you and Sara got back together. How that must have hurt her, Stu. Maybe you should try to call her, but don't be upset if she doesn't answer. She may try to put space between the two of you for a while," Amanda cautioned.

"That does make sense, and I'll bear it in mind. Just knowing that Sally was here makes me feel better. I couldn't do anything without you, Amanda," Stu said, looking into Amanda's eyes. She wanted him to say that to her and mean it. *That would come later, when she comforts him through another loss of love in his life*, she thought.

Back at Miss Marple's: "Sally, if you're free for a few minutes, please stay and visit with me here on the porch for a while," Miss Marple asked.

I would typically have come in the back door, but today I used the front porch door, and now felt trapped by her inquiries.

"Yes, of course, how are you today, Miss Marple?" I said as I sat down in one of her natural-colored wicker chairs. Just about that time my phone rang, and I couldn't believe my ears; it was Stu. I chose not to answer it just now here in front of Miss Marple; it would just spawn more questions from her.

"Wrong number, I take it," she said, looking over her glasses at me.

"Yes, I guess you can say that it wasn't someone I have time for now," I replied.

"So how has your day gone this far?" she asked. I would have to open and tell her something of interest. I filled her in on my stop at the Stain Cup and my lunch with Amanda but not my stop at the Hatfields. I didn't want that to get out until we knew more about the things found there. Not once did she ask me about Stu, nor did I offer anything on that subject. She filled me in on some local gossip that she picked up at lunch with the girls and about the next sailboat race. The races didn't seem to mean much to me anymore, other than the reporter's point of view. I listened as she talked while the sun began to set over the harbor.

"Miss Marple, it's been a very long day. Please forgive me, I think, I'll go to my room and retire a little early tonight," I said, getting to my feet and quickly moving up the stairs before she could think of something else to ask me.

No sooner had I gotten into my room than my phone rang; I took it out of my pocket and saw that it was Stu again. What could he want from me? He had the love of his life. I ignored it the best I could and got ready for bed before taking a seat in front of my computer. I turned it on and opened the file on the harbor and its people. I had compiled as much information on everyone that I could find. I was most interested in the spies that lived here at Miss Marple's. They had been gone most of the summer, but they were back now and watching the same people that I was. I noticed a person sitting in their car out in front of the Hatfields when I looked out through the peephole in the front door after sneaking in the back window.

Was this couple looking for a way to gain entrance, or had they already been in? I asked myself, while climbing back through the window I had entered, only to find their car was gone. Why were they interested in the Hatfields? This couple was a pair of world travelers, not small-town spies. This mystery is like a massive spiderweb—just about the time you think you know all the players, new ones appear.

I must get into their rooms at Miss Marple's while they are out. Hopefully I'll find something that will tell me what they're up to, I thought before my phone rang again.

"Oh, why, Stu, must you call me if there is no future in it for us?" I said aloud to myself. I turned off my phone and went to bed.

I tossed and turned all night long; when I did sleep, I saw the many faces of the people that were possibly involved in this mystery and how each of them might have done it. I couldn't get my mind wrapped around how the spies fit in. Had they been hired by the shooter?

CHAPTER 29

Unexpected Outcome

Knock, knock, knock. "Just a minute," I called out from the bathroom to someone at the door.

"Yes, how can I help you?" I asked Kenny when I opened it.

"Sally, I don't know what you've done, but I have never seen my aunt so upset. She sent me up here to get you. You better come quickly," he said as he turned and walked back downstairs.

"Okay, thanks," I managed to get out before he went out of sight. What have I done to make her upset? Maybe it's not about me. I grabbed my keys off the dresser and locked my door before going down to see her.

"Miss Marple, is something wrong? Kenny said that you needed to see me immediately," I said as I walked into her parlor.

"Sally, where have you been? No one has been able to get hold of you. I've already had five calls from people wanting to talk to you, dear. I wouldn't be so upset, but I am not an early riser, as you well know. Your callers have been ringing my number since seven this morning. There were three from Stu, one from Amanda, and one from our favorite cop. Didn't you pay your last phone bill or something?" she said, looking into my eyes with concern.

"Oh my, no!" I started laughing. "Miss Marple, I turned my phone off last night so I could sleep without it ringing, and I forgot to turn it back on. I am so sorry for the inconvenience I've caused you," I said.

"So that's why you aren't taking any of Stu's calls," she replied.

"Miss Marple, I went to see him a couple of nights ago and overheard him telling Sara that he loved her. I don't think I could stand looking into his face while he tells me about their love," I said as I sat down.

"Sally, you should have stayed a little longer. Amanda went over to see him yesterday after lunch and found him perplexed. He couldn't understand why you never came to see him after Bill gave you his message. There were flowers in his room that he thought came from Sara. Amanda walked over to check them out and found the flowers had a gift card pushed down in the middle of the vase. She took the card out and read it to herself first before offering it to Stu. His eyes lit up, knowing that you had been there, then told Amanda that Sara had called. You must have overheard them talking. Sally, when he called me looking for you, he confided talking to Sara about being friends, but nothing else, because he's in love with you."

I jumped up and ran back upstairs to find my phone and turn it on, then went back down to her parlor to apologize for my rudeness in not thanking her or saying goodbye. As I entered her room, I was stopped dead in my tracks. I had just left her seconds ago, yet standing only where I'd been seconds ago standing a dreamy six-foot suntanned blue-eyed heartthrob. His left shoulder was tightly bandaged and his arm in a sling. There he stood, with his right arm stretched out inviting me to come to his side. I couldn't remember if I walked or ran. All I knew is how it felt when his right arm encircled me and our lips met. No one else on earth was on our minds, not even the ladies in the room.

"Oh, Stu, please forgive me for doubting your love," I whispered in his ear once we came up for air. We laughed when we realized that we weren't alone. Stu took me by the hand and led me to the front porch where we sat facing each other.

"Sally, please," he said reaching into his pocket and pulling out a small box and opening it. "Darling, will you marry me?" I was in awe, not only because of the size of it but the man offering it. I looked into his eyes wanting to say yes but closed the box and handed it back to him.

"I am not saying no, Stu. There are things all couples should talk about before pledging their lives to each other. I pray you to ask me again after we talk over dinner, for there are things you don't know about me, things that may change your mind," I said. He closed the box and returned it to his pocket, now very quiet, and a bit withdrawn.

"All right, we'll do it your way," he said, standing up, then reaching down to help me to my feet. "But don't think for one minute that anything you have to say will drive me away. Sally, my heart can't be wrong about you. It just can't be! I'll be by to pick you up at five and not a second later. Then he kissed me goodbye before leaving me looking at him as he drove away. I turned to see three elderly women looking out the front-bay window at me, all with concerned looks on their faces.

"Had they watched and seen everything?" I wondered. I walked back in the door right smack into the trio in the hallway.

"How could have you done that to Stu?" Aunt Kitty asked.

"Come, there is something that the three of you should know about me," I said, leading them back to the parlor. Please sit down while I tried to put what I'm thinking into words.

"Miss Marple, you've always known that I have the DNA of a sleuth, as do you. I have never lied to you, but I have been selective with the truth," I said, reaching down and picking up the newspaper from the footstool and turning it to my column. "The three of you must promise to keep my secret for a few more weeks, and then everyone will know," I said, handing the paper to Aunt Kitty. She looked down at the paper and then handed it off to the other ladies.

"Sally, I don't understand what you are trying to tell us," she replied.

"I think I know," Miss Marple said. The other two women looked at her as she continued.

"Sally, are you telling us that you're Joe Bumgardner?" Without waiting for my answer, she added, "It all makes sense now." Then she started laughing. "Oh, girl, you fooled us all. This is going to be the talk of the summer season. How a pretty young thing like you was able to take this village by storm and do so much good for all. It is my honor to have shared this summer with you, Sally Crystal."

"Wow! That we are easier than I thought it would be. I only hope when I tell Stu tonight he takes it as well. I could not accept his proposal of marriage until he was aware that I am an investigative reporter and will be for many years to come. He may be a rich man, but I would never marry for money, and besides, I do enjoy what I do. All communities need someone at the helm looking out for danger," I said.

"Well, girl, you have made us very happy to know that you will truly be one of us soon. But there's another problem afoot, and that's keeping our lips sealed about all of this until you're ready to share it with our neighbors," Miss Marple said.

"Oh, you must! For my work isn't quite done here yet," I replied before going to my room to prepare for my date with Stu.

Several hours later I returned to sit on the porch with the ladies until Stu drove up.

"Don't worry, dear, he'll understand, everything will be all right," Aunt Kitty said. I just smiled in response to her remarks as I walked down the front steps to Stu's car. He got out and walked around it to open the car door for me; we exchanged a short kiss before I got in. He smiled and waved back at the ladies on the porch as he got back into the car, then we quickly drove away in his convertible.

We went up M119 past the golf course, farmland, and beautiful rolling hills. The road was narrow, just wide enough for two cars to pass one another, and sometimes not even that. It was little more than a paved footpath at times. We ended up on a very high hill that overlooked Lake Michigan and the village below, in an area with a set of park benches for those that might like to linger. It looked like a place used as a turnaround point as well. Stu got out of the car and walked around to help me out. We walked over to one of the benches and sat down.

"Okay, Sally, let's get the gorilla in the room out of the way first. You haven't said a word since I picked you up, and that's just not like you. Please, darling, I need to know that you feel as I do."

"Stu, I am a reporter who at this time is known as Joe Bumgardner," I said. "I took up a summer challenge offer from my bosses in hopes of getting my own column. I was ordered to move into the village and write on things that mattered to the people here. The newspaper tried for years in summers past to get news about the people here, but it was a tightly closed-off community to them. I moved into Miss Marple's, as a reporter on a summer hiatus from a small paper. Miss Marple didn't know then that I was Joe Bumgardner, but she does now, and so do Agatha and Kitty. I told them today because they wanted to know why I couldn't accept the ring. They promised me you'd understand and that I had nothing to worry about." I paused and took a deep breath.

Stu stood up and walked away, not speaking a word, to the wooden fence that acted as a barrier at the cliff lookout.

My mind rushed to protect my heart, for I knew we had gotten too close too fast. Maybe it wasn't meant to be after all, I thought. I stood up and walked over to his side and quietly looked out on the beauty of the scenery below.

"Stu, please, share with me what you're thinking. Is there anything that I can say?"

"Sally, I love you," Stu said as he turned and put his arm around me gently.

"Honey, my silence isn't because of you. I, too, have kept a secret. It's always been my policy to check out everyone I get close too. I serve a lot of rich people and must remain a man beyond reproach. I've known for some time who you are and what you do for a living. I must admit, I was first taken aback by the report I received. There's more you should know. A couple that lives in the same house you do are friends of mine, and they work for me from time to time. They too have gotten into many places without being seen by most, like the Hatfields' house." He paused to see my reaction.

"Stu, have you been having me followed?" I asked with a snip of concern in my voice.

"Oh no, not at all. They finished up at the Hatfield's before you arrived, using the front door key. A bit unique wouldn't you say?" he teased, with a big smile. "By the way, how did you jimmy up that window?" he asked.

"Sorry, not even if you take my life will I give up my secrets or the tools of my trade," I said, returning a smile.

"So you had lunch with Amanda and know that the tests that were taken on Sara came back inconclusive but only where it comes to Sara. Bonnie had been given morphine over an extended period and in copious amounts at the end because of the pain of cancer. There was no way to prove someone gave her a deadly amount that night. Yet there was something else the test showed that it was and put in the main report but not the one sent to my office. It is an ingredient that I only heard about once before in my life; it was used to take the life of my wife. As you well know, Sara would like to get her claws back in me. She was told by Amanda that I can't remember anything about the race or shooting, and her husband must believe that's true. Sally, your being on my arm may make you a target for whoever is trying to kill me. I want you to marry me, but making it known to others could be dangerous," Stu said as he looked into my eyes.

"I want the entire world to know you're going to be my one and only for a lifetime. So let's set a trap for the taking so we can get on with our lives," I said as Stu took the ring out of the box and slid it on my finger; my arms flew up around his neck as our lips found each other.

In Ohio: *Ring! Ring! Ring!* "Hello."
"Sam."
"What the hell! Why are you calling me here, and on our land phone, too, are you crazy? Sara could have answered the phone," Sam replied

"Oh, for God's sakes, Sam, I've been her friend longer than yours. She wouldn't think anything of my calling," the caller replied.

"I know that, but with friends like you who needs enemies?" Sam said.

"Oh, aren't you condescending. After you shot Sara and Stu, you pledged your love to her."

"Are you out of your mind? I never shot my wife or Stu. Where do you come up with this crap? I wasn't even in the village when it happened," Sam insisted.

"I suppose you're going to tell the police that when they come for you. I know for one thing that you had a friend fly you into the area that very night before dark, and if I know that so will they."

"I flew back up there so I could drive Sara back to Ohio after the race," Sam said.

"Then why didn't you stay? The police said they called you in Ohio to tell you about your wife being shot."

"They called my cell phone number, I was here at my home," Sam argued.

"You told everyone at the Stain Cup the following morning that you had just driven all the way from Ohio after getting a call from the police asking you to return."

"I understand why you're saying this now because it was of your doing, all of it. I accidentally stepped in your shit, and now I have it all over me. I should have known your fake friendship comes with a price. I am not sure yet how you killed Bonnie Gaiter, but I know you did. You had planned for my wife to take the fall for it. What did you hope to gain by doing it?" Sam asked. "Bonnie had been a good friend to you ever since Stu became her attorney."

"You fool! Can't you see how rich we would be if Sara were out of the picture? Stop acting like you love her. She was your meal ticket that's all. It's just a matter of time, and she will be out of the picture once and for all. You get in my way or turn on me, and I'll have you killed too, and you know I can do it. Keep your mouth shut, and you'll come out of all of this very rich, that is if you can convince the police of where you really were during the shooting. That's your headache, not mine," the caller said, then hung up without another word.

"Sam, who were you talking to?" Sara asked.

"Oh, I don't know, it was a wrong number. Is there something you need me for?" Sam asked.

"No, not me," Sara replied, just before the police walked into Sam's home office behind her.

"Sam Hatfield, you and your wife, are being arrested for the murder of Stu Baker," the officer said as he and his partner cuffed Sam and his wife.

"What are you talking about?" Sara yelled. "I was on that boat with Stu, and I was shot too. So why am I being arrested? We just had his funeral the other day in Black Hawk Harbor," she added, trying to sound shocked by the news they were just given. She had known for a couple of days that Stu was alive, because Amanda had called with his hospital phone number, and she had talked to him.

"My orders are to bring you both in, and that is what we are going to do. You can call your lawyer after booking, and before you go before the judge at nine in the morning, he'll decide if you can post bail.

"Can I get a few of my things like clean clothes and makeup?" Sara asked.

"No! Just what you're wearing is permitted for now. You will be wearing clothes provided for you there," replied the officer.

"Let me put the food away that I have out on the kitchen counter," Sara said.

"My officer will accompany you to the kitchen, so you can do that, then we will be on our way to Michigan."

Back in Black Hawk Harbor: *Ring! Ring! Ring!* "Hello."

"Stu, Bill here. You should know that the FBI has arrested Sara and Sam Hatfield, they're being brought back to Emmet County as we speak for trial. They've been charged with your murder," Bill said.

"Bill, I don't think for one minute that Sara had anything to do with the attempt, after all, she was with me and shot, too," Stu replied.

"That may be true, but I have known people to shoot themselves while trying to blame the deed on someone else. So for now, we'll let the story come to light as it will, and if you're right, she'll be freed. Sometimes the proof can indicate that there was more than one if you know what I mean. Yet on the other hand, they could be trying to play them off against each other to see if one of them gives up evidence of some kind. I understand that they have a lot of evidence against Sam. Stu, are you going to be working with the persecutor's office on the case?" Bill asked.

"I hope he'll let me, for I believe this trial is going to be a nail biter. Bill, there's another matter you should know about. It's the tests that came back on Bonnie's death. They were inconclusive, although there was an agent or ingredient found in her skin, hair, and blood that was also found in my late wife's body. It's a poison found in the Amazon jungle. Our country outlawed this poison to be used in fertilizer years ago. It was used in a minimal amount in the planting of plants in and about cemeteries to keep rodents and other animals from destroying them. If the poison is kept dry, it is of no danger to humans, but in a damp or wet stage, the properties of the toxin become deadly. The poison doesn't seem to harm plants at all in any arena, wet or dry, yet even a small amount of it in a house plant can be deadly to humans and animals. I believe but haven't yet proven that Lilian was murdered in this fashion, as was Bonnie," Stu informed Bill.

"Wow! That is something, I didn't know. You say that you're sure that Bonnie was murdered? Do you have any idea of who might have done it? Yes, I am sorry to say I think I do, but there's a piece of the puzzle I don't yet have to prove it. I am confident that it's just a matter of days before we'll be able to tie it all up," Stu said.

"When you say all tied up, do you mean that the murders and attempted murders are all connected?" Bill asked.

"Yes, I am sure they are, for they all have a common denominator," Stu replied. "Sally is going to help me set a trap. Oh, by the way, have you heard that Sally and I are now engaged to be married?"

"No, that's the most exciting news that I've heard all day. Congratulations!" Bill said, then added, "About the trap you're planning to set, will it endanger Sally's life? You must bear in mind that you're trying to trap an accomplished killer, someone who may be missing the human trait of fear. For some reason, a person like this thinks they have a right to take what they want with no repercussions for their actions," Bill said, with great concern.

"It was Sally's idea, she is a well-trained observer. We will take great care in how we pursue our target. Sally will wear a wire, of course, whenever she has to be alone with the person in question," Stu said.

"Are you telling me that you know the name of the killer and you're keeping it from your favorite cop?" Bill asked.

"As I told you before Bill, I am not yet sure of anything I can prove yet. When I am sure, you will be the first one I call, okay?" Stu promised before hanging up.

CHAPTER 30

Sweet Weapon of Desire

"Good morning, or should I say, good day, you're in bed before me and up later than most. How did you sleep? Well, I hope. You missed some exciting news last night. Sally came in late wearing a beautiful engagement ring," Kitty said, handing Miss Marple her first cup of tea.

"Great! That's the best news I could ever have gotten. Has Sally come down yet this morning?"

"Yes, before nine, she and Stu headed off to the courthouse," Agatha said.

"The courthouse! Why ever would they go there? Not to elope I hope?" No, the ladies laughed.

"Sara and Sam Hatfield were arrested yesterday afternoon at their home in Ohio and transferred back here. They were to be arraigned this morning before Judge Jackson at nine for attempted murder, so Stu and Sally wanted to beat the traffic," Kitty said.

"Well, when things start moving, one best not sleep or she'll miss everything," Miss Marple said laughing.

At the courthouse: "Mr. and Mrs. Hatfield, you stand before me today with the charge of attempted murder," Judge Jackson said as Sally and Stu entered the courtroom on cue. Sara's face showed no sign of surprise, but Sam's, on the other hand, turned white, as he looked at Stu and then back at the judge.

"Mr. Hatfield, are you feeling all right? You're as white as a sheet," the judge said. All Sam did was nod. "You both should know that Mr. Baker remembers everything about that night and he will be sitting at the prosecutor's table. He is a well-known lawyer around these parts, and he will also be asking questions from time to time. With that said, Mr. Hatfield, your bail is set at five hundred thousand and Mrs. Hatfield at two hundred thousand, and I am setting the first day of the trial at one week from today. To be able to make bail you must both promise not to travel out of this county for any reason. Do you understand what I am saying to you?" the judge asked.

"Yes, Judge," Sam said, and Sara nodded in agreement.

"Judge, I am not guilty of anything," Sam said.

"Mr. Hatfield, in this court you are innocent until proven guilty, so as of today, I tend to agree with you, but with that said, the FBI has a mountain of evidence to prove otherwise. I'll see you both back here next Monday at nine o'clock sharp," the judge said as he stood up, turned, and walked out the door behind his bench. The Hatfields stood talking to their lawyer and the bail bondsman, while Stu shared a few words with the prosecutor. I remained seated in the courtroom until Stu was done, then, as planned, we went to his office.

"Good afternoon, Amanda," Stu said as we entered his office. "Could you bring me the calls I need to return and the names of who I'll be seeing after lunch? The Hatfields are posting their bail and will be staying in their home here until the trial is over," Stu blurted out on purpose.

"Trial, what trial?" Amanda asked.

"Oh, you haven't heard? The Hatfields were brought back from Ohio last night to stand trial for attempted murder. The judge set their bail at two hundred thousand and five hundred thousand, the trial is due to start Monday, a week from today," Stu told her.

"Oh no! How did Sara seem to take it?" Amanda asked.

"She was very quiet but didn't seem surprised by any of it. I, for one, can't see how she can be involved in any of it. After all, we were both shots. Why would someone shoot her? I mean, if it was her husband who did it. He would've done it to keep her for himself, not to hurt her. Do you see what I mean? I know, all the evidence points at him and there's a lot of it, but things aren't always as they seem," Stu said pouring it on thick. Amanda listened intensely but gave no opinion of her own on the subject. While Stu got busy with his calls, I waited with Amanda in the outer office.

Amanda caught sight of the engagement ring on my finger and turned red. I thought, she'd blow her lid. She turned around and opened the window behind her as though she needed air, then after a few seconds, she turned back around and appeared to be her usual self again.

"Sally, that's a beautiful ring. Was it your mother's?" she asked.

"Oh no! Stu asked me to marry him last night, and of course, I said yes," I said, realizing that she wasn't having any of it.

"So how long will it be before you take your vows, and I am invited?" she said with a fake smile.

"Oh yes, of course, you're invited. There is no one closer to Stu than you, not even his aunt," I said, trying to get closer to her mentally.

"Well, I can hardly wait. I was at his and Lilian's wedding too, she was a beautiful lady. It's too bad what happened to her, and so soon after they said their vows," Amanda said with her back to me, making a cold chill run through me. Was she warning me or threatening me? I wasn't sure.

Stu finished, and we got out of there and none too soon. I explained to Stu what we had been talking about and what she had said, and he found it a bit strange too. The morning had quickly slipped away. We went to lunch, then he returned to his office after dropping me back off at Miss Marple's to write my column after I'd promised to go to dinner with him later.

"Not so fast young lady," Miss Marple said in the hallway outside her parlor. "Please, come join us for a minute. Did I just see Stu drop you off?" she asked, knowing he had. Miss Marple, Agatha, and Kitty had become almost inseparable. I pulled up the white wicker chair from across the room and sat down.

"Now let us get a better look at that rock you're wearing," Miss Marple said, pushing her glasses up on her nose as she examined it. "Wow! Who needs glasses? I don't think I've ever seen a stone that size. Be careful not to let it sprain your finger. What do you think Stu was thinking, putting something that big on your hand?" she said, and we all laughed.

"Miss Marple, it isn't all that big, and my finger will wear it well, I promise you."

"Sally, when you left this morning, you and Stu were headed to the courthouse. What happened?" Miss Kitty asked.

"Stu and I were just talking about it over lunch. We had never experienced anything like it before."

"What do you mean?" Miss Marple asked, leaning forward.

"The judge has cleared his calendar for this trial. Usually, it takes time, anywhere from six months to a year before a case makes it to the trial calendar, yet this trial will start next Monday. The Hatfields were just brought back yesterday from Ohio, and they appeared in court at nine this morning. Now that's fast, in anyone's book. I just feel that there's something else going on here that we are not aware of," Sally told the ladies.

"Sally, you didn't tell us if they were given a chance for bail," Agatha said.

"Yes, and it was high too, five hundred thousand for Sam and two hundred thousand for Sara, and believe it or not, they're both at home in the village already. You should have seen Sam turn sheet-white when Stu walked in the courtroom, where Sara didn't show any emotions at all. She had already been in contact with Stu before he got out of the hospital because Amanda told her he was still alive and gave her his number. Sara was talking to Stu when I went to the hospital to visit him and overheard them talking. I don't know what it is yet, but I think Amanda is up to something," I said as I stood up and hurried away before the ladies could come up with another question.

Back at Stu's office: "Hello, is this the greenhouse?"
"Yes, it is, how may I help you?"

"This is Amanda Grace. I am calling for Stu Baker, the attorney in Black Hawk Harbor. He has asked me to call you and have a wild pink orchid from the Amazon sent to Sara Hatfield, here in Black Hawk Harbor. Please add a gift tag to the plant with his name on it, would you? It would be appreciated by him if she were to receive it today."

"Miss Grace, the tag card, should we put the word love on it?" the greenhouse worker asked.

"Yes, thank you," Amanda said before hanging up.

Later: *Knock! Knock!* "Sara could you get that, I'm busy," Sam yelled out from the bedroom.

"Hello," Sara said after opening the door.

"Sara Hatfield?" the deliveryman from the greenhouse asked.

"Yes," Sara said.

"Please sign here," the man said, handing her a clipboard with an invoice on it. Then he ran out to his van and brought her back a beautiful pink orchid and gave her the plant and a copy of the invoice.

"Good day," he said as he turned to leave. Sara looked down at the invoice and noticed that it was sent by Stu. She hurried into the living room and hid it. She took the gift tag out and read it. "To my beloved Sara. Love, Stu forever." She could hardly believe her eyes; he had vowed his love for Sally. *Why now, would he be doing this? She would accept the plant for now until she could talk to him about it. Maybe it was meant to get back at Sam if he thought Sam had shot him,* she thought.

"Who was at the door, Sara?" Sam asked.

"A deliveryman from the greenhouse, he brought a plant that I ordered to dress up our bedroom. What do you think of it?" she asked.

"Gorgeous! An orchid, isn't it?" he replied.

"Yes. I didn't know you knew flowers, dear," she said nonchalantly, with a smile.

A week later: Everything else had taken a backseat for Stu this past week while he had worked with the prosecutor planning out the case and seating the jury; I hadn't seen him but twice myself. It was Monday morning, and it seemed like everyone was heading to Petoskey and the courthouse. Miss Marple and the other ladies drove in early so they could get a parking place. Stu and I were to park in the police parking lot across from the courthouse. This midsize town was full of people today; the city park was packed full, some sitting on lawn chairs and others on blankets on the ground. The city fathers had decided to put a large screen up in the park so more could watch the court proceedings as for the courtroom could only hold 120 viewers. They also allowed food vendors in the park while the trial was going on.

"See all of this, Sally, it's like a circus has come to town. I give most of the credit for this turn out to that writer, Joe Bumgardner," Stu said with a grin as we ran up the steps of the courthouse. I took a seat behind Stu, who sat at the prosecutor's table, and Miss Marple and the ladies sat right behind me. Miss Kitty tapped me on the shoulder and whispered, "Mr. Bumgardner was right when he wrote in his column last night that this trial would touch a lot of lives. Just look around here, I've never seen anything like it." I didn't look back at her, just nodded in agreement. Sara and Sam were brought in and seated at their table with their attorney. Sara didn't look so well, very tired, and pale.

"That unfortunate thing," I heard someone on the other side of the courtroom say.

"Martha, you know who she is, don't you?" her companion asked.

"No."

"That's Bonnie Gaither's daughter. Some say she had something to do with her mother's death."

"Oh, foolery, Bonnie died of cancer, everyone knows that. You can't believe anything you hear and only half of what you see. That's what everyone that came out today understands," Martha replied. Seconds later, everyone rose as the judge entered the courtroom and took his seat, then we did the same again as well. The judge called the attorneys forward and told them something in a secretive voice before they turned and returned to their tables in the front of the courtroom, then the first witness was called.

"The prosecution calls Sara Hatfield," the prosecutor said as he turned and looked at her.

"Can they do that? I mean, call someone to testify against themselves," Martha whispered to her companion.

"Please put your hand on the Bible and repeat after me: 'I promise to tell the truth the whole truth and nothing, but the truth so helps me, God." The court stenographer said. Sara repeated her, then the prosecutor stepped up to the front and asked in a compassionate toned voice, "Mrs. Hatfield, do you know that man over there sitting at my table?" he asked, pointing at Stu.

"Yes, I do," she replied.

"Did you conspire with your husband to kill him?" she was asked.

"No!" she said, with an uneasy tone in her voice.

"Could you tell this court what you did on the day that you and Stu Baker were shot? Please take your time and don't leave anything out," he instructed her.

"My alarm clock went off at five in the morning. I got up and hurried around getting ready, putting on my shorts outfit and my sweats over the top of it. We were promised normal Michigan weather, though of course, one never knows what the weather will be, especially out on the water," Sara said.

"What did your husband think about you going sailing with your ex-lover?" asked the prosecutor.

Sara's face flashed with a look of surprise at the prosecutor's question. "He didn't like it," she replied.

"So knowing he knew and didn't want you to go, you went anyways. Is that what you're telling this court? Are you saying he just stood by and watched your lover pick you up and drive away?" he asked.

"Sam had gone home to Ohio the night before the race," she replied.

"Wow! That must've really made him mad for him to leave and not even stay long enough to see the race. Maybe even mad enough to come back and try to get even?" the prosecutor replied.

"No! Sam wouldn't have done that. He's a loving idiot sometimes, I'll grant you that, but he's not a fool. If there's anything I know for sure, it's that he loves me, even when I act crazy at times, and believe it or not, I love him too," she said, looking over at her husband with tears rolling down her face. The court clerk took a small box of tissue over to Sara.

"Okay, continue, what else happened that day?"

"Stu picked me up at six, and we went to the airport that's owned by our association. There were about a dozen of our yacht club members flying to Traverse City where the sailboat race was to start at nine. After landing, we all went to breakfast together before getting onto our boats. Once onboard, Stu and I had more time to talk privately.

"He told me that he had invited me to be his first mate for two reasons. One, because he was waiting on some test to come back that would either convict or clear me of my mother's death. The other was to tell me that he intended to marry Sally Crystal," Sara said. Several people in the courtroom gallery took a shock-sounding breath, after hearing that Sara was being suspected of wrongdoing in her mother's death.

"How did that make you feel? After all, you've told your husband you want a divorce. Did it make you mad enough to kill, now knowing that your ex-lover not only suspected you of murdering your own mother but also told you he was in love with someone else? I can only imagine how I might have felt if it were me," the prosecutor asked.

"No! How would I do that? Do I look like a pistol-packing mama? What you see is all there was. I didn't come with a purse or backpack," she retorted.

"Please, continue," he said.

"We were lucky to get a warm breezy day and stayed ahead of everyone else. Stu was having some trouble with the boat's rudder and did what he could to move it back and forth, but it wasn't easy. During the race, we had to stop in Charlevoix, East Jordan, and Petoskey to pick up different-colored ribbons on our way to Black Hawk Harbor. We could see the other sailboats behind us in the distance as we got close to the last bend before the harbor. A motorboat came up fast on the starboard side, and when Stu stood up from working on the rudder to see who it was, he caught a bullet in his left arm and one in his chest. He fell back against the broom handle of the mask, hitting his head on his way down to the deck. I took a bullet in the upper part of my left thigh and fell on the deck, unable to move. The pain and heat that went through me caused me to pass out. The next thing I remember is waking up in the hospital." Sara paused.

"Did you see the shooter or the boat he was shooting from?" the prosecutor asked.

"The area we were in at the time was heavily shaded, and the person appeared to be dressed in black. I couldn't even tell you for sure if it was a man or a woman. I think the motorboat was red and white, a smallish four-seater, the kind many rents for water-skiing," she concluded, slumping back in her seat. She had been on the stand all morning. The judge excused Sara, and her husband moved quickly to her side. Then everyone stood up as the judge walked out the door behind his bench. The rest of the courtroom promptly emptied out as everyone went to lunch. It was clear now that all who heard the morning testimony were more than a little invested in the outcome. Stu and I crossed the street to the parking lot to sit in the car and eat our lunch, which I had packed earlier.

"Sally, did you notice how gray Sara's skin looked and how tired she seemed to be? It took all she had, even to testify," Stu said.

"Yes, I think everyone could see that she didn't look well. She's had a lot on her plate of late, and with all of this, she may not be getting much sleep," I replied.

"I don't know if that's it. Something just doesn't seem right," Stu said, rubbing his head. "Lilian, when she was ill also had gray-toned skin from lack of oxygen." Stu threw what was left of his sandwich back in the basket and told me to hurry. I did the same with my lunch and ran with him back into the courthouse; on our way in, he called for an ambulance. When we reentered the courtroom, Sara was lying on the front bench in the visitor seating area of the courtroom, waiting for the court to resume. Stu and I ran to Sara's side, where Sam was sitting near her.

"Sam, I've called for an ambulance for Sara. Sally and I were having lunch and talking about how ill Sara looked. Sam, her skin is gray like Lilian's was before she died," Stu said. Sam became very emotionally moved by the information.

"Oh my god, someone has gotten to her, but who would want my wife dead?" he cried.

The judge had been made aware that an ambulance was at the courthouse and removing Sara to the hospital. He hurried back to his bench and released Sam for the afternoon, so he could be with his wife, making it understood that we'd continue at nine in the morning. This case was now growing by the minute.

"Sam, before you leave, tell me what's new at your house. Has Sara been painting, new carpeting been laid, or modern furniture?" Stu asked.

"No, the only thing new at our house is the plant you sent Sara yesterday," Sam replied.

"Plant? I never sent Sara a plant. Who delivered it?" Stu asked.

"A man who works for Mary Beth's greenhouse," Sam said, running out. Once Sam was gone, Stu called the emergency room at the hospital and told a waiting doctor there what he expected from the tests that came back on her mother.

"Sally, honey, we have to get over to the greenhouse and talk to Mary. Someone is sending people plants using my name, and I want to know who it is," Stu said as we hurried out of the courthouse and back to the parking lot. The greenhouse in Black Hawk Harbor was seven miles from the courthouse, and Stu didn't say a word all the way there. Once we arrived, we hurried in to find anyone that could tell us who ordered the plant and what kind it was.

"Stu Baker, it's been a long time since you've come to see me," said a middle-aged woman, with a pencil stuck in a bun atop her head. Stu stepped forward and gave her a hug and a peck on the cheek, then stepped back.

"Mary, I would like to introduce my fiancée, Sally Crystal, to you."

"I don't understand," Mary whispered. "I was made to believe that you and Sara were back together."

"No! Who would have told you that?" Stu asked.

"Well, I took a call from Amanda yesterday. She had me send one of my very expensive Amazon pink orchids to Sara with a love card included," Mary replied, then she looked over at me.

"Miss Crystal, I am so sorry, I wish we would have met two days ago, and none of this would have happened," she said.

"None of what would have happened?" I asked.

"Well, Amanda told me to write, 'From Sara with my undying love.'"

"I accept your apology, Mary. Can you tell us something more about the plant? You said it came from the Amazon. It must have been expensive," I said.

"I order six of these plants each year for select customers. Amanda has already bought two of them from me this season at five thousand dollars apiece," Mary said, showing us her sales records.

"Look here, Sally! One of the plants went to Bonnie and the other to her daughter and both sent by Amanda. Mary, do you save all of your order books from year to year?" Stu asked.

"Yes, but they're in storage why?" she asked.

"I want you to find the book of two years back and see if Amanda sent Lilian a plant. Now back to this plant, how would one take care of an orchid?" Stu asked.

"It likes medium to bright morning sunlight and a chance to dry out between waterings, but when one does water, they should saturate it. Most ladies like to keep the plant in the window of their bedroom or sitting room, for these windows are usually found on the east side of the house," Mary replied.

"Thank you so much, Mary. You should also know that Sara has been taken to the hospital from the courthouse today, where she collapsed. We have to go now and find that plant before someone else does," Stu said.

"What! Are you saying a plant from my shop caused Sara to be ill?" Mary asked.

"No, not the plant but the poison someone added to it. Nevertheless, we must remove it from that home and see that it's taken to a poison control lab for examination," Stu replied as we hurried out of her shop. On the way to the car, Stu calls the police department and explained to Bill what we had just found out and that it should be someone with poison control to pick it up because it is now in its deadly state. Stu called the prosecutor and asked him to meet us at Stu's house so they could decide what to do next, for this case had just taken on a whole fresh look.

CHAPTER 31

Love Needs a Way

Knock, knock. "Hello, Fritz. Come in, we're in the office at the end of the hall," I said while hanging up the prosecutor's raincoat in the closet near the front door.

"Stu, what is it that you needed me for that I had to drop everything?" Fritz said as he entered the office. To his surprise, there were other people in the office with Stu already who picked up on his displeasure.

"Fritz, I am sorry, but I was sure you'd want to know immediately what we've uncovered. It's not something one would say over the phone. The FBI and our local police were also called, for there is a lot more at play here than just two people being shot at, and I believe these cases can be tied together," Stu said, handing the prosecutor a manila folder with sheets of paper that outlined what he believed had taken place; the how and when and who were all documented.

"This is crazy! Why would these people do such a thing?" the prosecutor asked.

"I can prove all of it with your help if we can find the missing piece of the puzzle. The plant I mentioned in that report didn't have poison in it before it arrived at the Hatfields, so who put it in and where did it come from? Once we answer this question, we'll find out why," Stu said. "Sara Hatfield lies in the hospital currently clinging to life, and I believe it's because of that poisonous plant. It was removed from the Hatfields' home by the poison control department of the FBI," Stu added.

"Fritz, we have more information on the motorboat used in the shooting and the pilot that flew Sam back to the harbor just before the shooting happened. We have the sniper gun that we believe was used in the shooting; it has recently been fire, and several empty cartages were also found in the Hatfields' home," the FBI agent said, then turned to Stu. "I can't see how you can tie these cases together unless you think that Sam put the poison in the plant himself to kill his wife. After all, he would stand to inherit millions of dollars for his trouble," the FBI agent added.

"Stu, do you really think that your secretary of over seven years would have something to do with trying to kill you, and if so, why?" Officer Bill asked. "I've known Amanda almost as long as I've known you and she has always been loyal to you. She even stood at your side night and day when you lost Lilian. I can understand, though, why you would have questions about her sending this plant to Sara with a love note from you. But if we can't put Amanda in the Hatfields' home after the plant was delivered there, then how could she be guilty of adding poison to it?" Bill asked.

"She had someone working with her, or she tricked someone into adding the substance, both Sam and Sara are friends of her," Stu replied.

"Well, if this is how she treats her friends, what would she do to someone she didn't like?" the prosecutor asked.

"Fritz, I'd like to cross-examine Sam after we hear from the boat owner, his pilot, and a maintenance person from Ohio, at the morning session of court tomorrow. Then you can take on Amanda with the note points I've given you and what you glean from the morning session. I do believe that we can close out these cases and get the community back to normal by the end of the afternoon session," Stu said with excitement.

"I for one won't miss court tomorrow," Bill said as he slipped on his coat that had been lying over the back of the chair he'd been sitting in. Everyone took their cue from him and moved toward the front door, everyone but Fritz. He remains seated waiting on Stu to return to his office after he saw his guests out. Once Stu stepped back into his office Fritz stood to his feet, and eye to eye with Stu, he spoke his mind loud enough for me to hear it in the living room where I was sitting.

"I am aware that you are a high-priced lawyer from New York, Stu, and you probably always get your way in such matters. Yet I am the head chief here, and I don't share my responsibilities with others so easy. I didn't want to burst your balloons in front of the FBI and police, but I'll be questioning Sam myself. If I should want any of your input, I'll ask for it," the prosecutor said, as he walked across the office to a nearby window, where he stood looking out waiting for Stu's reply.

"You're right, I was wrong. I don't have the right or freedom to examine anyone, and I do thank you for letting me sit at your table in the courtroom. I will only take the privileges you offer me," Stu promised as he tried to show Fritz the respect he was due. The two men nodded in agreement as they made their way to the front door. I handed Fritz his coat.

"Thanks, Sally," Fritz said.

"Stu, thank you for asking me over and sharing this information," he said, waving the folder Stu had given him. "By the way, I'll see you both in court tomorrow," he added while going down the front steps. He turned just long enough to let us see the smile on his face. We closed the door and turned to look at each other.

"Sally, please, you have my permission to pull back on the reins when it seems my emotions are taking over. What could have I thought when I told the prosecutor how to run the courtroom and this case? Well, I guess he knows one thing for sure," Stu said before kissing me. Once I regained my thoughts I had to ask what he meant.

"What's that?"

"Well, he knows what I would do," Stu said, with a grin on his face.

"Hay! Whattaya say, we go out and get a bite to eat?" Stu suggested.

"To tell you the truth, Stu, I'd rather stay here alone with you and have a pizza delivered, with maybe a salad and a bottle of wine. We can watch a chick flick and get our minds off the case for a while. We're engaged now, and we'll have to learn how to be alone together sooner or later," I said, almost whispering, making it necessary for him to get closer to me to hear.

"You know, you're right, we're usually surrounded by other people. Having you all to myself will be heavenly," Stu said as he pulled me to him with his one right arm and planted a passionate kiss on my lips. My passion broke free and my arms extended up to around his neck; I only came up from one kiss long enough to catch my breath before claiming another. The phone rang separating us long enough to answer it.

"Yes, hello," Stu said.

"Stu, it's Sam. The doctor just came into Sara's hospital room and told us that the poison Sara inhaled has done irreversible damage to her lungs and almost killed her. Stu, neither she nor I had anything to do with the shooting or her mother's death, I swear. Why would someone be trying to kill people in the harbor? None of this makes any sense," Sam said in tears.

"Sam, can you tell me where the plant food came from and who put it on the plant?" Stu asked.

"As I remember, I was agitated that you had the nerve to send my wife a pink orchid from the Amazon rain forest. We had just gotten back home, and things were starting to get back to normal, sort of. I didn't want to argue with her about it, so I made up a reason to go out to the store to get some fresh air and clear my mind. While I was at the store, I decided to look for plant food for Sara, when to my surprise Amanda Grace walked up behind me. She asked if she could help me find something. I told her what had happened and that I wanted to show my wife we could share this together too, so I was going to bring her back-plant food for a wild orchid. She informed me that she had some plant food for wild orchids at her house and if I wanted some I was welcome to it, so I followed her home. She got out of her car and went into her garage; minutes later she returned with several individually plastic packets of the fertilizer and handed them to me. She instructed me to tell Sara that she would need to use a pack a day on the plant, then cover it with plenty of water. I told Sara what she had said as she and Sara followed her instructions. Stu, was it the fertilizer or poison that Amanda gave us?" Sam asked.

"Sam, the plant and plant food, or fertilizer as you call it, have been picked up from your house by the FBI poison control division. We weren't sure of where the poison came from or who put it on the plant. Sam, you have just given me the missing piece of the puzzle. Take the stand tomorrow and tell the truth, no matter how it sounds, and if you're telling the truth to me now, all will be okay," Stu promised and then hung up.

"Now, where were we? Oh yes, we're practicing on how to be alone," Stu said, half laughing.

The whole night would prove to be one of a kind, one like we had never shared before nor would ever again; for the first time together can never be duplicated. The only time we allowed our minds to return to the outside world was at daybreak when the sound of the alarm clock woke us both.

"Good morning, beautiful," Stu said with a smile as I turned over next to him with a smile.

"Stu, forgive me, I must hurry over to Miss Marple's to shower and dress for court today," I said, jumping out of his bed and grabbed my things as I headed for the bathroom without as much as a hug or kiss. Stu laughed under his breath while thinking how embarrassed Sally was about waking up in his bed; it showed him she wasn't one who believed in casual hook-ups. Stu couldn't have been more pleased with the lady he had asked to be his wife.

"Stu, I am taking your car. I'll be back for you in about an hour after I shower and change for court," I heard Sally say as she ran out the door with my keys. Again, I laughed, but this time out loud.

I parked Stu's car behind mine in the driveway at Miss Marple's and hurried into the house and up the stairs. I entered my room and closed the door behind me, then put the keys and my purse on the table next to the door. I walked across my room, drew open the glass door, stepped out on the deck, and quickly sat down in a chair. While looking out onto Black Hawk Harbor, I relived the night I had just experienced. Wow! My life was about to take a turn that I had not previously considered. My work here would soon be don, and a column in the local paper seemed like an old dream, for I was marrying Stu and move to New York.

My heart was on cloud nine, but my mind was still in a state of flux. All this news will blow my boss's socks off; when he realizes that his brother will win the challenge, his brother's candidate would own the column. I hurried back into my room to prepare for the day and an hour later was picking up Stu.

The court in session: "Mr. Fitzpatrick, please step forward, I'd like to have a word with you and Mr. Hatfield's lawyer," the judge said. Both lawyers stepped forward, and the judge leaned forward over the front of his bench and spoke softly. "Have you or the police located the red-and-white motorboat?" the judge asked.

"The police are working on it as we speak, it is crucial to my client's case," the defendant's lawyer said.

"Prosecutor Fitzpatrick, please call your first witness," the judge said. Both lawyers walked back to their tables before the first witness of the day was called.

"Your Honor, the prosecution calls Carl Franks to the stand. The people in the courtroom grew curious as everyone looked around to see who'd stood up. We watched as a short oriental man in his late sixties or early seventies stood to his feet and strolled to the witness box. He put his right hand on the Bible and repeated the oath of truth than sat down. Mr. Franks, we'd like to thank you for making the long trip here from Ohio to testify today. Do you know Mr. Hatfield, and if so, what is he to you?" Fritz asked.

"Sam has been a friend of mine for about five years and my boss, kinda," Franks replied.

"Please explain, what you mean by 'kinda,'" the prosecutor instructed.

"When a friend needs your help, he calls, and you do what you can for him. No one needs to pay for this kind of help," Franks said.

"So you're telling this court that he called for your help? When was this?" Fritz asked.

"Friday afternoon, I'd say about three o'clock. He asked me to see that all the utilities and cable was turned on and fresh flowers put on the kitchen table, to make it look like someone was staying there," Franks answered.

"Is that what he told you, or did you come up with that conclusion on your own?"

"Yes, sir, that's what he said," Franks said.

"So you're saying that it was your job to follow up with his wishes to make the house look like it was being lived in. How soon did he need it done?"

"He said he was leaving for home about ten and would be in Ohio for breakfast," Franks replied.

"Your Honor, I am done with this witness for now," the prosecutor said. The judge excused the witness from the stand before the next one was called.

"Your Honor, we would like to call Art Goodall," the prosecutor requested.

Again, the courtroom went quiet and waited patiently as the witness stepped forward. We were all eager to hear what this stranger would have to say about Sam. After the oath, Mr. Goodall took his seat.

"Let me express my thanks again, as I did to Franks for your taking the time to come so far to be here. Now with that said, how is it you know Sam Hatfield?" Fritz asked.

"Sam and I served together in the Army in the sniper division and in the reserves once a month. Sam is one of those people that you thank God for as a friend, you know he'll have your back in trouble," he replied.

"The airport logs records tell us that you flew Sam into the club airport here the day of the sailboat race. Why?" Fritz questioned.

"Sam wanted to come back and drive his wife home. He was so upset the way things ended between them before he left," Goodall answered.

"What do you mean how things were left between them?" the prosecutor questioned.

"Sara and Sam are a couple of fickle emotional lovers. If I've heard them yell it once, I've heard it a dozen times—about getting a divorced, then within twenty-four hours, they're all over each other again. If you know what I mean," Goodall responded.

"Mr. Goodall, have you ever gone to the rifle-range with Sam with sniper guns?" the prosecutor asked.

"Yes, sir, many times," Goodall said.

"Would you say a good marksman always clean his gun?" asked the prosecutor.

"Yes, sir, always, we don't put our guns away dirty that's for sure," Goodall replied.

"Your Honor, I have no more questions at this time for Mr. Goodall."

"Mr. Goodall, you may leave the witness box for now," the judge said.

"Your Honor, I would like to call Sam Hatfield to the stand at this time," the prosecutor requested.

Everyone in the courtroom seemed to take a deep breath at the same time. Did the prosecutor believe that Sam would testify against himself? Sam stood to his feet and looked over at Stu. We could all see that they made eye contact. Sam took the oath and then sat down.

"Sam, how is your wife doing today?"

"It is touch and go, sir. The doctor said yesterday that her lungs have been damaged because of a poison she unknowingly inhaled. She's been shot and poisoned, how could anyone think she would be part of the shooting?" Sam questioned.

"Sam, I am sorry, and I promise before this case is closed, we will have the answers we both seek," Fritz said. "Now, with that said, let's get on with today's questioning."

"The prosecutor doesn't usually call the defendants to testify until he's put up all his witnesses; so why is Sam already on the stand?" Sally wondered.

"Sam, your wife told us about her day, on the day of the race. Please tell this court everything about yours," Fritz said.

"I arrived at the home in Ohio at eight in the morning the day of the race. My utilities were on, and the cable man was to come before noon. I unpacked the car and put things away, then ate my breakfast. I called Art, Mr. Goodall, and asked him to come over for coffee. I told him that I needed his help and why. He offered to fly me back to Black Hawk Harbor so I could be there waiting for my wife when the sailboat came into shore. We left Ohio at three in the afternoon on a small-engine plane arriving at a private airstrip in Michigan at five thirty, the day of the race. I then used my golf cart from my hangar area to drive down to my house in the harbor," Sam said.

"Your hangar area?" Fritz asked.

"Yes," Sam replied.

"So why did you have your friend fly you in if you fly?"

"Sir, I was coming to drive my wife home. I didn't want to leave my plane up here in Michigan for the winter when I'll be in Ohio."

"That makes sense, okay, please continue," Fritz said.

"Sailboats started coming in at seven, I was surprised that none of them were Stu's. All I could remember was the last word Sara and I shared, 'divorce.' Had she and Sam run off together? Was that the reason they hadn't arrive yet? We had fought before and often called for a divorce but never meant it. I waited an hour, then went back to our house and turned on the TV, knowing that there were news cameramen on sight, to report the outcome. At nine o'clock a reporter from the *News Review* said that a sailboat had been found at Crow's Landing and those aboard had been shot and taken by ambulance to the hospital."

"So you're telling the court that you knew at nine that your wife was taken to the hospital?" Fritz asked. "Why didn't you go to her then, if you loved her so much?"

"For the same reason you're thinking right now, all of you," Sam said, looking around the courtroom. "That I would be the one they looked at for doing this horrible thing; for I had a reason and the opportunity. But I tell you, I didn't do it! I couldn't sleep a wink between worrying about my wife's condition and when I could go to her. The state police department in Petoskey, Michigan, called my cell phone before midnight and told me my wife had been shot, and I should come back. They thought I was still in Ohio, and that was for the best. At eight in the morning, I went to the Stain Cup for breakfast and to hear if there was any other news on the shooting. Everyone was very supportive to me, and when I told them that the police had called me and asked me to come back to Michigan, not one of them doubted me," Sam said, then paused.

"Okay, Sam, you told us that you saw the first boat come in at about seven o'clock that night and continue watching till eight. Is that right?"

"Yes," he replied.

"Would you say that you and your wife are well-known around the harbor?" Fritz asked.

"Well, yes, of course, we are," Sam said proudly.

"Then why is it no one saw you pacing back and forth while you waited for the wife you love so much?" the Fritz asked forcefully.

"I didn't wait at the harbor docks. Our house sits on the water's edge, some two miles down the shoreline. I went out on the porch of my home when the first news was reported of the first sighting of boats nearing the harbor," Sam replied.

"You mean to tell us that you could see the boats pass by your home and you didn't see them at all?" Fritz asked.

"That's right, sir. They must've past by before I went out to watch."

"That would have made them the winner if they had made it all the way in," Fritz replied.

"Yes, sir, I do believe you're right," Sam said.

"So you weren't out on your porch to see the red-and-white motorboat go by either?" Fritz asked doubtfully, then added, "So you live right on the waterway and I am sure you own a boat or two, and now you tell me that you didn't even hear a boat's motor as it passed your house? That sounds quite convenient but hard to believe.

"Your Honor, the court would like to enter this sniper rifle into evidence," the prosecutor said, picking up a rifle off the evidence table to the right of his seat. He showed it to the court gallery and the judge, then walked over in front of Sam with it.

"Sam, is this your gun?" Fritz asked.

"I don't know, sir, may I get a better look at it?" Sam asked. Fritz handed him to examine.

"Yes, sir, it is, but it's been fired since I last held it. Sir, it would be clean and in two pieces if I were using it. Someone else had to have used it," Sam said with conviction.

"Sam, you said yourself, that you had reason and opportunity. Now we find you also owned the gun that shot your wife and her so-called lover. You really want us to believe you didn't do it?" Fritz asked, looking a bit confused.

"Your Honor, I am going to turn the questioning of this witness now over to Stu Baker, who is also a member of this court," the prosecutor said, then turned and saw the shocked look on Stu's face as he stood to his feet. The prosecutor took his seat. Stu slowly approached the witness box and collected his thoughts on what he would ask.

"Sam, I've known you ever since you met and married Sara, is that right?"

"Yes."

"In all that time, have you ever known me to try anything questionable with your wife?" Stu asked.

"No."

"So let's pick it up where the prosecutor left off. We know by your testimony that you own that sniper rifle, but do you also own an MP9 Shield?" Stu asked.

"No," Sam replied.

"Have you ever let anyone use your rifle, with or without you present?" Stu questioned.

"Yes, of course, I have, you know that. You used it at the rifle range," Sam replied.

"Do you remember the last time you took it to the rifle range, where other people used it?" Stu asked.

"Yes, it was in July at the Morhouses, the morning of their annual barbecue," Sam said.

"Can you tell this court who shot the rifle on that day?" Stu asked, already knowing the answer.

"Let me see. You, Homer Atkins, Beth Danial, Dave Bricker, Bill our local sheriff, myself, Sara and Amana Grace—they're all members of our club," Sam said.

"How many members does your club have?" Stu asked.

"As of now there's over sixty of us, from here and the surrounding counties, and we all share our guns," Sam said proudly.

"Do you ever have shooting contests?" Stu asked.

"Yes," Sam replied.

"You have men and women in your club?"

"Yes," Sam replied.

"What woman, would you say, is the best marksman in your club?" Stu asked.

"There's no question about it, Amanda Grace is the best by far," Sam responded.

"Wow, why didn't I even know that, and she's been my secretary for seven years. When I've been shooting with you, she was never there. Why do you think that was?" Stu asked Sam.

"I have no idea. Right there she is, ask her," Sam said, sounding a little impatient. Stu turned and looked Amanda in the eyes with a look of contempt on his face. Just about that time, a police officer came through the door of the courtroom, right up to the prosecutor's table where he whispered something to Fritz and Stu, then handed them a manila folder and a bag before leaving.

The prosecutor retook the floor and asked the judge to excuse Sam and call Amanda to the stand. She was asked to give her name and repeat the oath before sitting down.

"Amanda Grace, is that your whole name?" Fritz asked.

"No. It's Amanda Grace Billings, but no one has ever called me by my last name," she replied.

"That's interesting, why do you think that is? Maybe it's like the rest of your life, a mystery to most. Secrecy seems to be the way you hold power," Fritz said, not expecting a response.

"Amanda, being a marksman, you must own a gun or two yourself," Fritz said.

"Yes, sir, I do own a rifle, but not a sniper's," she freely said.

"Miss Billings, do you know Sam and Sara Hatfield?" Fritz asked.

"Yes, we've been friends for years," she said while flashing a smile over to Sam.

"Do you mean you're the kind of friend, one could trust to leave their house key with?" he asked.

"Yes, I have kept their keys on many occasions, to take in the mail or water plants," Amanda replied.

"Have you gone to the hospital to see your dear friend Sara this time or after she'd been shot?" Fritz asked.

"No, not yet," she replied.

"You heard her husband tell us this morning about her condition?" Fritz said, looking in her eyes.

"Yes, I am so sorry to hear she isn't better," Amanda said, looking over at Sam again while trying to avoid locking eyes with Fritz.

"Your Honor, we would like to excuse Miss Billings for now, but reserve the right to recall her and ask that she not be allowed to leave the courtroom until then," the prosecutor said. The judge nodded in agreement and excused Amanda to go back to her seat.

"At this time, Your Honor, the court would like to call Marybeth Cummings forward," Fritz said. Marybeth made her way to the stand before Fritz handed the questioning back over to Stu, then took his seat. Marybeth carried a black logbook in her hands and after being sworn in sat quietly until Stu asked her his first question.

"Marybeth, that book your carrying, what is it?" Stu asked.

"Stu, it's the book you asked me to find in my archives of business records of years past. I've made the copy of entries in it that you were interested in," she replied.

"Marybeth, what do you do for a living?" Stu asked.

"I own the Marybeth's greenhouse in Black Hawk Harbor," she said.

"How long have you owned this business?"

"Our family has owned the greenhouse for thirty years. When my parents had it, it was called Hawk Harbor greenhouse. I renamed it five years ago," she replied.

"You are a well-known and trusted business in the area, and I can vouch for that myself. Could you tell us what you found in your record book that might be of interest to this court?" Stu added.

"I am not sure how it is of interest to these proceedings, but this is what you asked me to find. On the sixth day of July 2015, a call was received by our store to deliver one of our pink orchids to Lilian Baker, your wife," she said.

The defense lawyer stood to his feet to object to the questioning of this witness: "Your Honor, how does any of this concern the court and this case?"

"Mr. Baker, don't lead this court down some rabbit hole. Get to the point!" the judge said.

"Yes, sir, I will bring it all together in just a few minutes, I promise."

"Marybeth, who ordered the plant in question?" Stu asked.

"You did, sir," she answered.

"What do you mean, I did?" Stu asked, sounding perplexed.

"Oh, sir, I mean your office. Amanda made the call and used your credit card to pay for it," she replied.

"Can I ask how much these plants cost?" Stu asked.

"Stu, these plants are costly. We can only get six of them a year from the Amazon rain forest, as it is hazardous to harvest them. They sell at five thousand each," she replied.

"Ouch! Why didn't I notice it on my credit card bill?" Stu said aloud.

"Stu, around the time you received that bill you were also mourning the death of your beautiful young wife, Lilian," Marybeth said.

"Yes, I am sure you're right, I kinda lost it for a while there," Stu replied.

"Marybeth, you say you've known Amanda for several years, is that right?"

"Yes, sir, ever since she started accompanying you to the harbor as your secretary," Marybeth replied.

"So would you say that you and she are friends?" Stu asked.

"No, sir. I am a country girl who's comfortable in sweatshirt and jeans with my hair pulled back in a ponytail. Amanda is all City, from her hair to her heels. She would never get her nails dirty. She's what we call here prim and proper," Marybeth said.

"Okay then, let's get back to what we were talking about. Have you sold any of those plants this summer season?" Stu asked.

"Yes, two in the harbor," she replied.

"Could you tell us who received them?" Stu asked.

"Yes, Bonnie, four weeks ago and Sara Hatfield, her daughter, just three days ago," she replied.

The gallery of people in the courtroom gasped in unison at such news.

"It sounds as though everyone who receives one of these plants gets sick or dies," Stu said.

"No, it is not our plants. No one in the store has become ill from them, or any of the other people who have purchased one," Marybeth said firmly.

"Okay, then what do these three plants have in common?" Stu asked Marybeth.

"Your office, Stu, they were all ordered by Amanda, using your credit card," she replied.

"Your Honor, I am done with this witness. Thank you, Marybeth," Stu said as she passed him on her way back to her seat in the gallery.

"Your Honor, we are putting the copies of Marybeth's records having to do with Amanda Grace Billings into the evidence files," Stu said. Then he looked down at the manila folder that had been brought into the court by a police officer then called Steve Fineout from the Fineout Marina to the stand.

Again, the courtroom went quiet as everyone glanced around to see who stepped up next. Steve Fineout, a twenty-something, good-looking, tanned, and blue-eyed wonder. As he walked forward, you could hear the ladies in the courtroom sounds like bees with their whispers. He took the oath and then sat down.

"The Fineout Marina rents out boats, is that right?" Stu asked.

"Yes, sir, we're a seasonal rental by the day, week, month, or season."

"Is there anyone in this courtroom that rented a red-and-white boat from you on or around the day of the race?" Stu asked.

"Yes, Amanda Grace has always been a good customer of ours."

"Did you rent it to her?"

"Yes, she rented it for four weeks, two days before the race. She told me that she was having company and wanted a boat while they were visiting. Many of our clients do this, it's cheaper than buying a boat," Steve said.

"Has she returned the boat yet?" Stu asked.

"No, sir, it's due back on Friday," Steve replied.

"Steve, the police will take possession of it and return it to you when they are done processing it for fingerprints and other evidence," Stu said.

"Your Honor, the court is done with this witness," Stu said, then walked over to Fritz and whispered something, then sat down and Fritz took over.

"Your Honor, we think we have enough evidence to have Amanda Grace Billings taken into custody right now," the prosecutor said.

"No, you can't! No! Don't let them do this, Stu. I've stood by you all these years," Amanda cried out in the courtroom as two female officers stepped up to help her to her feet and put the handcuffs on; then directed her to a gated area on the other side of the courtroom away from the others.

"Your Honor, it is already one, maybe this would be an appropriate time to take a lunch break, while Miss Billings is being booked and the police are checking on the red-and-white motorboat. I believe we can put this case to bed by the end of the day," the prosecutor said with assurance.

"Yes, I agree, we will break for lunch and meet back here at two o'clock," the judge said. We all got to our feet and waited for him to leave the courtroom.

CHAPTER 32

Death Has No Friends

"Sally, darling, please forgive me for being so quiet this past hour. Having a picnic lunch with you on a bright sunny day should be romantic and exciting. Yet my mind, I am afraid it's been off in space considering the unknown possibilities. The past has somehow taken first place, and until we clean up the why and who brought death to Black Hawk Harbor, no one is safe. To think that someone I've known and loved like a sister could have anything to do with it makes me a little ill. I guess, I counted on her too much and allowed her too far into my personal life. You know looking at it like that makes me think I may be an unknown accomplice. She seems to have had a secret desire for me to love her romantically. I swear, I never knew it. Let's go back into the courtroom before it starts filling up again with onlookers. Please pray that I can hold myself together until it's over. It's the hardest day of my life since mom died," Stu said. I put my arms around him and gave him a hug and kiss before we got out of the car.

"Stu, you are not responsible for someone else's mental disorder. There is no way that you led her on to believe that you were ever interested in her that way. After all, you married Lilian while Amana was working for you. I feel sorry for her too, but more for the people she hurt," Sally said.

"So we both see it the same way, having to prove it is another thing," Stu said. After we climbed the steps to the courthouse, he opened the door, and we both walk entered. We walked back to the front of the court and took the seats we had earlier. Minutes later the court was back in session and Stu was calling Sam back to the witness box, while Amana sat proudly off to the right side of the courtroom with two female police officers.

"Mr. Hatfield, you are still under oath," the judge reminded him.

"Yes, sir," Sam replied.

"Sam, you called me last night from the hospital to inform me of your wife's condition. Would you share that report with this court?" Stu asked. Big tears rose in Sam's eyes, his bottom lip started to quiver, as he tried to gather his thoughts, while those in the court waited.

"The poison that my wife unknowingly inhaled had been put on the plant. It has damaged her lungs, and there is little hope of reversing its effect," he responds.

"You're saying that the plant came to your home with poison on it? Is that what you want the court to think, and nothing was added to it once it entered your home?" Stu asked.

"No! That is not what I am saying. I went out shopping after the plant was delivered and ran into Amanda Grace in the store. She noticed me looking for something and asked if she could help. I told her about the beautiful plant that Sara had received, and where it came from, and who I thought sent it. She acted completely surprised and sympathetic to my feelings. Amanda said that she had some plant food for orchids at her house and if I would follow her home she would give Sara some. So I did as she suggested and followed her home. She pulled into her driveway, and I pulled in behind her. She hurried out of her car and into the garage, and seconds later, she was backhanding me seven separately sealed packets of the mixture, with about a half cup of plant food in each. She told me that Sara was to put one pack on the plant before thoroughly watering it once a week. This should be enough for her to care for the plant until we got back to Ohio. I thanked her for her kindness and drove away. Once back at home, I gave the packets to Sara and told her what Amanda had said."

Sam's tears broke loose, as he slumped back in his seat, looking like a whipped and broken man. The court clerk brought forward a box of tissues and handed it to him.

"Your Honor, we are done with this witness," Stu said. Sam was excused by the judge, and the court was ready for its next witness. The prosecutor stepped forward and call a police officer to the stand and waited as he was sworn in.

"You were sent out to find a boat and search it. Is that right?" Fritz asked.

"Yes, sir, we did locate the red-and-white motorboat belonging to the Fineout Marina. On the boat, we found hid under the wooden slat floorboard, a black hoodie sweat suit, and pair of gloves. We sent everything to the crime lab. We also found two spent shell rounds from a sniper's rifle and two spent rounds from an MP9 Shield pistol, but neither of the guns was found," the officer said.

"Did you have time to check and see if either of the defendants or Miss Billings owned a pistol?" Fritz asked the officer.

"Yes. Miss Billings does own a pistol of that make," he replied.

"Thank you," Fritz said to the officer, then turned to the judge.

"Your Honor, we are done with this witness, and the people wish now to call Miss Billings back to the stand." The judge looked over at Amanda and called her back to the stand. She stood to her feet proudly, wearing the orange jumpsuit was provided by the jail system, and she reentered the witness box like it was a seat at the king's table. The judge reminded her she was still under oath. She half-heartedly acknowledged him, as she sat up straight and crossed her legs at the knees. She placed a cloth handkerchief on her lap, then glanced out at the gallery like they were her subjects; she tossed her head back as though preparing herself to be crowned.

"Good afternoon, Miss Billings. You are a beautiful lady, even in orange. I myself have never looked good in that color. I believe you would look beautiful in anything you wore," he added. "You and I have never spoken before today, is that right?" Fritz asked.

"Yes, that's right," she replied in a soft tone voice.

"How do you really feel about your boss, Stu Baker? Please, feel free to be brutally honest about it. For this may be the only time you can do so," he told her, before stepping aside so she could look at him while talking.

"Seven years ago, I answered an ad as a personal professional law secretary at the law office of Baker and Stratton, in New York City. I was only twenty-four years old at the time. The man I met at my first appointment was in his late sixties, who told me I would be working for his partner Stu Baker. Stu had got tied up in court and couldn't see me just then. Stratton interviewed me for over two hours, leaving the room several times to check out the information I'd given him.

"When he returned the last time, he informed me that the job meant I would have to travel, and I may be away for several months at a time. He asked me if that would be a problem. I said no, for I was neither married nor had children. He said the job came with a salary that would remain the same no matter where we were. I asked him what that amount was and whether I would ever have to accompany Mr. Baker to court. He said the salary is 165,000 a year, and no, I wouldn't have to be in court.

"Of course, I jumped at the job, and I've enjoyed it for the past seven years," she said with a smiled, pausing before continuing. "For the first two years I had the time of my life working with Stu, we went everywhere together. We lived in separate houses even when we were away from New York. He's always been the perfect gentleman in every way, also when I wish he hadn't been. Then he met Sara Hatfield, and everything changed."

"What do you mean, changed?"

"She took up all of his free time. Sara looked at me like I was beneath her. I was only someone that worked for him. Before long they became engaged, and he became consumed by her and their so-called love. I decided to befriend her with the hopes of changing her mind about marrying him. She became very comfortable with our friendship and started confiding her secrets to me. When she told me, she was pregnant with Stu's baby. She hadn't planned on having one so soon. She said she wanted to have time before children to pursue her career. Not because she needed the money, her family was wealthy.

"She came to me with some papers from an abortion clinic and asked me what she should do about it? Why would she do that? Unless she wanted me to agree to it. I figured that she had already made up her mind, so I didn't try to talk her out of it. I knew how Stu wanted children, and if she didn't, then she wasn't the woman for him anyways. Once she had gone through with the abortion, I kinda let it slip what she had done, making it sound like I thought he already knew. Well, that ended those plans and Stu, and I was again enjoying our friendship away from work. Six months later, Lilian came into his life, and within two months, they were married. He only saw me in the office, we did nothing together anymore. He used to say that he didn't know what he'd do without me, but she changed everything. You can understand how I felt, can't you, Stu?" she said, looking down at him. He smiled back at her with a fake smile and nodded in response, she continued.

"Lilian was in the greenhouse, one day at the same time I was. I notice her eyeing a beautiful pink orchid that had just come in from Africa. I checked out the price on it and found it was way out of her price range. So I went to the office and used the business account credit card and had it sent to her from Stu. Then a couple of days later, I stopped in to see her and took some plant food that I had made up of rodenticide and dried black-spore-mold dust. I never told her what the plant food was made of. She seemed very happy to receive it and thanked me. Unfortunately, she passed away three weeks later.

"Again, I was there to help Stu through his pain. This time it took longer for him to respond to my attention, had I never given up. Life got back to normal for us for almost a year until we came back to this horrible place for the summer. Back here, not even a week, and he runs into a virtual nobody, by the name of Sally Crystal, and again our lives changed. Sally wasn't so easy for me to get close to. She always seemed to be busy, and for the longest time, they only referred to each other as friends. If they didn't take their relationship any further, then it would be okay, for Stu and I would be leaving for New York soon.

"Then Sara came into my office full of joy and singing, to tell me that she and Stu were getting back together. The thought of her marrying him almost blew my mind. I started to panic. I had to stop it one way or the other. I had already bought one of Marybeth's orchids, for Bonnie Gaither and couldn't go get another so soon. I had rented a boat, weeks before and hadn't returned it yet. So I decided to use it the night of the race. For there was no way to be sure that the tests would prove that Bonnie was poisoned by Sara, as I had hoped," Amanda said, then sat back in her chair, as though she were done.

"Are you saying that you also poisoned Bonnie Gaither?" asked the prosecutor.

"She was already near death because of cancer that ravished her body. I just helped her along in hopes of framing Sara, to save Stu," she replied.

"But that doesn't make sense. If I understand correctly, you poisoned Bonnie almost a week before Sara shared her news with you. Why was that?" the prosecutor asked, sounding a bit perplexed.

"Sara had been making advances toward Stu, even in front of his girlfriend Sally. That girl has no shame and being married too—poor Sam, he deserved better. Getting rid of her once and for all would have been a blessing. You can see that, can't you?"

"Seeing that you're talking about Sam. When did he give you his gun, and when did you give it back to him?" the prosecutor asked.

"He didn't. I used the key they gave me when they wanted me to look after their house. I knew where he kept it, it was no secret, we were all friends, you know. I put it back when he went to the Stain Cup for breakfast the morning after the race," she replied.

"Tell us, why did you shoot the only man you ever loved? You could have killed him."

"No, he was never really in danger of dying. I am an expert marksman. I would never do anything to hurt Stu," Amanda said, with a smile while glancing down at him again Stu sat almost motionless, the fake smile was gone, and his face was full of contempt for the woman before him.

"I think we've heard enough, Judge. I am done with this witness," the prosecutor said.

"Miss Billings, you will go with those two officers now, do what they tell, and I will see you back here tomorrow," the judge said.

"Yes, sir, thank you," Amanda replied. The courtroom stayed very quiet while she stepped down from the witness box and with a smile walked past everyone in the courtroom on her way out with her personal escorts.

"All rise," the officer of the court said as the judge stood up to leave the bench. Once he was out of the courtroom, we all started walking out. We talked while walking to the car.

"Stu, does Amanda have family that we could notify, or did she ever give you papers that would say what she wanted to be done if anything should happen to her? As much as this must hurt you, we must think of her. She needs a shrink. If we can't find any of her family to care for her, then you'll have to get her to sign papers, putting you in charge. I know that the court will probably assign her to a mental institution for years, if not for life. We've only got a few hours before court tomorrow and a lot to do," I said, trying to sound helpful.

"Sally, don't take this wrong. But I for one hope that she burns in hell. I have no intention of helping her in any way. Can't you see what she's done to me, and my life?" Stu asked angrily as we pulled out of the parking lot.

"Yes, I can. I can also see you need some time alone. You can drive me back to Miss Marple's, and I'll see you tomorrow morning," I said.

"Yes, I think that's a clever idea. I won't be much good at talking, I need time alone to think," Stu replied.

Once back at Miss Marple's, I went straight up to my room and wrote my column.

Death Has No Friends

Joe Bumgardner

Today, I write my column to all those people who read it over the summer religiously and spoke so well of it. The column started out as a challenge between two writers who wanted to have their own column but with only one opening. The owners of the *News Review* decided to see which one of us could draw the most readers to the paper over the summer; the winner would get their own weekly column. I am not sure which one of us would've been the winner, but my challenger will fill the opening and write the column, for I am planning to marry and move with my husband to New York. This is my last column as Joe Bumgardner.

If you've been watching the trial in the Petoskey Courthouse, about an attempted murder, you've seen the many ways that love can take a wicked turn and affect the lives of others. Some use marriage as a weapon and throw the word "divorce" around like it was a bargaining chip, never understanding the pain it may cause.

We were taken through the broken mind of a woman who didn't see anything she did as wrong, though she killed two people and seriously hurt others over seven years. After looking into Amanda Grace Billing's life, we found that she lost both of her parents before graduating from high school. She worked and put herself through college before going to work for the law firm that she is now with. We'll never know for sure if it was the loss of her parents or another lover that seeded the mental illness that led this person to attach herself and her life to this person, no matter what harm was done for her to obtain her secret love.

Today you had the chance to meet Amanda Grace Billings, who suffers from this illness, and you saw the carnage one person can do to so many others. By the time you have the chance to read this, the judge will have handed down his decision in this case. It may be too late for Amanda, but maybe someone who

SUMMER CHALLENGE

is listening will be helped. Perhaps they will realize that there is another way to pursue love.

Sincerely,

Your reporter Sally Crystal
Better known as Joe Bumgardner

I hurried and e-mailed my last column in knowing that my bosses would be scrambling to get it to press by the end of the day. Thank goodness, I have a small savings account to see me through the rest of the year or until I find work in New York.

I wanted to go to Stu's side. I couldn't get his last words out of my mind. "I need some time alone," he had said.

I can only hope that when times get tough, we don't seek our own corners or try to hide away from each other, I thought.

I called the local pizza parlor in the village and ordered one to be delivered. I would use this time to make some plans for my upcoming wedding. We were just weeks away from the end of the season here, and I know this is where we'll want to say our vows since this is where all our loved ones are. I would just take a couple of hours tonight before going to bed and write down some ideas to share with Stu tomorrow after court is over. Everything had been proven today in court; we will just get the judge's closing words and find out Amanda's outcome in the morning.

My phone rang while the alarm clock started sounding off. I reached over and turned off the clock before answering the phone.

"Who in the world would be calling this early?" I could only wonder.

"Hello," I said in a very sleepy voice.

"Sally, don't you think that you should have talked to my brother and me first before walking away from our challenge? The challenge didn't just involve you, it was a team effort. Your column has already been printed by the press crew last night and put into the paper for this afternoon's delivery, and it's too late to change it," Mr. Korn said.

"Mr. Korn, I am sorry if my column upset you. I knew you would be surprised, but I thought you'd be happy for me and pleased to know that Bates could take over the column," I said.

"Sally, we are happy for you and very surprised at the news. We hope to be the paper to print all the details of your marriage to Stu Baker. That is who your marrying, right?" Mr. Korn asked.

"Yes, yes, of course," I replied.

"Sally, you need to write one more column, you can call it the closer. I want you to write on what happens in court today, in your own words. I mean, share your opinion as Sally Crystal," he said.

"If that's what you want, you'll have it, and yes, we'll share our wedding plans with your paper, so you can be the first ones to print it, even before the *New York Times*," I promised him before saying goodbye and hanging up.

I jumped up and ran into the bathroom to shower and get ready for the day's events. Then I called Stu to find out what time he'd be by to pick me up.

"Sally, darling, I was just getting ready to call you. Whattaya say we go down to the Stain Cup for coffee and an order of toast before going to court. There's something I want to talk to you about before we see Amanda. I'll pick you up in five minutes or less," Stu said before hanging up.

"Wow, that's a change from last night. I wonder what he has on his mind. It must have something to do with Amanda," I surmised.

As I stepped out of the house, Stu was getting out of his car and hurried around it to open my door for me.

"Good morning, beautiful," Stu said as I slipped past him into the car. He closed the door and quickly got into his side. There was no thinking about it; we were in each other's arms as soon as his bottom hit the seat; our lips met, and all our pent-up emotions melted away. Minutes later, we were headed for the restaurant. As Stu drove, he apologized for how he had pulled away from me yesterday, agreeing without a word, from me that we must turn to, not away from each other in times of trouble. The day was already starting out to be very productive, and I could only hope that this was a sign of things to come as our car came to a stop in front of the Stain Cup. Again, Stu moved quickly to my side of the vehicle to open the door. It was starting to sprinkle as we hurried into the restaurant and went far back to sit, away from the other patrons and the busy doorway. The waitress followed us back to the table in the corner and took our order.

"Sally, now that we're finally sitting facing each other, I have to tell you that you were right for suggesting our helping Amanda.

I called my New York office and had my partner fax me everything we had on Amanda and her family. I stayed up late going through everything he sent me. I was very saddened by the fact I've never known her as well as I thought I did. I saw her as a well-educated and accomplished young woman who could mix well with any of our wealthy clients. She always dressed impeccably and cared for herself well. I only saw what she chose to reveal to me and the world in a well-packaged form.

"What she concealed was too painful for her to share with others. Her life started by her being left in a basket on someone's front step. She was raised mainly in orphanages, being adopted at the age of thirteen, only to be used as a free babysitter by her new parents. At the age of seventeen, she was raped by her foster father and ran away. She found help from an elderly woman who took her in and aided her with her education and became the closest thing to a real mother she would ever have. A week before graduating from college, the elderly lady died, and Amanda inherited everything from her, and by everything, I mean home, car, furniture, and close to a million dollars. But Amanda lost what she really needed, for that lady was the only person on earth that Amanda had.

"I believe Amanda believes that people can overcome any pain if they end up with someone by their side. I will do my best to help her if it means that she is kept safe and away from us. She will have the best care for the rest of her life if we have anything to do with it," Stu promised.

"Stu, you are the greatest joy of my life, and I am thankful every day you bumped into me," I said. We both laughed. "Now, there is a wedding to plan, if we're to marry here in the village," I said as the waitress approached our table with our order in hand.

CHAPTER 33

Respect from a Challenger

We all filed into the courtroom and took our seat, while those outside in the park watched the court proceedings on a large screen, sitting in lawn chairs or on the ground. Never had so many become interested in a court case as they did this time. Maybe it was because of Joe Bumgardner column that so many took an interest in it.

We were told to stand as the judge came in and entered the bench; then the jury was seated, and we remained standing until Amanda was led in by two female officers and seated left of the judge.

"You may all be seated," the officer next to the bench said. The Hatfields were seated at the defense table with their lawyer, while Stu and the Fritz sat at the other.

"Please, call your next witness," the judge said as Fritz stood to his feet.

"We would like to call the police officer that testified yesterday back to the stand," Fritz said. The young officer came forward and took the stand carrying a report from the FBI lab.

"Is that paper in your hands meant to be evidence for this court?" Fritz asked.

"Yes, sir," he replied, handing the report first to the judge to see who in turn handed it off to the prosecutor to be read.

"This report says that the black sweat suit and gloves belong to none other than Amanda Grace Billings and the pistol found in the water near the scene of the crime was also Amanda's. Where did the FBI find the poison used on the plant?" he asked the police officer.

"Sir, we went to Miss Billings home and found about one hundred small packets of the same poison, which contains rodenticide and dried black mold spores," the officer replied.

"Thank you, you are excused," Fritz said. As the officer made his way back to his seat in the gallery, the prosecutor called his next witness.

"Mr. Stu Baker, please take the stand," he said, taking everyone including me by surprise. The courtroom became so quiet that you could hear the dust settle. We all wanted eagerly to his first question for Stu once he was sworn in.

"Mr. Baker, Miss Billings has worked for you for seven years, is that right?"

"Yes, sir," Stu replied.

"Mr. Baker, would you tell us everything you know about Miss Billings?" the prosecutor asked. Stu shared with the court what he had told me at the restaurant earlier. I could now see that this was a plan between Stu and Fritz, in hopes of showing the court what kind of life Amanda had experienced in childhood and as a young woman and how she handled losing. Stu also took responsibility for her care, if the court was to put her into a mental institution in any State but New York. He promised that she would get the best of care that money could obtain for her.

"Mr. Baker, never before on the bench have I ever heard someone offer to care for someone who tried to kill them. She not only tried to kill you and Mrs. Hatfield, but you have also learned that she killed your wife and Mrs. Gaither. Most people in your position would look forward to her being imprisoned for life. Please tell this court why you feel any responsibility for this woman," the judge said.

"Your Honor, I had a wonderful mother and family to care for me. I never once had to wonder where I would sleep at night, and I have never felt alone in this world, but Amanda has. Yes, I agree she has done some horrible things to others and can never be allowed to be on her own again. She is mentally ill and needs to be in a mental institution for the rest of her life, and maybe she'll leave this life better than when she came into it. God has blessed me with enough money to see that it happens, with your help. Letting her be put to death won't bring back my wife, Lilian. I will soon marry Sally Crystal, and we agree that Amanda has the best life she can in an institution where she can live as normal a life as possible," Stu said.

I looked over at Amanda while Stu was talking and saw deep pain in her eyes, for she had just realized, I was sure, that she would never go home again. I almost started to cry for her.

She seemed for the first time to really be alone. No one would come forward to give her a hug or a touch of kindness before she was led away, I thought.

"Mr. Baker, you are excused," the prosecutor said. The judge turned to the jury and gave them their orders before them to deliberate the case. Once they were gone, the judge had Amanda moved away to a waiting area. Then the judge addressed the gallery and those watching on the screen outside.

"Because of Joe Bumgardner, the reporter, this case has been well-read about. This case will probably touch each one of you in diverse ways. Some of you won't feel anything for Miss Billings, others will see her childhood as the pain that fueled her actions, and still, others will see her as a broken, pathetic person that had everything—money, prestige, beauty—and wasn't happy unless she could have what wasn't hers. Today, we have become very self-indulgent and believe that we deserve whatever someone else has even if we haven't earned it. Our lives may not be so much different than Miss Billings if we feel we have the right to things that are not ours," the judge said with feelings before retiring to his chambers until the jury was in. No one in the court moved out of their seats for everyone believed the decision had already been made—so we thought. An hour later the judge sent out word that the jury was ready, and the court would continue in fifteen minutes.

"Please rise," the court officer said. We all did, and the judge entered the courtroom from his chambers and then the jury was escorted back into their seats.

"Have you in the jury come to your decision?" the judge asked.

"Yes, Your Honor," the foreman of the jury said.

"Please, read your findings," the judge said.

"We find Mr. Hatfield innocent. We find Mrs. Hatfield innocent. We find Amanda Grace Billings guilty of two counts of murder and two counts of attempted murder," he said.

"Thank you for your time and service in this case," the judge said to the jury before dismissing them.

"Please bring Miss Billings before my bench," he said to the two female officers with Amanda. You would think that she was dressed in a ball gown and diamonds the way she walked proudly up to stand before the judge.

"Miss Billings, do you know who I am?" he asked.

"Yes, Judge," she replied.

"Do you understand why you are here?" he asked.

"Yes, I do, and I am sorry, Your Honor, but you don't understand—none of you do," she said, turning to look at the rest of us.

"Miss Billings, you are not up here to address this courtroom. You are here to receive your sentence for two counts of murder and two counts of attempted murder. Do you understand what you did to be sentenced for these crimes?" the judge asked.

"Your Honor, I was protecting Stu from those gold diggers. I didn't move fast enough to save him from Lilian, but I took care of it as soon as possible. Sara wanted to abort his child even knowing that he was in love with her and wanted children—she was too selfish for him. Can't you see that? Bonnie Gaither was hours from death anyway because of cancer, so I tried to frame Sara for her death to keep her away from my Stu. I wouldn't have had to do it if she had been an honorable wife to Sam. I never tried to kill Sara or Stu on the sailboat, just wound them, and as far as poisoning Sara, I never did. Her husband is the one who gave the plant food to her and told her how to use it. Yes, Your Honor, I do know why I am here—it's because I wanted to keep my Stu safe. I've always stayed by his side during the tough times," she said.

"Miss Billings, you are the one that caused his greatest pain. You killed his wife, the love of his life. If I were to send you where I believe you should go to spend the rest of your life, you would go to prison with no chance of parole. Yet someone thinks we should take into consideration your life and how it started. His name is Stu

Baker. He's never been your lover, brother, or friend, but he was your boss, that's all, and for that, he was hurt. I've decided that you will serve out the rest of your life in a women's mental institution in the back hills of Washington State, and you will leave now," the judge said sternly.

No one moved an inch, and the courtroom remained silent until Amanda was escorted out by the two officers.

Was it true? Was this the last we'll ever see of her? I wondered, and I was sure many others did the same. The thought that there are people here, who genuinely believe that they have some unspoken right over other people's lives show that the judge was right when he said, "We're living in a self-indulgent society." Once the judge had left the bench the rest of us quickly scampered out of the courthouse, and the City of Petoskey's traffic was a bumper to bumper situation, as hundreds of people headed out.

Stu and I took the little-known backway to the village. As we drove, we started talking about our upcoming wedding and where it would be held, for it would be a well-televised one because of the promise I made to my boss. By the time we reached Black Hawk Harbor, we had agreed as to the wedding location. We would be married next to the same hall where the land preserve case was held in the small country church. It would be an outdoor reception here in the village so everyone who wanted to could attend. Only close family and friends would be in the church with us. We would have the Pier Restaurant serve it up like the last barbecue of the summer. I promised Stu that if he went along with my plans, I would agree to any he had for our wedding service in New York.

"Believe me, Sally, there will be no barbecue in New York, it will be an elegant affair. I will call my partner as soon as I get to my office and put the wheels into motion. Come to think of it, I'd better hurry to my office. I no longer have a secretary to pick up the slack and keep it in order," Stu said, pulling up in front of Miss Marple's. I kissed him goodbye and got out of the car then watched him drive away before going up to my room. I quickly got on the phone to the minister of the small church and told him the date and time we wanted to get married; he was thrilled with it. Then I called the Pier

Restaurant and hired them to do the chicken barbecue and everything that goes with it. With that done I will write my last column in the *News Review* and invite my readers and friends to the wedding.

I hurried and sent off my write-up to the paper and put this part of my life to bed.

Minutes later, I heard the ladies come into the house so, I shut my computer off and went downstairs to talk with them.

"Well, aren't you just the smartest one in the room," Kitty said with a wide smile on her face while waving the newspaper that she had in her hand. "You are going to be the talk of the town around every dinner table tonight," she added.

"Come, and sit with us, while we all have a cup of tea. I didn't think we would ever get out of Petoskey. What a traffic jam," Miss Marple said, placing the tea tray down on the large ottoman in front of our chairs. Please, help yourselves to some tea and scones," she said as she sat down and picked up her cup. "Kitty, what were you talking about, Sally being the talk of the town?" Miss Marple asked.

"I only got a glance at it, but the headlines say it all," Kitty said, opening the paper so we could all read it.

Joe Bumgardner Comes Clean
of Who He Really Is

This news, only known by a few, knotted the socks off her challenger and sent laughter through the pressroom. Please, if you run into Sally Crystal, thank her for an unbelievable summer of reading. We couldn't be happier with the many readers that joined our newspaper family over the summer. There will be one more write-up from Sally tomorrow, for she has another secret to share with all of you.

"Sally, what does that mean? What is he talking about? Do you have something that you want to share with us?" Agatha asked.

"My last write-up will tell of the day, time, and place of our upcoming wedding and invites all who want to come." Before I could make it all out, Kitty was pulling me out of my chair and to my feet; then she is wrapping me up tight in her arms.

"I knew it! I knew it! She blurted out with unbridled glee." Her face glowed with happiness as she looked into my eyes.

"He chose well! That boy is marrying up, and now I will have a niece and hopefully some little feet running around the house. So fill us in on your wedding plans, and don't leave anything out," Aunt Kitty said as she sat back down and picked up her teacup.

Miss Marple took the pencil from the bun that she often carried about in her hair and picked up a pad of paper as the others waited. We spent hours sharing all of Stu and my plans and what I (we) had yet to do to get ready for the wedding. For it was only two weeks away and I needed a wedding dress and much more. It was agreed that Mary Beth's greenhouse would be called to decorate the church with flowers. The bridal gown would come from the Petoskey Bridle Shop. Once this ceremony was done, Stu and I would fly to New York to repeat our vows there with his other friends, clients, and partners.

"It is settled, we'll all go shopping tomorrow for dresses, shoes, hats, and anything else we need for the wedding. Darling, you might as well tell Stu that you'll be very busy all day and half the night. This kind of shopping is a serious affair, and one has been known to get a bit tipsy doing it," Miss Marple said. It was very apparent that these ladies were having the time of their lives, and it tickled me to see it.

Wedding Bells Are Ringing

In my last column that was written to come out this afternoon, once the largest court case in the history of the county ended. It was a case that touched all the lives of those watching it on TV or listening to it on the radio. It was a case that not only represented those people involved in it but all of us as a society. I pray that everyone can take something from it that will improve their lives. Miss Billings allowed herself to live her life as a victim, no matter how much her life changed and improved. She believed she deserved anything even if it weren't given to her, poisoning and killing those that thought she was a friend. Remember, we may be victims for a brief time, if at all; it's not a career or a lifestyle one should aspire to.

There is another matter I would like to share with you all now.

On August the 24 at 4:00 p.m. Sally Crystal, your undercover reporter, and Stu Baker will be married at the small country church in Black Hawk Harbor. Large screens will be set up around the village so everyone will be able to view the wedding ceremony. This will all be followed by an old country barbecue, which will be catered by the Pier Restaurant.

Joe Bumgardner became your undercover reporter at the beginning of the summer, trying to keep you all informed on the important news of the harbor and county at large. This reporter took on a challenge by the News Review in hopes of getting a national byline column; there were only one opening and two reporters chosen to compete for it. I am happy to tell you that my challenger, Jake Bates, the sports reporter, will have the column being offered. See you at the wedding.

ABOUT THE AUTHOR

D'Maule, the author, was born in Charlevoix County, Michigan, raised in Boyne City, Michigan, and one of six children to Walter and Elnora Maule. She's written hundreds of pieces of poetry, five of which were published in *American Analog's 1989 Poetry of Our Time*. Her poetry also appeared in local newspapers and trade union papers and is framed in many homes. For years she wrote and read short stories for elementary school classes in Charlevoix, Michigan, and as a teen, she was a community organizer and helped start a teen center in Boyne City, Michigan. She also wrote letters to the *Boyne Citizen Newspaper* as Aunt Dee, calling for traffic lights for two corners of her community. She's raised her family and worked as a caregiver for the elderly for the past thirty years At the age of sixty-nine, she wishes to share her ability in storytelling. Future books on the horizon will be a trilogy—*Unraveling Mysteries of the Terrorist's Plan, Summer Challenge Mystery*, and *Coffee Table Poetry*, a poetry collection for the whole family.

CPSIA information can be obtained
at www.ICGtesting.com
Printed in the USA
LVHW090117200420
654092LV00005B/1259